Diagnosis of Neurological Disorders Based on Deep Learning Techniques

This book is based on deep learning approaches used for the diagnosis of neurological disorders, including basics of deep learning algorithms using diagrams, data tables, and practical examples for diagnosis of neurodegenerative and neurodevelopmental disorders. It includes applications of feed-forward neural networks, deep generative models, convolutional neural networks, graph convolutional networks, and recurrent neural networks in the field of diagnosis of neurological disorders. Along with this, data preprocessing including scaling, correction, trimming, and normalization is also included.

- Offers a detailed description of the deep learning approaches used for the diagnosis of neurological disorders.
- Demonstrates concepts of deep learning algorithms using diagrams, data tables, and examples for the diagnosis of neurodegenerative, neurodevelopmental, and psychiatric disorders.
- Helps build, train, and deploy different types of deep architectures for diagnosis.
- Explores data preprocessing techniques involved in diagnosis.
- Includes real-time case studies and examples.

This book is aimed at graduate students and researchers in biomedical imaging and machine learning.

Diagnosis of Neurological Disorders Based on Deep Learning Techniques

Edited by
Jyotismita Chaki

CRC Press
Taylor & Francis Group
Boca Raton London New York

CRC Press is an imprint of the
Taylor & Francis Group, an **informa** business

Designed cover image: © Shutterstock

First edition published 2023
by CRC Press
6000 Broken Sound Parkway NW, Suite 300, Boca Raton, FL 33487-2742

and by CRC Press
4 Park Square, Milton Park, Abingdon, Oxon, OX14 4RN

CRC Press is an imprint of Taylor & Francis Group, LLC

ISBN: 9781032325231 (hbk)
ISBN: 9781032325248 (pbk)
ISBN: 9781003315452 (ebk)

DOI: 10.1201/9781003315452

Typeset in Times
by codeMantra

Contents

Preface

Analyzing and diagnosing neurological disorders is difficult and time-consuming. Many of the same symptoms occur in various combinations among the various disorders. Many disorders do not have clear causes, indicators, or diagnostics. This can make a diagnosis much more difficult.

Several approaches have been developed in recent times to automatically diagnose different neurological disorders. These approaches can essentially be split into two types: hand-crafted features and classifier approaches based on standard instruction. The second solution is focused on completely automatic approaches based on deep learning. The first type uses manually segregated characteristics and is given to classifiers as data. In training, the classifiers do not change the functions. However, in the second category of attributes, parameters may be modified to execute unique training data activities. Deep learning does not use hand-crafted features and have successfully been adapted to solve the medical diagnostic problems. As a result, deep learning is now playing an important role in the advancement of medical diagnostics.

This is basically the need for a new book in the field of neurological disorder diagnostics based on deep learning. To my knowledge, this is the first book to offer a detailed description of the deep learning approaches used in the field of neurological disorder diagnostics. This book demonstrates the core concepts of deep learning algorithms that, using diagrams, data tables, and examples, are especially useful for deep learning-based human neurological disorder diagnostics. After introducing the basic concepts of deep learning-based diagnosis for neurological disorders, this book will examine deep learning techniques for modeling the diagnosis and the properties and merits of the deep learning network models. This book will cover two major areas of human medical diagnosis: neurodegenerative disorders and neurodevelopmental and psychiatric disorders. A particular focus is placed on the application of feed-forward neural networks, deep generative models (e.g., stacked auto-encoders, deep belief networks, deep Boltzmann machine, and generative adversarial networks), convolutional neural networks, graph convolutional networks, and recurrent neural networks in the field of diagnosis of neurological disorders. Along with this, the focus is also on data preprocessing which will include scaling, correction, trimming, and normalization of data. The theory behind each deep learning architecture will be supported by practical examples (case studies) in this book. This book will also cover the technique to select the most effective deep model for the diagnosis of neurological disorders as well as the deep learning-based effective treatment for the same. Lastly, highlights will be on how the use of deep neural networks can address new questions and protocols, as well as improve upon existing challenges in diagnosis of neurological disorders. This book will assist scholars and students who might like to learn about this area as well as others who may have begun without a formal presentation. It is comprehensive, but it prohibits unnecessary mathematics. The subject's coverage is exceptional and has much of the principles needed to understand deep learning if anyone is searching for depth. This book is intended for professionals looking to gain proficiency in these technologies but is turned off by the complex mathematical equations.

This book can be useful for a variety of readers, but I have considered three target audiences in mind. Some of these target audiences are university students (undergraduate, graduate, or postgraduate) learning about deep learning, including those who are beginning a career in deep learning research. The other target audiences are researchers and practitioners who do not have a deep learning background but want to rapidly acquire one and begin using deep learning in their product or platform.

MATLAB® is a registered trademark of The MathWorks, Inc. For product information, please contact:
The MathWorks, Inc.
3 Apple Hill Drive
Natick, MA 01760-2098 USA
Tel: 508-647-7000
Fax: 508-647-7001
E-mail: info@mathworks.com
www.mathworks.com

About the Editor

Jyotismita Chaki, PhD, is an Associate Professor in School of Computer Science and Engineering at Vellore Institute of Technology, Vellore, India. She gained her PhD (Engg.) from Jadavpur University, Kolkata, India. Her research interests include computer vision and image processing, pattern recognition, medical imaging, artificial intelligence, and machine learning. Jyotismita has authored more than 40 international conference and journal papers and is the author and editor of more than eight books. Currently, she is the Academic Editor of *PLOS One* journal and *PeerJ Computer Science* journal and Associate Editor of *IET Image Processing* journal, *Array* journal, and *Machine Learning with Applications* journal.

List of Contributors

Pelin Alcan
Industrial Engineering Department,
 Faculty of Engineering and Natural
 Sciences
Istanbul Okan University
Istanbul, Turkey

Ahsan Ali
Department of Applied Mechanics
Indian Institute of Technology Madras
Chennai, India

Athar Al-Azzawi
School of Science and Engineering
Altınbas University
Istanbul, Turkey

Saif Al-Jumaili
School of Science and Engineering
Altınbas University
Istanbul, Turkey

H.B. Anita
Department of Computer Science
Christ (Deemed to be University)
Bangalore, India

Febin Antony
Department of Computer Science
Christ (Deemed to be University)
Bangalore, India

J. Arunnehru
Department of Computer Science and
 Engineering
SRM Institute of Science and
 Technology
Chennai, India

Ravi Kant Avvari
Department of Biotechnology and
 Medical Engineering
NIT Rourkela
Odisha, India

Yalın Baştanlar
Department of Computer Engineering
Izmir Institute of Technology
Urla, Turkey

R. Chandraprabha
Department of Electronics and
 Communication
BMS Institute of Technology and
 Management
Bengaluru, India

G. Chemmalar Selvi
School of Information Technology and
 Engineering
Vellore Institute of Technology
Vellore, India

P. Chitra
Department of Computer Science
 and Engineering, School of
 Engineering and Technology
Dhanalakshmi Srinivasan University
Trichy, India

Emre Dandıl
Department of Computer Engineering
Bilecik Seyh Edebali University
Bilecik, Turkey

Adil Deniz Duru
Faculty of Sport Sciences, Coaching
    Education Department
Marmara University
Istanbul, Turkey

Jincy A. George
Department of Life Sciences
Christ (Deemed to be University)
Bangalore, India

Zerrin Işık
Department of Computer Engineering
Dokuz Eylul University
Izmir, Turkey

Alex Noel Joseph Raj
Department of Electronic Engineering
Shantou University
Shantou, China

C. Keerthika
School of Computer Science and
    Engineering
Vellore Institute of Technology
Vellore, India

Y. Laasya
School of Information Technology and
    Engineering
Vellore Institute of Technology
Vellore, India

G.G. Lakshmi Priya
VIT School of Design
Vellore Institute of Technology
Vellore, India

Anisha M. Lal
School of Computer Science and
    Engineering
Vellore Institute of Technology
Vellore, India

Vijayalakshmi G V Mahesh
Department of Electronics and
    Communication
BMS Institute of Technology and
    Management
Bengaluru, India

Deepthi K. Oommen
Department of Computer Science and
    Engineering
SRM Institute of Science and
    Technology
Chennai, India

Subha D. Puthankattil
Department of Electrical Engineering
National Institute of Technology
Calicut, India

M. Sabrina
School of Information Technology and
    Engineering
Vellore Institute of Technology
Vellore, India

S. Sharanya
School of Information Technology and
    Engineering
Vellore Institute of Technology
Vellore, India

N. Sunaina
School of Information Technology and
    Engineering
Vellore Institute of Technology
Vellore, India

Osman Nuri Uçan
School of Science and Engineering
Altınbas University
Istanbul, Turkey

K. Usha
School of Information Technology and
   Engineering
Vellore Institute of Technology
Vellore, India

Marrapu Vynatheya
Department of Electrical Engineering
National Institute of Technology
Calicut, India

Altuğ Yiğit
The Graduate School of Natural and
   Applied Sciences
Dokuz Eylul University
Izmir, Turkey

Mehmet Süleyman Yıldırım
Department of Computer Technology
   of Sogut Vocational School
Bilecik Seyh Edebali University
Bilecik, Turkey

1 Introduction to Deep Learning Techniques for Diagnosis of Neurological Disorders

Jyotismita Chaki
Vellore Institute of Technology

CONTENTS

INTRODUCTION

Deep learning is being used by researchers to train algorithms to spot neurological disorders at a level equivalent to that of trained doctors. Compared to numerous domain experts, deep learning has demonstrated the ability to achieve greater diagnostic accuracy results. While this may be a point of disagreement among physicians, many potential victims can't wait for the technology to arrive. This book demonstrates the core concepts of deep learning algorithms that, using diagrams, data tables, and examples, are especially useful for deep learning-based human neurological disorder diagnostics. After introducing the basic concepts of deep learning-based neurological disorder diagnostics, this book will examine deep learning techniques for modelling the diagnosis and the properties and merits of the deep learning network models. A particular focus is placed on the application of different types of deep neural networks, which is useful for detecting different types of neurological disorders. In this book, the theory behind each deep learning architecture is supported by practical examples. Also, the pre-processing techniques needed to enhance the digital neurological disorder data for proper identification of human diseases is included here. Lastly, highlights will be on how the use of deep neural networks can address new questions and protocols, as well as improve upon existing challenges in neurological disorder diagnosis.

This book is organized as follows: Chapter 2 delivers the data pre-processing techniques for the deep learning-based diagnosis of neurological disorders. In this chapter, the extremely important data pre-processing techniques are studied based on the Alzheimer's disease detection using deep learning techniques.

DOI: 10.1201/9781003315452-1

These pre-processing techniques are explained using the benchmarking Alzheimer's Disease Neuroimaging Initiative (ADNI) dataset. The detailed list of datasets used in the recent research works and mapping of dataset with the appropriate data pre-processing techniques are drawn as the concluding remarks for the new researchers to begin their journey in the early detection of neurological disorder diseases.

Chapter 3 deals with the case study related to the classification of the level of Alzheimer's disease using anatomical magnetic resonance images based on a novel deep learning structure. In this chapter, the authors propose a novel 2D deep convolutional neural network to classify four stages of Alzheimer's disease. The dataset consists of four types, namely Non-Demented, Very Mild Demented, Mild Demented, and Moderate Demented subject MR images. First, we applied a pre-processing technique to resize the image for compliance with our models. Then, Reduce Atmospheric Haze technique is performed that can decrease the atmospheric haze, making all images sharp and clear to feed to the model. The authors implemented the model 30 times and obtained more than 99.46% for evaluation metrics. The proposed method shows an outstanding performance compared with other papers reported in the literature.

Chapter 4 is devoted to a case study related to the detection of Alzheimer's disease stages based on deep learning architectures from MRI images. In this chapter, advanced deep learning (DL) architectures with brain imaging techniques were employed to maximize the diagnostic accuracy of the model developed. The proposed method works with convolutional neural networks (CNNs) to analyse the MRI input–output modalities. The method is evaluated using Alzheimer's Disease Neuroimaging Initiative (ADNI) dataset. Binary classification is done on Alzheimer's disease (AD) and Mild cognitive impairment (MCI) subjects from CN. This method is efficient to analyse multiple classes with a less amount of training data.

Chapter 5 introduces the reader to a case study of analysing the detection of Alzheimer's using deep neural network. This chapter discusses the detection of AD in human brain images. Generally, researchers train a neural network to categorize patients using diagnostic criteria and medical conditions with the dataset of images. This chapter investigates deep neural networks (DNNs) for retrieval of features and categorizes them for the detection of AD with papers from the recent 4 years. It visualizes the number of papers according to networks utilized for the detection system. Many recent research projects that employed brain MRI images and CNNs to diagnose Alzheimer's disease found encouraging outcomes. As a result, this research provides an end-to-end CNN-based architecture for AD detection. Detecting Alzheimer's disease reduces anxiety of the symptoms, lessens the family burden, and provides peace of mind for the person.

Chapter 6 deals with a case study related to the detection and classification of Alzheimer's disease with predictor variables. The researchers used the Open Access Series of Imaging Studies (OASIS) dataset to determine whether the labels were demented or not. The novelty comes from conducting considerable experimentation to identify critical predictor factors before selecting DNN architecture and precisely set hyper-parameters to achieve remarkable results. The proposed approach is a promising way for assisting early prediction of Alzheimer's diseases using neuroimaging data.

Chapter 7 presents and analyses the main research about classification of brain tumour using optimized DNN models. The chapter's objective is to investigate the overall performance of this DNN architecture in the brain tumour category. The accumulation of cells in an abnormal position in specific brain tissues is called a brain tumour. The early detection of tumour cells is essential for the care and recovery of patients. A brain tumour is typically recognized after a prolonged and time-eating system. There are numerous styles of function extraction and category strategies used to discover brain tumours from MRI images. This overall performance singularly and in the aggregate is implemented and evaluated in the dataset with a T1-weighted MRI image of the Internet Brain Segmentation Repository (IBSR). The outcomes were recorded in Precision, Recall, F1-Score, and Accuracy phrases. The results and discussions of this study's outcomes could convey the merits and pitfalls of this DNN architecture so that you are free to add information inside the area of deep neural network.

The focus of Chapter 8 is on how to perform the fully automated segmentation of brain stroke lesions using mask region-based convolutional neural network. In this chapter, the authors propose a fully automated method based on mask region-based convolutional neural network (Mask R-CNN) for segmentation of brain stroke lesions using MR images. ATLAS v2.0, a publicly available stroke dataset comprising of T1-weighted MR scans, is used in the chapter. Within the scope of the experimental studies in the dataset, automatic segmentation of stroke lesions using the proposed Mask R-CNN method is achieved with a dice similarity coefficient of 78.50%. The findings obtained in the study show that the proposed Mask R-CNN method can be utilized as an assistant tool for segmentation of stroke lesions with accurate boundaries.

Chapter 9 deals with a case study related to the efficient classification of schizophrenia EEG signals using deep learning methods. This work is an attempt to evaluate the deep learning methods of VGG-16 and AlexNet over the long short-term memory (LSTM) network in detecting schizophrenia efficiently as deep learning methods are able to identify the subtle patterns hidden in the data. VGG-16, a CNN architecture, is widely used in many learning applications due to the ease with which it can be implemented, while AlexNet, also being a CNN, could learn the representation of features from the data. The results of VGG-16 and AlexNet are compared with that of the classification efficiency of LSTM in detecting schizophrenia. The resting state EEG signals obtained from a publicly available database were sampled at a frequency of 250 Hz. Detection of schizophrenia using LSTM was carried out by extracting non linear features, such as Katz fractal dimension (KFD) and approximate entropy (ApEn) along with the statistical time domain measure of variance, from the acquired EEG signals. The LSTM model gave an accuracy of 99% in classifying schizophrenia from healthy controls, while 99.81% and 99.61% were obtained for VGG-16 and AlexNet, respectively. The CNN models outperform the classification efficiency of the feature input LSTM model in detecting schizophrenia, which could be of assistance to the clinicians for an expeditious diagnosis.

The focus of Chapter 10 is on implementation of a DNN-based framework for actigraphy analysis and prediction of schizophrenia. This chapter focuses on using the DNN-based framework to study and analyse the data obtained from actigraphy that records activity cycles to predict the presence of schizophrenia. The methodology proposed is quantitatively evaluated and assessed to measure its performance.

Chapter 11 deals with an ensemble approach towards evaluating psychomotor skills in autism spectrum disorder through deep learning. Existing modalities of diagnosis are qualitative and do not provide the comprehensive evaluation over a long period of time. Further, there is an increased risk of missing the detection at an early stage, having long-lasting health implications on the motor and cognitive skills. Deep learning algorithms have emerged as a potential tool for exploring possible association of the data with the symptoms that are clinically relevant for ASD diagnosis. Owing to higher accuracy in detecting the disorder, techniques such as CNN, RNN, DBN, LSTN, and AE have become very popular in assessing the level of risk in developing the disorder. However, due to non-corroboration of the morphological and behavioural specifics to the features extracted using deep learning techniques, effective diagnosis has been a challenge. This chapter delves into the reasons as to why the effective diagnosis is not possible and presents author speculations that may direct future investigations towards improved accuracy using deep learning models.

Chapter 12 deals with dementia detection with deep networks using multi-modal image data. This chapter first introduces a broad review of multi-modal imaging approaches proposed for dementia diagnosis. Then it presents DNNs, which extract structural and functional features from multi-modal imaging data and are employed to diagnose Alzheimer's and mild cognitive impairments. While MRI scans are safer than most types of scans and provide structural information about the human body, PET scans provide information about functional activities in the brain. Thus, the setup has been designed to make experiments using both MRI and FDG-PET scans. Performances of multi-modal models were compared with single-modal solutions. The multi-modal solution showed superiority over single modals due to the advantage of focusing on assorted features.

Chapter 12 provides an overview of the importance of the Internet of Things (IoT) in neurological disorders. IoT and information technologies applied in the improvement of healthcare operations have reached an important point. In the days we live, especially after the pandemic, it has become even more important to research various technologies under the title of health4.0 to strengthen health services. IoT was improved to combine existing medicinal sources and ensure individuals with the most trustworthy and most efficient healthcare services. One of the greatest opportunities IoT has to offer is hidden in immanent connectivity. Thus, smart services such as remote patient tracing/monitoring, home therapy, and assisted living platforms are possible. In recent years, neurological diseases have come to the fore more than all other diseases. When the literature is searched, it is seen that the number of articles examining the studies on neurology and IoT is quite limited. In recent years, the interpretation of large volumes of complex electronic data, especially in health systems, is of great importance. Interpreting this data can also introduce important challenges. Deep learning is well suited to tackling these challenges. The motivation and the contribution of the chapter proceed precisely from this point. The purpose of this chapter is to summarize the most fundamental practices of IoT in neurology.

2 A Comprehensive Study of Data Pre-Processing Techniques for Neurological Disease (NLD) Detection

G. Chemmalar Selvi, G.G. Lakshmi Priya,
M. Sabrina, S. Sharanya, Y. Laasya,
N. Sunaina, and K. Usha
Vellore Institute of Technology

CONTENTS

DOI: 10.1201/9781003315452-2

2.1 INTRODUCTION

Neurological disorders are diseases that cause damage to the nerves in the brain and throughout the human body. The main reason for such diseases will be different in each case; however, it will even include hereditary problems, congenital disorders, contaminations, and several other problems related to environmental health [1,2]. Examples of symptoms include paralysis, muscle weakness, poor coordination, loss of sensation, seizures, confusion, pain, and altered levels of consciousness. Due to the malfunctioning of the brain, there are three neurological diseases which are Alzheimer's disease (AD), Parkinson's disease (PD), and schizophrenia (SZ) causing severe threat to the human lives. To find the right medication to increase the high chance of living, various methods are being used gradually and the earlier detection of these diseases can help the affected patients to be cured faster by determining the cause and medication in the early development stage.

Recent developments in advanced machine learning (ML) algorithms especially using deep learning (DL) techniques are becoming increasingly important [3,4]. The most important phase in the early detection of cognitive damages is derived studying the critical patterns in detection and management of neurodisorders. Hence, certain ML techniques such as data classification in examining the various critical conditions of the patient are highly crucial when it comes to selecting the very strong discriminatory factors that are hugely monitored for performance result. Thus the proper preparation of patient information before examining the disease is highly imperative to avoid the data noise and inconsistencies leading to the ambiguity in examining the disease.

There are different pre-processing techniques such as image resizing (IRE), scaling, correction, stripping, and trimming. Normalization, filtering, and smoothing are used to remove the noise and enhance the properties of MRI image data. The recent research works carried out based on NLD disease detection focus on various filtering such as Gaussian, median, frequency, Weiner, skull stripping, and normalizations such as spatial normalization, intensity normalization, Z-score normalization, numerical normalization, histogram normalization, CLAHE normalization, and spatial smoothing, and nonsharp filters have been applied [5–12]. It has been shown that these methods greatly enhance the features of the image data by holding essential information using the benchmarking Alzheimer's Disease Neuroimaging Initiative (ADNI) dataset.

In this work, an extensive study of data pre-processing techniques is performed in the diagnosis of neurological disorders based on machine and deep learning algorithms. The organization of the work is presented in the following sections. Section 2.2 discusses various literatures examining the detection of NLD diseases. In Section 2.3, the open-access datasets available for the NLD disease prediction are presented with links to access it directly for the benefit of the new researchers starting their work in this domain. In addition to it, a comprehensive summary table of the different machine learning (ML) models and DL models used in NLD disease prediction are presented. In Section 2.4, the results of applying various data pre-processing techniques using ADNI dataset are demonstrated. Finally, Section 2.5 concludes the work by summarizing the various data pre-processing techniques used with the NLD disease detection.

2.2 RELATED WORKS

Saladi et al. [11] proposed an effective way to remove noise from magnetic resonance imaging (MRI) data to enhance the features and image resolution quality. The authors have employed various denoising algorithms such as principal component analysis (PCA) and spatially adaptive nonlocal means (SANLM) filters for pre-processing the image data thereby improvising the image quality. The metrics including signal-to-noise ratio, peak signal-to-noise ratio (PSNR), mean squared error, root mean squared error, and structure similarity (SSIM) are used for measuring the performance of the experimental results. The result analysis compared SANLM with conventional denoising methods which yielded the best performance by reducing the highest noise present in the image data. It presented a PSNR value of 2.07% for all the processed images which helped to enhance the accuracy for proper MRI brain image segmentation.

Ben George et al. [12] presented an approach for the enhancement of MRI images by using the modified tracking algorithm (MTA) and data pre-processing techniques such as center-weighted median (CWM) filter. The primary method MTA is applied to discard the film artifacts, skull sections, and labels, which are followed by CWM filtration. For this work, the data was taken from the Brain Web Database in McGill University. The data consisted of 80 images, and the statistical measures such as variance or entropy were used to measure the local contrast enhancement. The experimental results show that PSNR and ASNR values for each filtering method were calculated in which for Weighted Median filter, the highest value of PSNR was 0.92667, and ASNR value for the CWM was highest at 0.9280. Thus, the authors presented the novel data pre-processing technique for enhancing the image quality.

Suhas et al. [13] explained the importance of noise removal in medical imaging and discussed the experimental performance evaluation using various MRI de-noising approaches. Filters such as median, Gaussian, Max, Min, and arithmetic mean were used, which were applied on the MRI scans of the brain and spinal cord. The authors aimed to remove the Rician, Gaussian, and salt-and-pepper noise as well from the MRI images. Additionally, the existing median filter has been modified using extra features as the effective data pre-processing techniques which employs a combination of median and means filtering together. The proposed method was also analyzed with the other filters to validate its performance results, and the results proved that the proposed method retains the structural details of the MRI scan images very well without losing many essential details even after clearing the noise present in the image.

Alakörkkö et al. [10] focused more on spatial smoothing which is one of the standard pre-processing methods for removing noise present in the fMRI image data. The authors have tried to apply spatial smoothing on fMRI data which ensures any kind of variation introduced through the functional networks in the brain. Hence, it showcased the degree of spatial smoothing which measures the variations of functional network nodes. Hence, the authors concluded that the application of spatial smoothing must be avoided when the network analysis of the fMRI data is required for experimentation.

López-González et al. [14] aimed to evaluate the different methods of intensity normalization which is the most widely used method for quantification output of brain fluorodeoxyglucose (FDG)-positron emission tomography (PET) image data generated using the Monte Carlo (MC) simulation technique. This work presents some challenges related to semi-quantification methods of the FDG-PET and MRI subject data that are obtained to generate activity maps which in turn were modified by adding hypometabolism to generate hypometabolic patterns used for brain functionalities. The activity maps generated and their respective attenuation maps using MC simulation are illustrated in the experimental results where the simulated data was subjected to image reconstruction using image pre-processing technique known as spatial normalization. At the end, the voxel-based quantification and the data analysis results are presented in the form of activity maps and other visual comparisons such as the total volume of the detected hypermetabolic voxels and unspecific hypometabolic areas and finally concluded the serious concern in terms of false positive results due to abnormal use of normalization.

2.3 METHODS

2.3.1 Open-Access Data for NLD Disease Detection

This section presents the most widely used dataset in the recent research studies for NLD disease detection such as Alzheimer's disease (AD), Parkinson's disease (PD), and schizophrenia (SZ). Table 2.1 shows the list of publicly available datasets with their official link to download the dataset for their research study.

2.3.1.1 ADNI

The US-based ADNI database is made available at their official ADNI database and launched in with $60 million for the research study. The dataset contains the magnetic resonance imaging (MRI), positron emission tomography (PET), and other biological markers used for the detection of neurological diseases. The ADNI dataset can be used for detecting the AD, PD, and SZ diseases.

TABLE 2.1

Dataset summary for ADNI disease

S. No.	Dataset Name	Dataset Link
1.	Alzheimer's Disease Neuroimaging Initiative (ADNI)	ADNI – Alzheimer's Disease Neuroimaging Initiative (usc.edu)
2.	Open Access Series of Imaging Studies (OASIS)	www.oasis-brains.org
3.	Center for Biomedical Research Excellence (COBRE)	www.mrn.org/common/cobre-phase-3
4.	Function Biomedical Informatics Research Network (FBIRN)	www.nmr.mgh.harvard. edu/~greve/fbirn/fips/

2.3.1.2 OASIS

The Open Access Series of Imaging Studies (OASIS) is the neuroimaging data freely available for detecting neurological diseases such as AD and PD. The three forms of OASIS data are:

1. OASIS-Cross-sectional
2. OASIS-Longitudinal
3. OASIS-3

2.3.1.3 COBRE

The Center for Biomedical Research Excellence (COBRE) is comprised of both anatomical and functional MR data. Other diagnostic information from 72 patients is collated from the MRI image data, and this dataset is used for detecting AD and PD diseases.

2.3.1.4 FBIRN

The Function Biomedical Informatics Research Network (FBIRN) is the open-source dataset containing the functional MRI data used for studying the neurological diseases such as AD and PD to support the data management services.

2.3.1.5 PPMI

The Parkinson's Progression Markers Initiative (PPMI) is the biomarker-defined cohorts used for Parkinson's disease (PD) detection which has 423 patient data registered in 24 different sites.

Table 2.1 presents the official link to download and extract the patient details for neurological disorder prediction.

2.3.2 ML MODELS FOR NLD DISEASE DETECTION

Machine learning is one of the techniques used for analyzing the patients' information in detecting the presence of critical diseases. A substantial number of ML algorithms exist, and neuroimaging is the first area of neurology to benefit from the application of these ML techniques [15,16,17,18,19]. Their applications provide promising results for early detection of neurological disorders, prognosis, and development of new therapies. The summary in Table 2.2 lists the robust ML architecture used for detecting the neurological degenerative disease such as AD, SD, and PD disease types and the appropriate data pre-processing technique used in the respective research work along with the dataset used for the experimental result analysis.

The support vector machine (SVM) was mostly used for detecting the Parkinson's disease where the data pre-processing technique used in this work was skull stripping and normalization, and the experimental results show that the overall mean accuracy as 85.8% which yields promising results in PD detection [9]. In this paper [20], Alzheimer's disease was detected using the SVM architecture and the data was taken from ADNI which is pre-processed using the data pre-processing techniques known as image re-orientation and skull stripping for improvising the image quality. Different variations of SVM were used in [21–23] to detect Alzheimer's disease using the OASIS dataset which was pre-processed using the key slice selection and shape registration methods, and the overall accuracy of 92.75% was achieved. The neural networks like convolutional neural networks (CNNs) and its variations were used as multiclass classifiers for diagnosis and prognosis of Alzheimer's disease. For optimal feature selection, image texture and shape were extracted from the OASIS dataset which resulted in a trained weighted model [24–28]. In the work in Ref. [29], SVM was used for SD disease prediction using the ADNI dataset, and the data pre-processing techniques such as slice trimming, correction, and normalization were used to study the physiological signs from the MRI brain images.

2.3.3 DEEP LEARNING MODELS FOR NLD DISEASE DETECTION

In the recent years, the deep learning (DL) models were developed to solve the limitations of ML-based techniques. The most popular and robust deep learning architecture is the CNN architecture having several benefits over the conventional ML-based approaches. The CNN has multilayer architecture to deal with large-scaled dataset and handles the imbalanced data samples. Recently, various CNN-based architectures have shown satisfying results in detecting neurodegenerative disorders [30–35]. Table 2.3 summarizes the different deep learning techniques used in the detection of neuro diseases such as AD, SD, and PD. In Table 2.3, the deep learning architecture used to diagnose the disease is presented along with the dataset used for the experimental analysis. The data pre-processing technique used for preparing the data enabling to identify the optimal feature is determined which is mandatory for the model construction.

2.4 EXPERIMENTAL DISCUSSION OF DATA PRE-PROCESSING TECHNIQUES FOR BRAIN ANALYSIS

Data pre-processing is the necessary technique which when used makes the image suitable for further processing by enhancing the image quality and removing the noise present in the image. It aims at increasing the image resolution

TABLE 2.2

Machine learning architecture for AD, SD, and PD detection

S. No.	ML Architecture	Disease Prediction and Classification	Data Pre-processing	Feature	Dataset	Dimensions	Results	Reference Paper
1.	Support vector machine	Parkinson's disease (PD) progressive supranuclear palsy (PSP)	Skull stripping, normalization to MNI space	PCA coefficients for the PSP versus PD binary labeled group	Clinical data taken from 56 patients and 28 healthy control subjects	PD patients (28), PSP patients (28), and healthy control subjects (28)	PD vs controls :overall mean accuracy=85.8, PSP vs. controls: overall mean=89.1 PSP vs PD: overall mean=889.9	[19]
2.	Support vector machines (SVM)	Alzheimer's disease – AD	Image re-orientation, cropping, skull-stripping, image normalization to MNI standard space	PCA coefficients.	ADNI	137 AD, 76 MCIc, 134 MCInc, and 162 healthy controls (CN)	Accuracy – 76% AD vs CN 72% MCIc VS CN 66% MCIc vs MCInc	[20]
3.	Support vector machine (SVM), generalized eigenvalue proximal SVM (GEPSVM), and twin SVM (TSVM).	Alzheimer's disease (AD)	Key slice selection, shape registration	DF was treated as the AD-related features, reduced by principal component analysis (PCA),	OASIS	28 ADs and 98 NCs	Accuracy=92.75±1.77, sensitivity=90.56±1.15, specificity=93.37±2.05, precision=79.61±2.21.	[21]

(*Continued*)

TABLE 2.2 (*Continued*)
Machine learning architecture for AD, SD, and PD detection

S. No.	ML Architecture	Disease Prediction and Classification	Data Pre-processing	Feature	Dataset	Dimensions	Results	Reference Paper
4.	Neural network is used as multiclass classifier	Alzheimer's disease (AD)	Shape registration	Texture and shape features of the hippocampus region	OASIS	—	Training phase output with adjusted weights	[22]
5.	Support vector machine (SVM)	Alzheimer's disease (AD)	Slice-timing correction, normalization, resampling, detrending, smoothing	Graph measures	ADNI	Four patients with AD	Accuracy of 88.4%	[23]
6.	Convolutional neural network support vector machine	Alzheimer's disease – AD	Bias field correction, affine registration.		ADNI		Accuracy	[24]
7.	Convolutional neural network	Alzheimer's disease – AD	Skull stripping and gray matter segmentation spatial normalization bias correction	JPEG slices. Slices which contain no information are discarded. Gray matter slice	Nifti	33 AD, 22 LMCI, 49 MCI patients, and 45 healthy controls which makes a total of 355 MRI volumes.	Class-wise performance comparison, classification performance accuracy	[25]

(*Continued*)

TABLE 2.2 (*Continued*)

Machine learning architecture for AD, SD, and PD detection

S. No.	ML Architecture	Disease Prediction and Classification	Data Pre-processing	Feature	Dataset	Dimensions	Results	Reference Paper
8.	Convolutional neural network	Alzheimer's disease – AD	dcm2nii software package was used to convert DICOm to NifTI correction using FSL–MCFLIRT		ADNI	10,722 for training	Accuracy	[26]
9.	3D ConvNet	Alzheimer's disease – AD	Motion correction and normalization		ADNI	340 subjects 1,198 MRI brain scans	Accuracy	[27]
10.	Convolutional neural network AlexNet architecture	Parkinson's disease – PD	Normalization filtering	Uniform contrast	PPMI	100 subjects	Accuracy loss specificity	[28]
11.	Support vector machine	Schizophrenia disease – SD	SPM8 software used for spatial normalization	PCA	None	542 healthy and 558 schizophrenic patients	Accuracy	[29]

TABLE 2.3
Deep learning architecture for AD, SD, and PD detection

S. No.	DL Architecture	Disease Prediction and Classification	Data Pre-processing	Feature	Dataset	Dimensions	Results	References
1	Recurrent neural network	AD Prediction	Filtering	Longitudinal cerebrospinal fluid (CSF)	ADNI	A total of 1,618 ADNI participants which include 415 (CN), 307 MCI converter, 558 MCI nonconverter, and 338 AD patients	Accuracy – 81%	[30]
2	Two frameworks based on CNN	Prediction of Parkinson's disease	Normalization	Wavele and concat	ADNI	252 individuals	Accuracy – 86.9% F-measure – 91.7%. MCC – 63.2%	[31]
3	CNN architectures employing transfer learning. DenseNet121, MobileNet, InceptionV3 and Xception neural networks	Detection of Alzheimer's disease	Scaling	Fine tuning	OASIS	2,565 images as mild dementia, moderate dementia, nondementia, and very mild dementia categories	99% of training accuracy, 97% of validation accuracy, and accuracy of 91% on test data.	[32]
4	AlexNet architecture in CNN	Detection of neurodevelopmental disorders including autism, ADHD, and schizophrenia	Skull stripping, motion correction, slice timing correction, smoothing and band-pass filtering	Functional connectivity matrix, volume, time series	COBRE	fMRI data	71.15% accuracy, 70.13% precision, 69% sensitivity, 80.30% specificity, and 69.56% F1 – score.	[33]

(Continued)

TABLE 2.3 (*Continued*)
Deep learning architecture for AD, SD, and PD detection

S. No.	DL Architecture	Disease Prediction and Classification	Data Pre-processing	Feature	Dataset	Dimensions	Results	References
5	DCNN	Detection of schizophrenia	Normalization	Z-score	Dataset collected in psychiatry and neurology institute	14 patients EEG signals	Accuracy using average pooling layer – 98.07% accuracy using convolution, max pooling, and fully connected layers –81.26%	[34]
6	Feedforward back propagation neural networks	Detection of schizophrenia	Use of statistical parametric mapping software, motion correction, normalization,	Friston 24 motion parameter, cerebrospinal fluid, and white matter signals	Dataset collected from Xinxiang medical university	A total of 39 EOS patients and 31 healthy patients were recruited for the dataset. Functional images were collected transversely using an echo-planar imaging (EPI) sequence.	79.3% accuracy, 87.4% sensitivity, 82.2% specificity	[35]

without losing the essential information from the image. The primary reasons for the image imperfection are low-contrast and low-resolution properties which are then processed using the data pre-processing techniques. Hence there are numerous data pre-processing techniques available to improve the brain image quality of which filtering and normalization are the most popular techniques with brain MRI image classification which are discussed as follows.

2.4.1 FILTERING

Image filtering techniques are used to modify the image when deploying an application. Using these techniques, the characteristics or its appearance is changed to remove any noisy features and improvise the images by smoothing, sharpening, and edge enhancement. In particular, in image processing, the Gaussian filtering, box filtering, median filtering, and other variations among them are explored in great detail. In this work, the experiments were conducted using the ADNI dataset, and Python code was written using the Jupyter Notebook.

2.4.1.1 Gaussian Filter

Gaussian filtering introduces blurring to an image in an asymmetric fashion, ignoring image brightness, and helping in smoothing the images significantly by performing nonlinear low-pass filtering. The 2-D convolution filter known as the Gaussian smoothing operator applied over the image data, blurs and removes the noise from it as shown in Figure 2.1.

2.4.1.2 Output

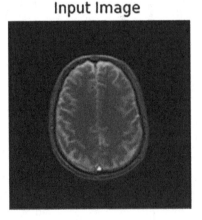

FIGURE 2.1   Gaussian filter.

2.4.1.3 Median Filter

Median filtering uses neighborhood operations to remove noise, as well as fine image details using maximum-likelihood-based operations. The median filter retains the details of the image pixels by considering the surrounding details of the information present in the image data. In addition to removing noise, median filtering also tends to remove sharp, small features from a picture as shown in Figure 2.2.

2.4.1.4 Output

Input Image   **Median Filter**

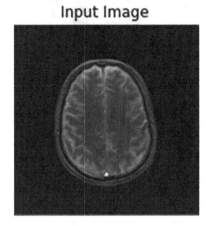 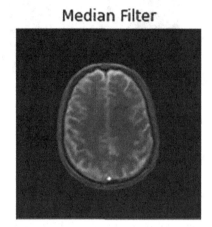

FIGURE 2.2 Median filter.

2.4.1.5 Weiner Filter

Wiener filtering was one of the first methods developed to reduce additive random noise in images. It works on the assumption that additive noise is a stationary random process, independent of pixel location; the algorithm minimizes the square error between the original and reconstructed images. Wiener filtering is a low-pass filter, but instead of having a single cutoff frequency, it is a space-varying filter designed to use a low cutoff in low-detail regions and a high cutoff to retain detail in regions with edges or other high-variance features. The window size determines the overall frequency cutoff: larger windows correspond to lower cutoff frequencies, and therefore more blurring and noise reduction as shown in Figure 2.3.

2.4.1.6   Output

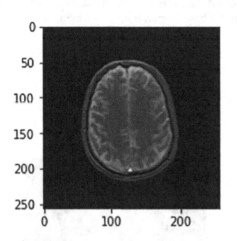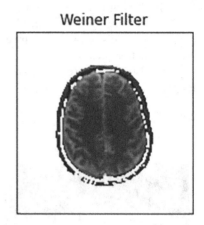

FIGURE 2.3   Weiner filter.

2.4.1.7   Frequency Filter

The frequency filter pre-processes the image in the frequency domain which is used for smoothing and sharpening of the images by reducing the high-frequency and low-frequency components. There are three types of filters, namely low-pass filter, high-pass filter, and band-pass filter. Low-pass filter removes the high-frequency components that means it keeps low-frequency components. It is used for smoothing the image. It is used to smoothen the image by attenuating high-frequency components and preserving low-frequency components. High-pass filter removes the low-frequency components that mean it keeps high-frequency components. It is used for sharpening the image. It is used to sharpen the image by attenuating low-frequency components and preserving high-frequency components. Band-pass filter removes the very low-frequency and very high-frequency components that means it keeps the moderate range band of frequencies. Band-pass filtering is used to enhance edges while reducing the noise at the same time as shown in Figures 2.4 and 2.5.

2.4.1.8 Output

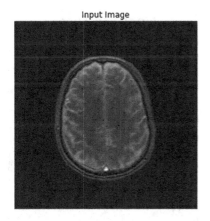
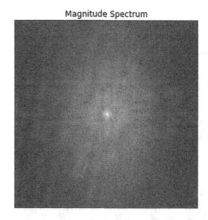

FIGURE 2.4 Frequency filter.

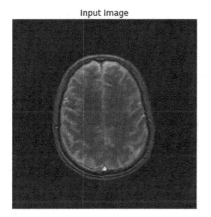
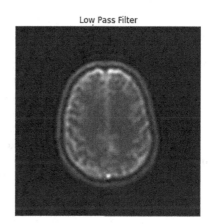

FIGURE 2.5 Low-pass filter.

2.4.1.9 Unsharp Filter

The unsharp filtering technique has been widely used to enhance high-frequency details such as edges by subtracting its local blurriness involved in pre-fixed low-pass filter mask operations and adding high-frequency weighting elements to the original image. Here, the filter is used to improve the image edges by masking it with parameters such as radius, percentage, and threshold as shown in Figure 2.6.

2.4.1.10 Output

Input Image

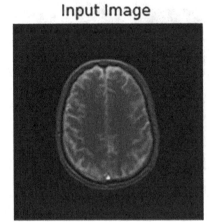

Unsharp Filter

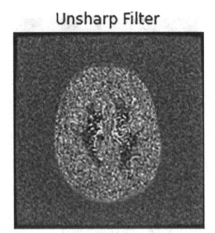

FIGURE 2.6 Unsharp filter.

2.4.2 Normalization

Normalization is used for comparing the data by scaling down the different combinations of dataset which is always the classical pre-processing step in the ML model. In image processing, this normalization is applied to study the complex patterns generated with the pixel intensity of the image to match the different brain shapes as one unique pattern. Data normalization is an important step which ensures that each input parameter (pixel, in this case) has a similar data distribution. This makes convergence faster while training the model. Normalization is done by subtracting the mean from each pixel and then dividing the result by the standard deviation. The distribution of such data would resemble a Gaussian curve centered at zero.

2.4.2.1 Spatial Normalization

Spatial normalization is the obvious phase wherever fMRI data are used which actually analyze the one-to-one correspondence between-subject-level of different individuals' brain against the common template. It is an important technique used for image registration that matches the images' subjects to the reference brain space to perform comparisons across subjects with varied brain morphologies. As the human brain varies in size and shape, the image registration can never be perfect as there is no correspondence between one subject to another spatial reference.

2.4.2.2 Intensity Normalization

Intensity normalization applied on the brain magnetic resonance image (MRI) data is acquired for detecting the subjects present in the images at irregular time intervals resulting in large intensity variations. It ensures optimal comparisons across data acquisition methods and texture instances by contrast stretching and histogram stretching of the image as shown in Figure 2.7a and b.

2.4.2.3 Output

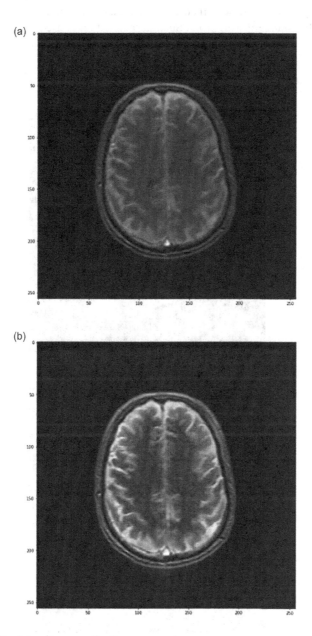

FIGURE 2.7 Intensity normalization.

2.4.2.4   Histogram Normalization

Histogram normalization is a technique to distribute the frequencies of the histogram over a wider range than the current range for enhancing the contrast of poor contrasted images. The general idea is to make pixel distribution uniform. This makes X-rays appear a little darker. This generates view, which radiologist would not see in his standard workplace. Such normalization is used in popular opensource X-ray datasets, such as CheXpert as shown in Figure 2.8a and b.

2.4.2.5   Output

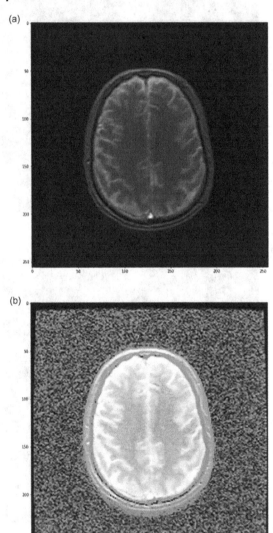

FIGURE 2.8   Histogram normalization.

2.5 CONCLUSION

Data are inconsistent and noisy which needs to be cleaned before processing with any machine learning algorithm. For the successful detection and treatment of neurological disorders, an efficient and error-free processing pipeline is required, and data pre-processing poses an essential step in this pipeline. To be able to extract essential information from images, removal of noise is important as it extremely enhances the accuracy of the model performance. Filtering helps in removing noise and keeps valuable information intact. In this work, the authors have used ADNI dataset and examined the most popularly used data pre-processing techniques such as filtering and normalization. It has been shown that these approaches seek for the essential image information and yet clears out much of the noise present in the image. Normalization, a scaling technique, is one of the most important pre-processing steps. The types of normalization presented in this study are spatial normalization, intensity normalization, and so on. Spatial smoothing using Gaussian and median filters was done, and the results showed that spatial smoothing should be avoided whenever possible as the sharp edges of the images were blurred which has a chance of affecting the degrees of fMRI which is not usable for detecting the disease. Hence, a detailed examination of these pre-processing techniques such as filtering and normalization was applied to the benchmarking dataset taken from ADNI website, and the corresponding results were presented. Hence, the future scope of using data pre-processing would be highly vital and crucial step in the process of model building process which involves hybridizing the pre-processing technique according to the requirement of the problem statement.

REFERENCES

[1] Bassett, D. S., & Sporns, O. (2017). Network neuroscience. *Nature Neuroscience*, *20*(-3), 353–364.

[2] Mott, M., & Koroshetz, W. (2015). Bridging the gap in neurotherapeutic discovery and development: the role of the national institute of neurological disorders and stroke in translational neuroscience. *Neurotherapeutics*, *12*(3), 651–654.

[3] Noor, M.B.T., Zenia, N.Z., & Kaiser, M.S., et al. (2020). Application of deep learning in detecting neurological disorders from magnetic resonance images: a survey on the detection of Alzheimer's disease, Parkinson's disease, and schizophrenia. *Brain Informatics*, *7*, 11.

[4] Islam, J., & Zhang, Y. (2018). Brain MRI analysis for Alzheimer's disease diagnosis using an ensemble system of deep convolutional neural networks. *Brain Informatics*, *5*(2), 1–14.

[5] Ali, H.M., Kaiser, M.S., & Mahmud, M. (2019). Application of Convolutional Neural Network in Segmenting Brain Regions from MRI Data. In: Liang, P., Goel, V., Shan, C. (eds) *Brain Informatics. BI 2019. Lecture Notes in Computer Science* (vol. 11976, pp. 136–146). Springer, Cham.

[6] Fan, Y., Resnick, S.M., Wu, X., & Davatzikos, C. (2008). Structural and functional biomarkers of prodromal Alzheimer's disease: a high-dimensional pattern classification study. *Neuroimage*, *41*(2), 277–285.

[7] Noor, M. B. T., Zenia, N. Z., Kaiser, M. S., Mamun, S. A., & Mahmud, M. (2020). Application of deep learning in detecting neurological disorders from magnetic resonance images: a survey on the detection of Alzheimer's disease, Parkinson's disease and schizophrenia. *Brain Informatics*, *7*(1), 1–21.

[8] Fan, Y., Batmanghelich, N., Clark, C.M., Davatzikos, C., & Alzheimer's Disease Neuroimaging Initiative. (2008). Spatial patterns of brain atrophy in MCI patients, identified via high-dimensional pattern classification, predict subsequent cognitive decline. *Neuroimage*, *39*(4), 1731–1743.

[9] Benson, C.C., & Lajish, V.L. (2014). Morphology based enhancement and skull stripping of MRI brain images. In: *2014 International Conference on Intelligent Computing Applications* (pp. 254–257). Coimbatore, India. IEEE.

[10] Alakörkkö, T., Saarimäki, H., Glerean, E., Saramäki, J., & Korhonen, O. (2017). Effects of spatial smoothing on functional brain networks. *European Journal of Neuroscience*, *46*(9), 2471–2480.

[11] Saladi, S., & Amutha Prabha, N. (2017). Analysis of denoising filters on MRI brain images. *International Journal of Imaging Systems and Technology*, *27*(3), 201–208.

[12] George, E.B., & Karnan, M. (2012). MRI brain image enhancement using filtering techniques. *International Journal of Computer Science & Engineering Technology (IJCSET)*, *3*, 2229–3345.

[13] Suhas, S., & Venugopal, C.R. (2017). MRI image preprocessing and noise removal technique using linear and nonlinear filters. In: *2017 International Conference on Electrical, Electronics, Communication, Computer, and Optimization Techniques (ICEECCOT)* (pp. 1–4). Mysuru, India. IEEE.

[14] López-González, F.J., Silva-Rodríguez, J., Paredes-Pacheco, J., Niñerola-Baizán, A., Efthimiou, N., Martín-Martín, C., & Aguiar, P. (2020). Intensity normalization methods in brain FDG-PET quantification. *Neuroimage*, *222*, 117229.

[15] Salvatore, C., Cerasa, A., Battista, P., Gilardi, M.C., Quattrone, A., & Castiglioni, I. (2015). Magnetic resonance imaging biomarkers for the early diagnosis of Alzheimer's disease: a machine learning approach. *Frontiers in Neuroscience*, *9*, 307.

[16] Liu, L., Zhao, S., Chen, H., & Wang, A. (2020). A new machine learning method for identifying Alzheimer's disease. *Simulation Modelling Practice and Theory*, *99*, 102023.

[17] Zhang, Y., & Wang, S. (2015). Detection of Alzheimer's disease by displacement field and machine learning. *Peer J*, *3*, e1251.

[18] Mirzaei, G., Adeli, A., & Adeli, H. (2016). Imaging and machine learning techniques for diagnosis of Alzheimer's disease. *Reviews in the Neurosciences*, *27*(8), 857–870.

[19] Khazaee, A., Ebrahimzadeh, A., & Babajani-Feremi, A. (2016). Application of advanced machine learning methods on resting-state fMRI network for identification of mild cognitive impairment and Alzheimer's disease. *Brain Imaging and Behavior*, *10*(3), 799–817.

[20] Payan, A., & Montana, G. (2015). Predicting Alzheimer's disease: a neuroimaging study with 3D convolutional neural networks. *arXiv preprint arXiv:1502.02506*.

[21] Dakka, J., Bashivan, P., Gheiratmand, M., Rish, I., Jha, S., & Greiner, R. (2017). Learning neural markers of schizophrenia disorder using recurrent neural networks. *arXiv preprint arXiv:1712.00512*.

[22] Basaia, S., Agosta, F., Wagner, L., Canu, E., Magnani, G., Santangelo, R., & Alzheimer's Disease Neuroimaging Initiative (2019). Automated classification of Alzheimer's disease and mild cognitive impairment using a single MRI and deep neural networks. *NeuroImage: Clinical*, *21*, 101645.

[23] Spasov, S., Passamonti, L., Duggento, A., Lio, P., Toschi, N., & Alzheimer's Disease Neuroimaging Initiative (2019). A parameter-efficient deep learning approach to predict conversion from mild cognitive impairment to Alzheimer's disease. *Neuroimage, 189*, 276–287.

[24] Ramzan, F., Khan, M.U.G., Rehmat, A., Iqbal, S., Saba, T., Rehman, A., & Mehmood, Z. (2020). A deep learning approach for automated diagnosis and multi-class classification of Alzheimer's disease stages using resting-state fMRI and residual neural networks. *Journal of Medical Systems, 44*(2), 1–16.

[25] Zeng, L.L., Wang, H., Hu, P., Yang, B., Pu, W., Shen, H., & Hu, D. (2018). Multisite diagnostic classification of schizophrenia using discriminant deep learning with functional connectivity MRI. *EBioMedicine, 30*, 74–85.

[26] Lee, G., Nho, K., Kang, B., Sohn, K.A., & Kim, D. (2019). Predicting Alzheimer's disease progression using multi-modal deep learning approach. *Scientific Reports, 9*(1), 1–12.

[27] Liu, S., Liu, S., Cai, W., Pujol, S., Kikinis, R., & Feng, D. (2014). Early diagnosis of Alzheimer's disease with deep learning. In: *2014 IEEE 11th International Symposium on Biomedical Imaging (ISBI)* (pp. 1015–1018). Beijing, China. IEEE. doi: 10.1109/ISBI.2014.6868045.

[28] Sarraf, S., & Tofighi, G. (2016). Deep learning-based pipeline to recognize Alzheimer's disease using fMRI data. *2016 Future Technologies Conference (FTC)* (pp. 816–820). San Francisco, USA. IEEE. doi: 10.1109/FTC.2016.7821697.

[29] Gunduz, H. (2019). Deep learning-based Parkinson's disease classification using vocal feature sets In: *IEEE Access*, Duzee, Turkey, vol. 7, pp. 115540–115551, doi: 10.1109/ACCESS.2019.2936564.

[30] Vásquez-Correa, J.C., Arias-Vergara, T., Orozco-Arroyave, J.R., Eskofier, B., Klucken, J., & Nöth, E. (2019). Multimodal assessment of Parkinson's disease: a deep learning approach. In: *IEEE Journal of Biomedical and Health Informatics, 23*(4), 1618–1630, doi: 10.1109/JBHI.2018.2866873.

[31] Jahan, N., Nesa, A., & Layek, M.A. (2021). Parkinson's disease detection using CNN architectures with transfer learning. In: *2021 International Conference on Innovative Computing, Intelligent Communication and Smart Electrical Systems (ICSES)* (pp. 1–5). Chennai, India. IEEE. doi: 10.1109/ICSES52305.2021.9633872.

[32] Chaihtra, D., & Vijaya Shetty, S. (2021). Alzheimer's disease detection from brain MRI data using deep learning techniques. In: *2021 2nd Global Conference for Advancement in Technology (GCAT)* (pp. 1–5). Bangalore, India. IEEE. doi: 10.1109/GCAT52182.2021.9587756.

[33] Boppana, L., Shabnam, N., & Srivatsava, T. (2021). Deep learning approach for an early stage detection of neurodevelopmental disorders. In: *2021 IEEE 9th Region 10 Humanitarian Technology Conference (R10-HTC)* (pp. 1–6). Bangalore, India. IEEE. doi: 10.1109/R10-HTC53172.2021.9641691.

[34] Oh, S.L., Vicnesh, J., Ciaccio, E., Yuvaraj, R., & Acharya, U.R. (2019). Deep convolutional neural network model for automated diagnosis of schizophrenia using EEG signals. *Applied Sciences, 9*(14), 2870, 10.3390/app9142870.

[35] Han, S., Huang, W., Zhang, Y., Zhao, J., & Chen, H. (2017). Recognition of early-onset schizophrenia using deep-learning method. *Applied Informatics, 4*, 10.1186/s40535–017–0044–3.

3 Classification of the Level of Alzheimer's Disease Using Anatomical Magnetic Resonance Images Based on a Novel Deep Learning Structure

Saif Al-Jumaili, Athar Al-Azzawi, and Osman Nuri Uçan
Altınbas University

Adil Deniz Duru
Marmara University

CONTENTS

DOI: 10.1201/9781003315452-3

3.1   ORGANIZATION OF THE CHAPTER

Chapter 3 is structured as follows, starting with the Abstract of the research. In the following section, a literature review is presented to explain the current implementations of deep learning techniques on Alzheimer's disease. This section is followed by the Motivation and Contribution sections. Then, technical information about the implementation is described in the Materials and Methods section. This section includes the mathematical primitives of the evaluation metrics. The Results and Discussion sections consist of the findings and the comparison of these findings with the current literature, respectively. In the Conclusion part, mechanical structure of the deep learning and the implementation results are emphasized. Finally, the Future Scope part is proposed.

3.2   INTRODUCTION

Alzheimer's disease (AD) is a chronic progressive neurodegenerative disease that affects the elderly and has a significant effect on brain degeneration, cognitive functions, quality of life, memory functions, and progressive dementia [1]. Based on the World Health Organization (WHO) report, AD is ranked the fifth leading cause of death. The number of deaths will be increasing exponentially to approximately 152 million by 2050 [2]. Until now the etiology of AD is still vague, and there are no specific drugs that can treat dementia completely [3]. While the first stage before the patient has categorized, an AD is mild cognitive impairment (MCI) which is the middle between normal aging and AD [4].

Based on the American Academy of Neurology, about 15% of patients who show symptoms of the initial stage (MCI) may eventually have AD [5], while just 2% of all patients suffer from normal aging. Regrettably, because of the difficulty to understand AD by patients and people around them, the patients suffer from different stages such as (moderate and severe), till the time of discovering they have AD which leads to missing the perfect time of intervention [6]. Thus, it is very important to identify the AD at the early stage as possible. Normally, the doctors make some medical tests for patients such as neuroimaging and neuropsychological examinations to recognize dementia at the early stage and how much develops, which is an essential stage to start the treatment and restrain it from getting worse [6].

From a computer science view, one of the most important technologies that can help doctors to observe patients with AD is the neuroimage, which can show the characteristic change in the brain including prodromal and pre-symptomatic states, which can provide more information to get an accurate diagnosis [7]. Many neuroimaging techniques have been introduced to detect AD such as magnetic resonance imaging (MRI) [8], MRI voxel-level [9,10], computed tomography (CT) [11], and positron emission tomography (PET) [12–14]. CT is a technique that combines different types of X-ray images from multiple angles to create three-dimensional (3D) images [15]. The advantage is low cost and rapid test, whereas, the quality of images generated to the medial temporal lobe is not good enough to diagnose MCI accurately [16]. PET can provide reliable information about the distribution of positron nuclide markers for metabolic processes [17]. The use of MRI enables us to achieve high-resolution 3D brain tissue images [18–20]. Thus, it is widely used in clinical tests of AD.

One can use the advantage of deep learning in medical image diagnosis for several types of diseases [21]. Especially, convolutional neural networks (CNNs) have varying usages such as classification [22,23], recognition [24], and segmentation [25,26]. It can extract the intricate features from the images to diagnose Covid-19 [27,28], breast cancer [29], AD [22], histology images [30], tumor detection [31], etc.

There are many papers published to classify and detect the early stage of AD. Since there is no existing remedy that can recover and cure the brain, it is extremely important to detect AD in the elderly, especially at the MCI [32]. In particular, different types of methods are proposed to classify AD using neuroimaging techniques and deep learning. Among these proposed methods, Suriya Murugan et al. [33] balanced the dataset with the synthetic minority over-sampling technique in a new CNN model to perform AD classification.

In another study, Fuadah et al. [34] proposed a method based on the pre-trained network model of AlexNet to classify MR images of AD of subjects. Moreover, Zhu et al. [35] proposed a new method based on anatomical landmarks and performed a CNN model for the classification. Similar to that study, Taher M. Ghazal et al. [36] proposed a system that can be used for the detection of Alzheimer's disease by using an MRI dataset. The backbone of the system utilizes a CNN; they applied a pre-trained network that was AlexNet. The highest accuracy reached was 91%.

Likewise, Ahmed Abdullah Farid et al. [37] applied a two-step approach; a composite hybrid feature selection method to reduce the features and increase the accuracy and a hybrid classification technique by combining JRip and random forest classifiers. In addition to the previous studies, Shereen A. El-Aal and Neveen I. Ghali [38] used two types of pre-trained models (ResNet-101 and DenseNet-201) to extract features from MRI images of Alzheimer's and then utilized two types of an optimal subset (Rival Genetic algorithm [RGA] and Pbest-Guide Binary Particle Swarm Optimization [PBPSO]) to improve classification accuracy further. Furthermore, Suganthe et al. [39] proposed to use a hybrid deep learning convolutional neural network based on the Inception-ResNet-v2 architecture.

In addition, Badiea Abdulkarem Mohammed et al. [40] used two types of common CNN models (AlexNet and ResNet-50) to classify MRI datasets. The authors used the t-distributed stochastic neighbor embedding algorithm (t-SNE) to represent the dimensionality of features, and they applied different types of classifiers, namely support vector machine (SVM), decision tree, random forest, and K-nearest neighbors (KNNs).

Besides, Ben Nicholas et al. [41] compared different types of multiple feature descriptors such as local binary pattern (LBP), local wavelet pattern (LWP), histogram-oriented gradients (HOGs), and local bit plane decoded pattern (LBDP). Since many methods have been used in recent papers published to classify AD using MRI images, we summarized the ones that used CNN in Table 3.1.

TABLE 3.1

Summary previous papers published to classify AD using MRI images

Authors	Dimension	Data Type	Classes	Model	Accuracy (%)
Gunawardena et al. [42]	2D	MRI	4	2D-CNN	96.00
Jain et al. [43]	2D	MRI	3/binary	2D-CNN(Vgg16)	95.73
Hosseini et al. [44]	3D	MRI	3/Binary	3D-CNN	94.80
Korolev et al. [45]	3D	MRI	Binary	3D-CNN	80.00
Basheera et al. [46]	2D	MRI	3/Binary	2D-CNN	90.47
Yagis et al. [47]	3D	MRI	Binary	3D-CNN(Vgg16)	73.40
Oommen et al. [48]	2D	MRI	Binary	2D-CNN(Vgg19)	90.02
Sarraf et al. [49]	2D	MRI	Binary	2D-CNN(LeNet-5)	96.85
Wang et al. [50]	2D	MRI	Binary	2D-CNN	90.60
Pathak and Kundaram [51]	2D	MRI	3	2D-CNN	91.75
Pan et al. [52]	3D	MRI	Binary	3D-CNN	89.00
Forouzannezhad et al. [53]	2D	MRI	Binary	2DCNN	73.10
Escudero et al. [54]	2D	MRI	Binary	SVM	89.20
Altaf et al. [55]	2D MRI	MRI	3/Binary	SVM	97.80
Li et al. [56]	3D	MRI	Binary	3D-CNN	88.31
Kim et al. [57]	3D	MRI	Binary	Hierarchical	92.10
Payan and Montana [58]	3D	MRI	Binary	3D-CNN	95.39
Adaszewski et al. [59]	2D	MRI	4	SVM	80.30
Tong et al. [60]	2D	MRI and PET	3	Nonlinear graph fusion	91.00
Ahmed et al. [61]	2D	MRI	Binary	SVM	83.70
Ge et al. [62]	3D	MRI	Binary	3D-CNN	94.74
Hosseini-Asl et al. [63]	3D	MRI	3	3D-CNN	97.60
Tong et al. [64]	2D	MIR	Binary	Multiple instance learning	88.80

3.2.1 MOTIVATION

Based on the aforementioned papers, the accuracy values obtained in the previous studies were fairly acceptable. Thus, we tried to increase the accuracy further by developing a novel method using deep convolution neural network to classify four levels of AD based on the MRI. The dataset used is publicly available on Kaggle that consists of more than 5,000 images.

3.2.2 CONTRIBUTION

As a novelty, in the development part, we designed a novel deep learning structure that can extract features from MRI and classify them. Moreover, our design enables shrinking the number of layers and reduces the computational cost. Furthermore, Reduce Atmospheric Haze technique has been implemented on

MRI. The strength of the model lies in three main advantages; first, a small number of layers with high-accuracy results, second, high ability to concentrate on the region that has the most features and suppress irrelevant regions in images, and third, it reduces the computational burden. Thus, the accuracy obtained was perfect compared with state-of-the-art methods.

3.3   MATERIALS AND METHODS

3.3.1   DATASET

In this section, we explain the dataset type that we used to classify AD. The dataset consists of an axial slice of MRI images. The dataset is formed by four types of category classes (non, very mild, mild, and moderate). The dataset is divided randomly into training and testing with ratio of 90%–10%. Training data has around 5,121 images, and testing data has 1,279 images. Figure 3.1 illustrates a sample of the four classes that we used in this study. The dataset is publicly available on Kaggle [65].

3.3.2   PROPOSED METHOD

3.3.2.1   Images Processing

This section presents the structure of the model that we developed to detect and classify four early types of Alzheimer's disease. The diagram of the model is shown in Figure 3.2. Before the implementation of the data into the model, all images underwent two stages of preprocessing. The first one was to resize all the images (train and test) to have a size of 224×224×3. To increase the accuracy further, we applied Reduce Atmospheric Haze technique called imreducehaze which is a combination of two different types of dehazing algorithms, simpledcp and approxdcp. The "simpledcp" is a method that uses per-pixel dark channel assessment of the haze, and then uses a quadtree decomposition which can help to assess the atmospheric light. After that, the second part of the algorithm, namely "approxdcp," was applied using only per-pixel and spatial blocks to compute the dark channel. The result of reducing atmospheric haze makes all images sharper.

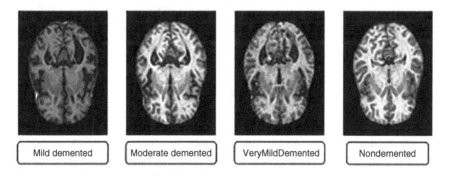

| Mild demented | Moderate demented | VeryMildDemented | Nondemented |

FIGURE 3.1   Sample AD MRI.

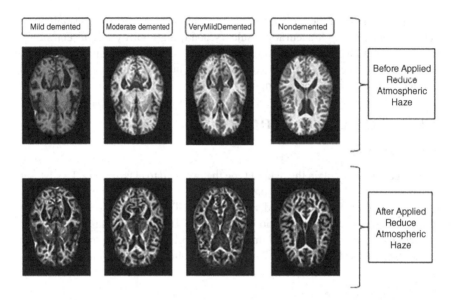

FIGURE 3.2   MRI images before and after "Reduce Atmospheric Haze" techniques.

3.3.2.2 CNN Design

The advantages of using deep learning in medical fields are plentiful. It uses several types of medical images for classification of several types of diseases. The architecture of CNN is based on layers, where each has an individual learning mechanism. CNN is a hierarchical learning technique that is based on the raw input images. The traditional architecture of CNN is divided into two major concepts. The former one is feature extraction, while the latter is classification. The aim is to extract features using several types of layers from the given input images. The extracted features will be redirected to the classifier in order to split it into its class. There are essential steps in CNN algorithms, the first step is called "convolution," which enables us to find features and perform filters. Whereas strides and the number of filters are considered most important among the parameters that play an essential role in obtaining the convolutional operation output; stride is defined as the distance between two pixels, and the number of filters represents the features map number [66]. The mathematical operation of convolution on two functions is given in Eq. (3.1) [67].

$$H(t) = \int_{-\infty}^{\infty} f(T)G(t-T)dT \tag{3.1}$$

where convolution between two functions referred to as $H = f * G$.

The mechanism of the convolution operation is shown in Figure 3.3. The process mechanism of convolution is regarded as the Hadamard product (element-wise).

As shown in Figure 3.4, our proposed method consists of six blocks of convolution layers. Each block has a convolution layer, batch normalization layer,

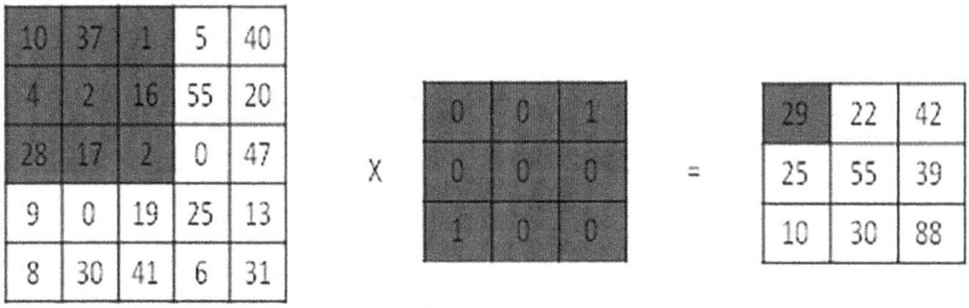

10	37	1	5	40
4	2	16	55	20
28	17	2	0	47
9	0	19	25	13
8	30	41	6	31

X

0	0	1
0	0	0
1	0	0

=

29	22	42
25	55	39
10	30	88

FIGURE 3.3 Kernel used in the proposed method for feature extraction in convolutional layers.

clipped ReLU layer, and MaxPooling layer. The first one starts from the left upper, where the kernel matrix we used was 3×3, fixed for all convolution layers. Next, the process continues with the kernel matrix 3×3 shifted one column to the right because of the stride set (1×1). This process is repeated to cover all the image input. To speed training and reduce the sensitivity to the network, we used batch normalization techniques. It standardizes inputs which makes an effect of stabilizing the learning process and decreases the number of epochs in the model.

In the convolution layer, there are different types of activation functions used as rectified linear unit (ReLU), leaky ReLU, sigmoid, Maxout, exponential linear unit (ELU), and tan$h$. The activation function works in the conversion of the input data from linear to nonlinear. ReLU is considered one of the most common activation functions that were recently used. To prevent the output from becoming larger, we applied a clipped rectified linear unit (clippedReluLayer) that has a thresholding method. We applied MaxPooling with stride (2×2) that can reduce the dimensionality and retain the important information of features extracted. Moreover, applying MaxPooling provided the highest possible average value through the pooling. In the classification part, after all features were extracted by convolution layers, we fed features into the three blocks of fully connected layers where each one was followed by a dropout layer to prevent overfitting. Finally, we used a fully connected layer followed by SoftMax layer and classification layer.

3.3.3 Evaluation Metrics

We used several evaluation metrics to check the performance of our proposed model based on the confusion matrix outcome from different types of tests after 30 rounds. We averaged the accuracy, sensitivity, and specificity over 30 rounds. Accuracy is calculated as the number of correct predictions from the whole dataset as shown in Eq. (3.2). The recall or sensitivity is calculated as the number of correct positive predictions from the total positive number as shown in Eq. (3.3). Precision or confidence is the rate of correct number that can be expected as positive to the total number of expected positives as shown in Eq. (3.4). The combination of precision and recall means a harmonic which is also called F1-score

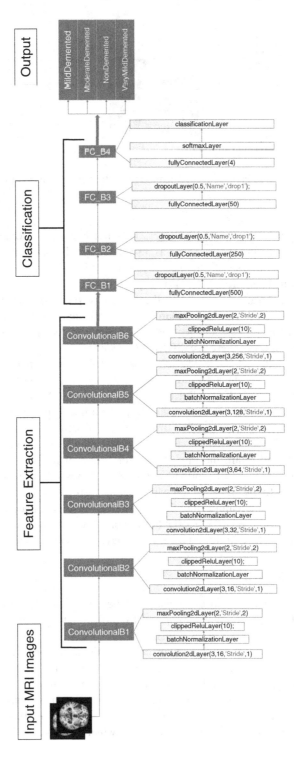

FIGURE 3.4 Block diagram that shows the proposed model. There are six blocks of convolutional layers; convolution layer, batch normalization layer, clipped ReLU layer, and MaxPooling layer.

that illustrated the balance of precision and recall as shown in Eq. (3.5). F1-score reassured to get a perfect impression about the results we achieved.

We used the outcomes from the confusion matrix to calculate the evaluation metrics, whereas the true positive (TP) denotes the number of positive values classified correctly from the validation data. The true negative (TN) indicates the number of the negative values classified correctly from the validation data. Whereas the false positive (FP) denotes the number of positive values classified wrongly from the validation data. The final value used is a false negative (FN), which refers to the number of negative values that are falsely classified.

$$\text{Accuracy} = \frac{TP + TN}{TP + FP + TN + FN} \tag{3.2}$$

$$\text{Recall} = \text{Sensitivity} = \frac{TP}{TP + FN} \tag{3.3}$$

$$\text{Precision} = \text{Confidence} = \frac{TP}{TP + Fp} \tag{3.4}$$

$$F1 - \text{score} = \frac{2 \times TP}{2 \times TP + FP + FN} \tag{3.5}$$

3.4   RESULTS

The main idea behind this study was to classify four different stages of AD based on the MRI images. The CNN was the backbone of our model proposed. The architecture of the proposed model consists of six blocks for extracting discriminatory features from MRI images and five blocks for classification of the most relevant features of the four stages as shown in Figure 3.4. We trained and tested our model 30 times to check the results from the proposed method to verify the accuracy, efficiency, and efficacy (with a fixed epoch size of 20). Figure 3.5 shows all accuracy results that we achieved after implementing 30 times (training and testing). Based on these results, the proposed model yielded superior results to classify an Alzheimer's disease using MRI images.

More specifically, based on the confusion matrix that we achieved from 30 times (training and testing) to the proposed model and to be more precise for each round, we used several types of performance evaluation criteria. As shown in Table 3.2, every round (train and test) was evaluated. All the results obtained were perfect for the classification of four stages of AD. The highest value results achieved were 100% for all evaluation criteria within rounds R1, R8, R18, R22, and R26, respectively, whereas all other rounds obtained acceptable accuracies which were over 99%. In the precision results, the highest result value achieved was 100%, whereas in the R17 and R20, the lowest performance was obtained within 97%. Recall and F1-scores were also obtained successfully (100%) in different rounds, however, the lowest results were in R23 as 89% and 92%, respectively.

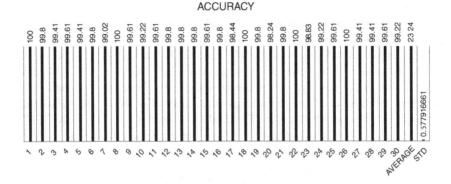

FIGURE 3.5   Accuracy results of 30 different.

Deep transfer learning has been used for classifying different types of diseases. So, we implemented two common types of deep transfer learning methods (GoogleNet and VGG16). And we compared them with our model results. In Table 3.3, we have shown that our method still obtained superior results.

To evaluate the model performance in an intuitive way, gradient-weighted class activation mapping (Grad-CAM) or (HeatMap) was used, which can provide a visual performance of the model exactly where the model has extracted features from the MRI images. It represents how accurate the model is in terms of extracting accurate features compared with other methods that were applied using the same MRI images. The red color represents the utmost important regions that the model used to extract discriminatory features that can aid in the classification decision that is used in the model. As shown in Figure 3.6, it is obvious that our model concentrates on the regions inside the image that can provide accurate features to classification compared with the GoogleNet and VGG16.

3.5   DISCUSSION

In this study, we designed a novel deep learning structure that will increase the accuracy of the classification of different stages of AD. As shown in the result section, we trained and tested our model 30 times to ensure of the outcome. The reason for our obtained astonishing results can be summarized as follows; first, we used a batch normalizing technique that keep the expressivity of our proposed model and that able to fix the issue which can be happened during training and affected by the change of layers. Second, we solved overfitting by using dropout techniques that can shrink the neural network.

For the sake of a clear view, Table 3.3 shows a comparison of the results achieved by the proposed method to the two pre-trained models namely GoogleNet and VGG16, although the pre-trained models have many layers, but the results were somewhat acceptable, it was of 93.7% and 92.4%, respectively, whereas our method increased classification accuracy by at least 7% compared with the pre-trained models.

TABLE 3.2

Results achieved for 30 times implementation

Round	Accuracy	Precision	Recall	F1
R1	100	100	100	100
R2	99.9	99.72	100	99.75
R3	99.61	99.5	99	99
R4	99.8	99.75	99.25	99.75
R5	99.7	99.75	94.25	96.75
R6	99.9	100	99.75	99.75
R7	99.51	99.25	98.5	98.75
R8	100	100	100	100
R9	99.8	99.25	99.75	99.75
R10	99.61	99	99	99
R11	99.8	99.75	99.75	99.75
R12	99.9	100	99.75	99.75
R13	99.9	100	99.75	99.75
R14	99.9	100	99.75	99.75
R15	99.8	99.25	99.5	99.75
R16	99.71	99.25	99.5	99.25
R17	99.22	97.75	98.75	98.25
R18	100	100	100	100
R19	99.9	100	99.75	99.75
R20	99	97.25	98.25	100
R21	99.9	100	99.75	99.75
R22	100	100	100	100
R23	99.41	98	89.5	92.5
R24	99.61	99.5	98.5	99
R25	99.8	99.75	99.25	99.75
R26	100	100	100	100
R27	99.7	99.25	99.5	99.25
R28	99.7	99.75	99	99.25
R29	99.8	99.75	99.25	99.75
R30	99.61	99	99	99

Finally, there are many different types of papers published to classify AD, but comparing results with other papers is related to different types of criteria such as the number of subjects, number of images, modality type used, etc. So, in order to be more precise and more reassured, we compared our result with other methods that were published recently; they used the same MRI images dataset. In comparison, only 12 state of the art used the same dataset with applied different approaches, whereas most papers published the focus was on using pre-trained models and others proposed new models; the accuracies were 79%, 94%, 99%, and 70%, receptively [38-40-68-69]. And even for the papers that proposed a new model, our model outperforms them with all evaluation metrics [1-41-70-71].

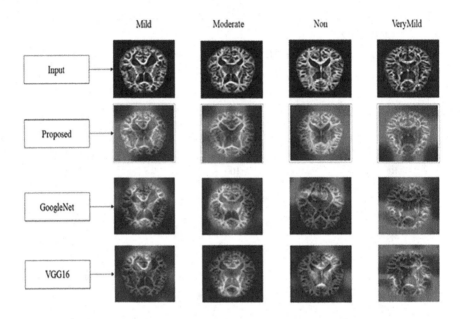

FIGURE 3.6 Comparison of our model using grad-cam visualization method with different types of deep transfer model, where the mild = mild demented, moderate = moderate demented, non = nondemented, and very mild = very mild demented.

TABLE 3.3
Comparison of deep transfer learning with our model results

Method	Accuracy
VGG16	92.4
GoogleNet	93.7
Proposed	99.46

Also, we compared our model with papers that used two classes to classify AD; it can be clearly stated that 2D-DCNN obtained higher results in all evaluation metrics they obtained [72] and [73]. As shown in Table 3.4, our model obviously produced an excellent performance compared with other methodologies.

As shown in Table 3.4, our model obviously produced an excellent performance compared with other methodology.

3.6 CONCLUSION

AD as a neurodegenerative disease leads to intellectual disability, which is called dementia. So far, no remedy or medical treatment has been discovered to recover

TABLE 3.4

Compare our results with other results that were recently published in the literature using a similar dataset

Authors	Dataset	Number of Classes	Accuracy	Recall	Precision	F1-Score
Suganthe [39]	Kaggle	4	79	28.22	70.64	39.91
Shuang Liang [1]	Dataset	4	99	99.5	99.63	99.61
Manu Subramoniam [68]	[65]	4	99	NV	NV	NV
Mohammed [40]		4	94	98	97.75	96
Murugan [33]		4	95.23	95	96	95.27
Nicholas [41]		4	91	85.32	74.1	78.3
Shereen A El-Aal [38]		4	94	91	96	93
Mggdadi [69]		4	70	NV	NV	NV
Islam [70]		4	73	NV	NV	NV
Rajawat [71]		4	99.3	NV	NV	99.5
Shahwar [72]		2	97.3	92	89	87
Olabi [73]		2	75	84	NV	NV
Proposed		4	99.74	99.48	98.93	99.22

from dementia. The disease goes through different stages of development, where detecting AD in early stages plays a valuable role to prevent the progress and development of AD. That is why scientists use several types of deep learning methodology in order to find a method that can provide accurate results to detect and classify AD using MRI or PET data. The CNN is one of the parts of deep learning, that is extensively used to classify neurological diseases. It has the ability to intricate and discern subtle patterns. Thus, we used CNN in our study to develop a new method that provides a high-accuracy result. In this study, we used 2D MRI images to classify four early stages of AD, which consist of more than 6,400 images. Based on the experimental results and validation of our proposed model and with a holistic view analysis of the model, we trained and validated our model 30 times. Our model outperformed two models of deep transfer learning namely GoogleNet and VGG16. The results indicate that our proposed method can provide aid to health sector by diagnosing the people that suffer from AD at the early stages.

3.7 FUTURE SCOPES

For future work, we plan to use a different type of deep learning mechanism by applying a quantum convolutional neural network to MRI images to classify the multiclass AD stages and increase the number of images and compare the result with a classical convolutional neural network.

REFERENCES

[1] S. Liang, and Y. Gu, "Computer-aided diagnosis of Alzheimer's disease through weak supervision deep learning framework with attention mechanism," *Sensors*, vol. 21, no. 1, p. 220, 2021.

[2] D. Australia, S. Baker, and S. Banerjee, "Alzheimer's disease international. World Alzheimer Report 2019: attitudes to dementia," *Alzheimer's Disease International; Alzheimer's Disease International*: London, UK, 2019.

[3] A. D. Korczyn, "Why have we failed to cure Alzheimer's disease?" *Journal of Alzheimer's Disease*, vol. 29, no. 2, pp. 275–282, 2012.

[4] A. M. Sanford, "Mild cognitive impairment," *Clinics in Geriatric Medicine*, vol. 33, no. 3, pp. 325–337, 2017.

[5] R. C. Petersen, J. C. Stevens, M. Ganguli, E. G. Tangalos, J. L. Cummings, and S. T. DeKosky, "Practice parameter: early detection of dementia: mild cognitive impairment (an evidence-based review): report of the quality standards subcommittee of the American Academy of Neurology," *Neurology*, vol. 56, no. 9, pp. 1133–1142, 2001.

[6] A. Alberdi, A. Aztiria, and A. Basarab, "On the early diagnosis of Alzheimer's disease from multimodal signals: a survey," *Artificial Intelligence in Medicine*, vol. 71, pp. 1–29, 2016.

[7] S. Trombella, F. Assal, D. Zekry, G. Gold, P. Giannakopoulos, V. Garibotto, J.-F. Démonet, and G. B. Frisoni, "Brain imaging of Alzheimer'disease: state of the art and perspectives for clinicians," *Revue Medicale Suisse*, vol. 12, no. 515, pp. 795–798, 2016.

[8] J. Venugopalan, L. Tong, H. R. Hassanzadeh, and M. D. Wang, "Multimodal deep learning models for early detection of Alzheimer's disease stage," *Scientific Reports*, vol. 11, no. 1, pp. 1–13, 2021.

[9] V. Jayanthi, B. C. Simon, and D. Baskar, "Alzheimer's disease classification using deep learning, " *Computational Intelligence and Its Applications in Healthcare*, pp. 157–173: Elsevier, 2020.

[10] C. Yang, A. Rangarajan, and S. Ranka, "Visual explanations from deep 3D convolutional neural networks for Alzheimer's disease classification." In *AMIA Annual Symposium Proceedings*, vol. 2018, p. 1571, 2018.

[11] P. Scheltens, "Imaging in Alzheimer's disease," *Dialogues in Clinical Neuroscience*, vol. 11, no. 2, p. 191, 2009.

[12] B. Dubois, H. H. Feldman, C. Jacova, H. Hampel, J. L. Molinuevo, K. Blennow, S. T. DeKosky, S. Gauthier, D. Selkoe, and R. Bateman, "Advancing research diagnostic criteria for Alzheimer's disease: the IWG-2 criteria," *The Lancet Neurology*, vol. 13, no. 6, pp. 614–629, 2014.

[13] M. Liu, D. Zhang, and D. Shen, "Relationship induced multi-template learning for diagnosis of Alzheimer's disease and mild cognitive impairment," *IEEE Transactions on Medical Imaging*, vol. 35, no. 6, pp. 1463–1474, 2016.

[14] M. A. Ebrahimighahnavieh, S. Luo, and R. Chiong, "Deep learning to detect Alzheimer's disease from neuroimaging: a systematic literature review," *Computer Methods and Programs in Biomedicine*, vol. 187, p. 105242, 2020.

[15] J. Beaulieu, and P. Dutilleul, "Applications of computed tomography (CT) scanning technology in forest research: a timely update and review," *Canadian Journal of Forest Research*, vol. 49, no. 10, pp. 1173–1188, 2019.

[16] B. Zhang, G.-j. Gu, H. Jiang, Y. Guo, X. Shen, B. Li, and W. Zhang, "The value of whole-brain CT perfusion imaging and CT angiography using a 320-slice CT scanner in the diagnosis of MCI and AD patients," *European Radiology*, vol. 27, no. 11, pp. 4756–4766, 2017.

[17] C. R. Jack Jr, H. J. Wiste, C. G. Schwarz, V. J. Lowe, M. L. Senjem, P. Vemuri, S. D. Weigand, T. M. Therneau, D. S. Knopman, and J. L. Gunter, "Longitudinal tau PET in ageing and Alzheimer's disease," *Brain*, vol. 141, no. 5, pp. 1517–1528, 2018.

[18] I. Domingues, G. Pereira, P. Martins, H. Duarte, J. Santos, and P. H. Abreu, "Using deep learning techniques in medical imaging: a systematic review of applications on CT and PET," *Artificial Intelligence Review*, vol. 53, no. 6, pp. 4093–4160, 2020.

[19] S. Debette, S. Schilling, M.-G. Duperron, S. C. Larsson, and H. S. Markus, "Clinical significance of magnetic resonance imaging markers of vascular brain injury: a systematic review and meta-analysis," *JAMA Neurology*, vol. 76, no. 1, pp. 81–94, 2019.

[20] G. Battineni, N. Chintalapudi, F. Amenta, and E. Traini, "A comprehensive machine-learning model applied to magnetic resonance imaging (MRI) to predict Alzheimer's disease (AD) in older subjects," *Journal of Clinical Medicine*, vol. 9, no. 7, p. 2146, 2020.

[21] J. B. Bae, S. Lee, W. Jung, S. Park, W. Kim, H. Oh, J. W. Han, G. E. Kim, J. S. Kim, and J. H. Kim, "Identification of Alzheimer's disease using a convolutional neural network model based on T1-weighted magnetic resonance imaging," *Scientific Reports*, vol. 10, no. 1, pp. 1–10, 2020.

[22] F. E. Al-Khuzaie, O. Bayat, and A. D. Duru, "Diagnosis of Alzheimer disease using 2D MRI slices by convolutional neural network," *Applied Bionics and Biomechanics*, vol. 2021, no. 2, p. 9, 2021.

[23] D. Agarwal, G. Marques, I. de la Torre-Díez, M. A. Franco Martin, B. García Zapiraín, and F. Martín Rodríguez, "Transfer learning for Alzheimer's disease through neuroimaging biomarkers: a systematic review," *Sensors*, vol. 21, no. 21, p. 7259, 2021.

[24] S. Sarraf and G. Tofighi, "Deep learning-based pipeline to recognize Alzheimer's disease using fMRI data." In *2016 Future Technologies Conference* (FTC), pp. 816–820, IEEE, San Francisco, CA, USA, 2016.

[25] X. Chen, L. Li, A. Sharma, G. Dhiman, and S. Vimal, "The application of convolutional neural network model in diagnosis and nursing of MR imaging in Alzheimer's disease," *Interdisciplinary Sciences: Computational Life Sciences*, vol. 14, no. 1, pp. 34–44, 2021.

[26] N. Yamanakkanavar, J. Y. Choi, and B. Lee, "MRI segmentation and classification of human brain using deep learning for diagnosis of Alzheimer's disease: a survey," *Sensors*, vol. 20, no. 11, p. 3243, 2020.

[27] S. Al-Jumaili, A. D. Duru, and O. N. Uçan, "Covid-19 Ultrasound image classification using SVM based on kernels deduced from Convolutional neural network." In *2021 5th International Symposium on Multidisciplinary Studies and Innovative Technologies (ISMSIT)*, IEEE, Ankara, Turkey, pp. 429–433.

[28] S. Al-Jumaili, A. Al-Azzawi, A. D. Duru, and A. A. Ibrahim, "Covid-19 X-ray image classification using SVM based on Local Binary Pattern." In *2021 5th International Symposium on Multidisciplinary Studies and Innovative Technologies (ISMSIT)*, IEEE, Ankara, Turkey, pp. 383–387.

[29] S. R. A. Ahmed, O. N. UÇAN, A. D. Duru, and O. Bayat, "Breast cancer detection and image evaluation using augmented deep convolutional neural networks," *Aurum Journal of Engineering Systems and Architecture*, vol. 2, no. 2, pp. 121–129, 2018.

[30] A. Echle, N. T. Rindtorff, T. J. Brinker, T. Luedde, A. T. Pearson, and J. N. Kather, "Deep learning in cancer pathology: a new generation of clinical biomarkers," *British Journal of Cancer*, vol. 124, no. 4, pp. 686–696, 2021.

[31] J. S. Paul, A. J. Plassard, B. A. Landman, and D. Fabbri, "Deep learning for brain tumor classification." In *Medical Imaging 2017: Biomedical Applications in Molecular, Structural, and Functional Imaging*, SPIE, vol. 10137, pp. 253–268, 2017.

[32] G. Lee, K. Nho, B. Kang, K.-A. Sohn, and D. Kim, "Predicting Alzheimer's disease progression using multi-modal deep learning approach," *Scientific Reports*, vol. 9, no. 1, pp. 1–12, 2019.

[33] S. Murugan, C. Venkatesan, M. Sumithra, X.-Z. Gao, B. Elakkiya, M. Akila, and S. Manoharan, "DEMNET: a deep learning model for early diagnosis of Alzheimer diseases and dementia from MR images," *IEEE Access*, vol. 9, pp. 90319–90329, 2021.

[34] Y. Fu'adah, I. Wijayanto, N. Pratiwi, F. Taliningsih, S. Rizal, and M. Pramudito, "Automated classification of Alzheimer's disease based on MRI image processing using convolutional neural network (CNN) with AlexNet architecture." *Journal of Physics: Conference Series*, vol. 1844, IOP Publishing Ltd, p. 012020.

[35] T. Zhu, C. Cao, Z. Wang, G. Xu, and J. Qiao, "Anatomical landmarks and DAG network learning for Alzheimer's disease diagnosis," *IEEE Access*, vol. 8, pp. 206063–206073, 2020.

[36] T. M. Ghazal, S. Abbas, S. Munir, M. Khan, M. Ahmad, G. F. Issa, S. B. Zahra, M. A. Khan, and M. K. Hasan, "Alzheimer disease detection empowered with transfer learning," *Computers Materials and Continua*, vol. 70, no. 3, pp. 5005–5019, 2022.

[37] A. A. Farid, G. Selim, and H. Khater, "Applying artificial intelligence techniques for prediction of neurodegenerative disorders: a comparative case-study on clinical tests and neuroimaging tests with Alzheimer's disease," 2020.

[38] N. I. G. Shereen A El-Aal, "A proposed recognition system for Alzheimer's disease based on deep learning and optimization algorithms," *Journal of Southwest Jiaotong University*, vol. 56, no. 5, 2021.

[39] R. Suganthe, M. Geetha, G. Sreekanth, K. Gowtham, S. Deepakkumar, and R. Elango, "Multiclass classification of Alzheimer's disease using hybrid deep convolutional neural network," *NVEO-Natural Volatiles & Essential Oils*, vol. 8, no. 5, pp. 145–153, 2021.

[40] B. A. Mohammed, E. M. Senan, T. H. Rassem, N. M. Makbol, A. A. Alanazi, Z. G. Al-Mekhlafi, T. S. Almurayziq, and F. A. Ghaleb, "Multi-method analysis of medical records and MRI images for early diagnosis of dementia and Alzheimer's disease based on deep learning and hybrid methods," *Electronics*, vol. 10, no. 22, p. 2860, 2021.

[41] B. Nicholas, A. Jayakumar, B. Titus, and T. Remya Nair, "Comparative study of multiple feature descriptors for detecting the presence of Alzheimer's disease," *Ubiquitous Intelligent Systems*, pp. 331–339: Springer, 2022.

[42] K. Gunawardena, R. Rajapakse, and N. Kodikara, "Applying convolutional neural networks for pre-detection of Alzheimer's disease from structural MRI data." In *2017 24th International Conference on Mechatronics and Machine Vision in Practice (M2VIP)*, IEEE, Auckland, New Zealand, pp. 1–7.

[43] R. Jain, N. Jain, A. Aggarwal, and D. J. Hemanth, "Convolutional neural network based Alzheimer's disease classification from magnetic resonance brain images," *Cognitive Systems Research*, vol. 57, pp. 147–159, 2019.

[44] E. Hosseini-Asl, G. Gimel'farb, and A. El-Baz, "Alzheimer's disease diagnostics by a deeply supervised adaptable 3D convolutional network," *arXiv preprint arXiv:1607.00556*, 2016.

[45] S. Korolev, A. Safiullin, M. Belyaev, and Y. Dodonova, "Residual and plain convolutional neural networks for 3D brain MRI classification." In *2017 IEEE 14th International Symposium on Biomedical Imaging (ISBI 2017)* IEEE, Melbourne, VIC, Australia, pp. 835–838.

[46] S. Basheera, and M. S. S. Ram, "Convolution neural network–based Alzheimer's disease classification using hybrid enhanced independent component analysis based segmented gray matter of T2 weighted magnetic resonance imaging with clinical valuation," *Alzheimer's & Dementia: Translational Research & Clinical Interventions*, vol. 5, pp. 974–986, 2019.

[47] E. Yagis, L. Citi, S. Diciotti, C. Marzi, S. W. Atnafu, and A. G. S. De Herrera, "3D convolutional neural networks for diagnosis of Alzheimer's disease via structural MRI." In *2020 IEEE 33rd International Symposium on Computer-Based Medical Systems (CBMS)*, IEEE, Rochester, MN, USA, pp. 65–70.

[48] L. Oommen, S. Chandran, V. Prathapan, and P. Krishnapriya, "Early detection of Alzheimer's disease using deep learning techniques," *International Journal of Research in Engineering and Technology*, vol. 7, 2020.

[49] S. Sarraf, D. D. DeSouza, J. Anderson, and G. Tofighi, "DeepAD: Alzheimer's disease classification via deep convolutional neural networks using MRI and fMRI," *BioRxiv*, p. 070441, 2017.

[50] S. Wang, Y. Shen, W. Chen, T. Xiao, and J. Hu, "Automatic recognition of mild cognitive impairment from MRI images using expedited convolutional neural networks." In *International Conference on Artificial Neural Networks*, Springer, Cham, pp. 373–380.

[51] K. C. Pathak, and S. S. Kundaram, "Accuracy-based performance analysis of Alzheimer's disease classification using deep convolution neural network," *Soft Computing: Theories and Applications*, pp. 731–744: Springer, Singapore, 2020.

[52] D. Pan, A. Zeng, C. Zou, H. Rong, and X. Song, "Early detection of Alzheimer's disease using 3D convolutional neural networks," *Alzheimer's & Dementia*, vol. 17, p. e053169, 2021.

[53] P. Forouzannezhad, A. Abbaspour, C. Li, M. Cabrerizo, and M. Adjouadi, "A deep neural network approach for early diagnosis of mild cognitive impairment using multiple features." Orlando, FL, USA, pp. 1341–1346.

[54] J. Escudero, J. P. Zajicek, and E. Ifeachor, "Machine Learning classification of MRI features of Alzheimer's disease and mild cognitive impairment subjects to reduce the sample size in clinical trials." In *2011 Annual International Conference of the IEEE Engineering in Medicine and Biology Society*, IEEE, Boston, MA, USA, pp. 7957–7960.

[55] T. Altaf, S. M. Anwar, N. Gul, M. N. Majeed, and M. Majid, "Multi-class Alzheimer's disease classification using image and clinical features," *Biomedical Signal Processing and Control*, vol. 43, pp. 64–74, 2018.

[56] F. Li, D. Cheng, and M. Liu, "Alzheimer's disease classification based on combination of multi-model convolutional networks." In *2017 IEEE International Conference on Imaging Systems and Techniques (IST)*, IEEE, Beijing, China, pp. 1–5.

[57] J. P. Kim, J. Kim, Y. H. Park, S. B. Park, J. San Lee, S. Yoo, E.-J. Kim, H. J. Kim, D. L. Na, and J. A. Brown, "Machine learning based hierarchical classification of frontotemporal dementia and Alzheimer's disease," *NeuroImage: Clinical*, vol. 23, p. 101811, 2019.

[58] A. Payan, and G. Montana, "Predicting Alzheimer's disease: a neuroimaging study with 3D convolutional neural networks," *arXiv preprint arXiv:1502.02506*, 2015.

[59] S. Adaszewski, J. Dukart, F. Kherif, R. Frackowiak, B. Draganski, and A. s. D. N. Initiative, "How early can we predict Alzheimer's disease using computational anatomy?" *Neurobiology of Aging*, vol. 34, no. 12, pp. 2815–2826, 2013.

[60] T. Tong, K. Gray, Q. Gao, L. Chen, D. Rueckert, and A. s. D. N. Initiative, "multi-modal classification of Alzheimer's disease using nonlinear graph fusion," *Pattern Recognition*, vol. 63, pp. 171–181, 2017.

[61] O. B. Ahmed, M. Mizotin, J. Benois-Pineau, M. Allard, G. Catheline, C. B. Amar, and A. s. D. N. Initiative, "Alzheimer's disease diagnosis on structural MR images using circular harmonic functions descriptors on hippocampus and posterior cingulate cortex," *Computerized Medical Imaging and Graphics*, vol. 44, pp. 13–25, 2015.

[62] C. Ge, Q. Qu, I. Y.-H. Gu, and A. S. Jakola, "Multi-stream multi-scale deep convolutional networks for Alzheimer's disease detection using MR images," *Neurocomputing*, vol. 350, pp. 60–69, 2019.

[63] E. Hosseini-Asl, R. Keynton, and A. El-Baz, "Alzheimer's disease diagnostics by adaptation of 3D convolutional network." In *2016 IEEE International Conference on Imaging Processing (ICIP)*, IEEE, Phoenix, AZ, USA, pp. 126–130.

[64] T. Tong, R. Wolz, Q. Gao, R. Guerrero, J. V. Hajnal, D. Rueckert, and A. s. D. N. Initiative, "Multiple instance learning for classification of dementia in brain MRI," *Medical Image Analysis*, vol. 18, no. 5, pp. 808–818, 2014.

[65] S. Dubey. "Alzheimer's Dataset: Images of MRI Segmentation," https://www.kaggle.com/tourist55/alzheimers-dataset-4-class-of-images.

[66] J. Gu, Z. Wang, J. Kuen, L. Ma, A. Shahroudy, B. Shuai, T. Liu, X. Wang, G. Wang, and J. Cai, "Recent advances in convolutional neural networks," *Pattern Recognition*, vol. 77, pp. 354–377, 2018.

[67] H. Wang, and B. Raj, "On the origin of deep learning," *arXiv preprint arXiv:1702.07800*, 2017.

[68] M. Subramoniam, "Deep learning based prediction of Alzheimer's disease from magnetic resonance images," *arXiv preprint arXiv:2101.04961*, 2021.

[69] E. Mggdadi, A. Al-Aiad, M. S. Al-Ayyad, and A. Darabseh, "Prediction Alzheimer's disease from MRI images using deep learning." In *2021 12th International Conference on Information and Communication Systems (ICICS)*, IEEE, Valencia, Spain, pp. 120–125.

[70] J. Islam, and Y. Zhang, "A novel deep learning based multi-class classification method for Alzheimer's disease detection using brain MRI data." In *International Conference on Brain Informatics*, Springer, Cham, pp. 213–222.

[71] N. Rajawat, B. S. Hada, M. Meghawat, S. Lalwani, and R. Kumar, "Advanced identification of Alzheimer's disease from brain MRI images using convolution neural network." In *Proceedings of 2nd International Conference on Artificial Intelligence: Advances and Applications*, Springer, Singapore, pp. 219–229.

[72] T. Shahwar, J. Zafar, A. Almogren, H. Zafar, A. U. Rehman, M. Shafiq, and H. Hamam, "Automated detection of Alzheimer's via hybrid classical quantum neural networks," *Electronics*, vol. 11, no. 5, p. 721, 2022.

[73] N. OLABI, A. YILMAZ, and Z. ASLAN, "Automated detection of Alzheimer's disease using wavelet transform with convolutional neural networks," *EURAS Journal of Health*, p. 129.

4 Detection of Alzheimer's Disease Stages Based on Deep Learning Architectures from MRI Images

Febin Antony, Anita H B, and Jincy A George
Christ (Deemed to be University)

CONTENTS

4.1 INTRODUCTION

Alzheimer's disease (AD) can be referred to as a neurodegenerative illness that causes memory loss in an individual. It adversely impacts the living skills of the individual and delimits their progression. An AD patient not only feels confused all the time but also faces diffuse cortical function difficulties (Aderghal et al., 2018). In such conditions, it is vital to introduce intervention measures so that

DOI: 10.1201/9781003315452-4

the disease can be detected at the earlier stage itself and proper treatment procedure can be initiated. The present research focuses on analyzing the different deep learning architectures that can be used for the examination of MRI images and the early identification of AD symptoms. It includes using a deep learning algorithm that is based on deep beliefs networks (DBNs) so that there is the development of a neural network. It will help in composing several hidden layers so that there is the determination of interconnection between the different units that lie under the hidden layers. It facilitates the adoption of a bioinspired model that is known to work based on the human brain mechanism. It will not only provide better insights about human brain mapping but also ensure precise and early determination of AD symptoms (Ahmed et al., 2017). The present research focuses on analyzing this aspect to bring improvement in the treatment process of AD patients.

The rest of the paper is organized as follows: Section 4.2 discusses various existing literary works related to classification of AD and dataset details. Section 4.3 discusses the research gaps. Section 4.4 provides a brief description about the proposed research methodology including implementation of deep learning classifier for AD classification and the steps involved in the design of the classifier. Section 4.5 discusses the experimental results and performance evaluation. Section 4.6 concludes the paper with experimental observations and future scope.

4.2 OBJECTIVES OF THE STUDY

The prominent research objectives of this study are as follows:

- To examine the early diagnosis of AD using a deep learning approach.
- To examine the efficacy of the transfer learning model in terms of detecting AD stages from MRI images at an earlier stage.
- To employ a hybrid approach comprising CNN for classifying AD stages from MRI images.
- To ensemble DL-based neural networks for the early detection and diagnosis of AD.

4.3 LITERATURE REVIEW

4.3.1 Early Diagnosis of Alzheimer's Disease Using DL-Based Approaches

According to Liu et al. (2014), AD is a fundamental type of dementia which results in the loss of memory among individuals. It impacts different parts of the brain and affects its ability to comprehend language, think, and memorize. Due to AD, the individual often faces issues of declining memory and poor functioning of other cognitive functions. Brookmeyer et al. (2007) examined that the strength of individuals suffering from Alzheimer's disease has increased over years and reached more than 26.6 million in 2006. It is expected that the strength of AD patients will increase and double every 20 years. As a result, it is expected that 1.2% of the global population will be suffering from AD by 2046.

Gauthier et al. (2006) examined that early diagnosis of AD is essential so that there is recognition of comorbidities and mild cognitive impairment (MCI) related to the prodromal stage. In MCI, the patients experience symptoms of memory loss and deficiency, but it does not impact their daily activities. However, MCI is highly related to the risks of AD progression and other symptoms or forms of dementia. By diagnosing AD at an early stage, there is the identification of the risk of progression and severity of AD. Roberson and Mucke (2006) analyzed that varied machine learning (ML) methods such as positron emission tomography (PET), subclass MRI, and neuroimaging biomarkers can be used for the diagnosis of AD and its symptoms. The use of machine learning apparatus helps in the early identification of AD patients and forecasts the risks of MCI to them.

Zhang et al. (2011) analyzed that the use of binary classification tasks also plays an important role in simplifying the problem and determining AD modalities. In this process, a workflow is developed in which the combined features of Alzheimer's disease are identified with the help of the multi-kernel SVM classifier. Liu et al. (2013) examined that the optimized graph cut algorithm can be used for the diagnosis of AD. In this process, there is the distribution of specific classes for the training database so that there is the attainment of insights about specific parameters that are required for the distribution of classes in the training dataset. Hence, the focus must be given to developing new tools so that there is early detection of AD symptoms and the patient could be given appropriate treatment therapies for curing symptoms.

4.3.2 A TRANSFER LEARNING APPROACH FOR EARLY DIAGNOSIS OF AD ON MRI IMAGES

Mehmood et al. (2021) examined that Alzheimer's is a brain disease that causes memory loss in people. The symptoms of the disease could not be identified easily, and it almost takes 15–20 years before the real identification of symptoms of the disease. Alzheimer's symptoms get aggravated over time and create issues in the execution of daily activities such as walking, skills loss, or planning. Bi et al. (2019) analyzed that different techniques such as functional magnetic resonance imaging (fMRI) and single-photon emission computed tomography (SPECT) are used for the diagnosis of AD. Chaddad et al. (2018) conducted a study to highlight the different advancements that took place in the segment computer vision for the extraction of data in the medical and healthcare segment. It includes the use of ML algorithms for the identification of features and categorization of AD.

Hosseini-Asl et al. (2016) examined that the deep learning (DL) tool can be used for the early detection of AD symptoms. The DL technique will help in overcoming the limitation that is faced in the medical sector for the execution of computer-aided diagnosis (CAD) systems. It will help in the extraction of the discriminative features that are essential for ascertaining the AD symptoms from the raw image data. It forecasts extracting insights about different features such as segmentation, skull-stripping, smoothing segmentation, feature extraction, and normalization. Kingma and Ba (2014) proposed a new technique known as deep residual network (DRN) to determine the symptoms of disease and predict their outcomes. This technique can be used to solve the issues related to training accuracy and degradation that are mostly faced at the time of execution of the feature extraction process. However, the use of the DRN process gets restricted because CNN requires large dataset volumes for the training of data because of which it often becomes difficult to implement the DRN process for medical imaging purposes.

4.3.3 CLASSIFICATION OF AD MRI IMAGES USING A HYBRID CNN TECHNIQUE

Yildirim and Cinar (2020) conducted a study to determine early symptoms of AD by making use of MRI images with a hybrid CNN model. In the CNN-based hybrid model, the MRI images are categorized into four parts which are demented, mild demented, moderate demented, and non-demented. Çinar and Yıldırım (2020) examined that in CNN-based hybrid method, major emphasis is given to the structuring of the system so that all the insights are gained in a streamlined manner. In this method, there is avoiding training of a network from scratch, and the benefits are supposed to be taken from the knowledge acquired from Resnet50 architecture. It leads to the enhancement of the hybrid model that not only helps in removing the five layers of Resnet50 but also plays a prominent role in enhancing the performance of the model.

Ruuska et al. (2018) ascertained that once the testing is done there is determination of facts related to performance metrics. It includes the use of several processes for the scaling of the efficacy of classification. All these assessments are carried out by making use of a confusion matrix. The study suggested other metrics such as accuracy, precision, recall, and F-score accuracy so that there is determination of outcomes by proper analysis. For example, by using a confusion matrix, there is categorization of the process by including the data in CNN architecture. It helps in the estimation of the outcome by executing the classification process accurately. Hence, it was concluded from the study that the Resnet50 model that is based on CNN architecture can be used for the early detection of AD symptoms.

4.3.4 ENSEMBLES OF DL-BASED NETWORK MODELS FOR THE EARLY DIAGNOSIS OF THE AD

Ortiz et al. (2016) analyzed different deep learning architectures that are based on unsupervised and supervised learning algorithms for the early detection of AD symptoms. The deep learning algorithm is based on deep belief networks (DBNs) that play an important role in developing a neural network for the composition of several hidden layers. All these layers are interconnected so that there is no connection between the units that are laid down under the layers. It leads to the mimicking of the bioinspired model that is believed to work based on the human brain mechanism.

Hinton (2002) examined that there is a use of an unsupervised learning method for the setting of the visible units so that there is training of the vector by making use of contrastive divergence (CD). A major benefit of this process is that it is based on error detection by updating the weights and computing the errors. As a result, there is training of data and restructuring of the current state of the hidden units by making out data labels.

Hinton et al. (2006) analyzed that in the case of DBN, there is a formulation of RBM layers that plays an important role in determining the layer-wise algorithm values by making use of the model introduced by Hinton and Osindero. It includes the use of the greedy layer-wise algorithm for the identification of the training data that play an important role in the training RBMs in the hidden layer. As a result, by making use of deep learning architecture, there is the determination of valuable insights about AD and its symptoms.

Petersen et al. (2010) examined that Alzheimer's Disease Neuroimaging Initiative (ADNI) has been introduced by the US and Canadian universities and medical centers to standardize the biomarker procedures for imaging techniques for mild Alzheimer disease. ADNI's major goal is to develop improved methods for the attainment of uniform and standardized information from PET data and multisite MRI imaging for AD patients. It will help in the development of a data repository for cognitive, clinical, and biochemical data. By using ADNI, there is the development of a longitudinal and naturalistic perspective for early detection of AD along with the identification of symptoms such as MCI, normal cognitive aging, and MCI & AD biomarkers. By using ADNI, there will be successful use of cognitive normal subject cohorts that are showing mild symptoms of MCI. As a result, there is a determination of anticipated characteristics of Alzheimer's disease.

4.4 GAP ANALYSIS

Based on the above facts, it can be said that several studies have been conducted in the segment of AD to propose methods for its early detection. However, specific studies that highlight the use of machine learning in the identification of AD and its symptoms have been limited. It created a gap that is addressed in the present research by analyzing the facts related to the use of DL for the AD stages. It includes focusing on the different deep learning architectures that can be used to extract data from MRI images and provide précised patient outcomes. The present research also identified that several methods have been introduced by scholars in the past for the early detection of AD. However, these methods had certain limitations because of which the data acquired from them was not accurate and could not be used widely in the medical field for detecting AD. Hence, this gap is analyzed in the present research, and relevant insights are provided about classification techniques that apply DL-based models to brain regions.

4.5   RESEARCH METHODOLOGY OF THE STUDY

The proposed research employs a DL-based convolutional neural networks (CNNs) with brain imaging techniques for enhancing the diagnostic accuracy. The CNN model is trained using the training data which incorporates MRI input output modalities, and the proposed detection model is evaluated using an ADNI dataset. Especially, the T1-weighted MRI data was selected from the ADNI dataset which comprises validated neurological data.

The steps involved in the design of the proposed approach are listed below.

Data Collection and Dataset Details: The data for the experimental analysis is taken from the ADNI dataset. A T1-weighted MRI data from ADNI dataset is used wherein the ADNI study provides an observational analysis of the health condition of the elderly individuals with CN, MCI, or AD. An unbalanced dataset is used with 2,600 MCI images, 1,500 CN images, and 1,000 AD images. The National Institute of Health (NIH) funds the ADNI study which accurately assesses the information collected from MRI images. Individuals from ADNI were selected from the website for CN, MCI, and AD. T1-weighted MRI data was processed by the members of the neuroimaging challenge for the automatic classification of MCI. The sample MRI image data from the dataset is shown in Figure 4.1.

The ADNI study is an observational analysis of the health condition of the elderly individuals with CN, MCI, or AD. The National Institutes of Health (NIH) funds the ADNI study which accurately assesses the information collected from MRI images. Individuals from ADNI were selected from the website for CN, MCI, and AD. T1-weighted MRI data was processed by the members of the neuroimaging challenge for the automatic classification of MCI.

CNN is a neural network and feed-forward type which is mainly used for image recognition and processing. One of the prominent advantages of employing CNN for segmentation is the best use of the shared weight of the conventional layers and their efficiency in image recognition and in the sorting process. The ability of the CNN in extracting relevant features from images is effective use of

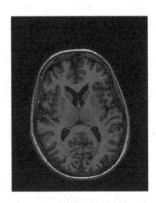

FIGURE 4.1   Sample image from the ADNI dataset.

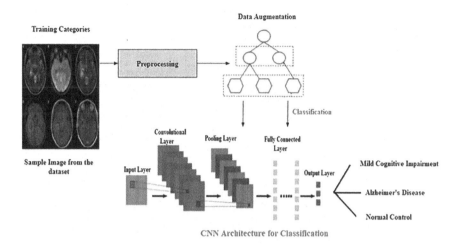

FIGURE 4.2 Block diagram of the CNN-based AD classification model.

the image filters which is a common phenomenon in most of the classification and detection applications. A CNN-based model called Inception V3 which is a top-end version of Inception V1 was used for image classification. In Inception V3, improvements can be done in label smoothing, dense layers, and auxiliary classifier and in batch normalization which will give 2,048-dimensional vector output. The block diagram and flowchart of the classification approach is illustrated in Figure 4.2.

In this research, skull-stripping is done to take only the brain images and to remove the skull part. CNN is trained for segmenting MRI images automatically, and the images were classified using a modified Inception V3 model for maximizing the efficacy and accuracy of the CNN. The changes in the batch normalization and dense layers were done with 100 epochs to get the trainable and non-trainable parameters. This research intends to maximize the efficiency of the detection mechanism by incorporating performance measures such as accuracy and precision. The flowchart depicting the proposed classification framework is shown in Figure 4.3.

4.6 FINDINGS AND DISCUSSIONS

Early detection is considered a critical task for effective management of AD and its streaming for mild cognitive impairment which is known as a common practice in the medical field. There are various deep learning techniques that are useful for examining the structural brain changes on MRI and CNN because of their efficient use of automated feature learning that also includes a variety of multilayer perceptron. In the current study, the main focus of the researcher is to detect the stages of AD that are based on deep learning architecture from MRI images.

The potential capability of the CNN-based approach is determined using a confusion matrix as shown in Figure 4.4. In this research, the accuracy is

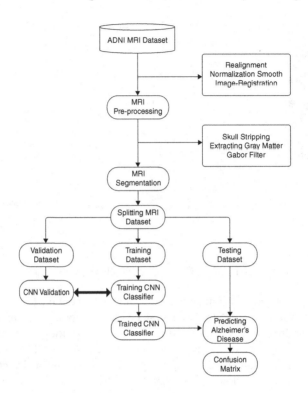

FIGURE 4.3   Flowchart of the AD classification process.

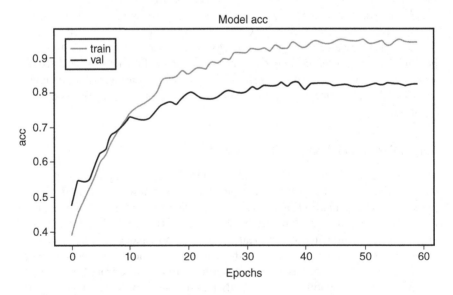

FIGURE 4.4   Confusion matrix.

measured using four different classification elements, namely true positives (TP), true negatives (TN), false positives (FP), and false negatives (FN). These terms are used for constructing a confusion matrix. The confusion matrix is mainly used for solving the problems related to classification accuracy where the output can be two or more classes.

Accuracy defines the percentage of number of correctly detected Alzheimer's stages and is calculated as shown in the below equation:

$$\text{Accuracy} = \frac{TP + TN}{TP + TN + FP + FN} \tag{4.1}$$

The recall score for a learning model is calculated as:

$$\text{Recall} = \frac{TP}{TP + FN} \tag{4.2}$$

F1-score measures the model's accuracy, and the value of this score ranges between 1 and 0. Here, 1 and 0 denote the best and worst values, respectively. The F1-score is calculated as:

$$\text{F1 score} = \frac{2 * \text{Precision} * \text{Recall}}{\text{Precision} * \text{recall}} \tag{4.3}$$

Precision is defined as the number of accurate positive predictions. It is defined as:

$$\text{Precision} = \frac{TP}{TP + FP} \tag{4.4}$$

Support is the number of actual occurrences of the class in the specified dataset. It defines the total number of samples of the true response in the training data which is used to evaluate the performance of the classification process.

The results of the experimental analysis as obtained from the classification report are discussed in Table 4.1.

The graphs of the accuracy, AUC, and loss are illustrated in Figures 4.5–4.7, respectively.

It can be inferred from the simulation results that the testing accuracy of the Inception V3 model is 80.82%.

From the confusion matrix, the TP value of CN, AD, and MCI are 192, 215, and 246, respectively. The validation of the research matches with the testing accuracy of the Inception V3 model 80.82%.

4.7   CONCLUSION AND RECOMMENDATIONS

The present research concluded that the use of deep learning architecture will help in bringing improvement in the diagnosis of AD and its symptoms. It includes focusing on the use of the Hinton and Osindero model that is based on the RBM layers formation. Through this layer, there is the determination of the layer-wise algorithm values that provide intrinsic insights about feature extraction from the

TABLE 4.1

Inception V3 classification report of the proposed model

	Precision	Recall	F1-Score	Support
CN	0.75	0.74	0.74	260
AD	0.81	0.74	0.77	289
MCI	0.86	0.95	0.90	259
Micro avg	0.81	0.81	0.81	808
Macro avg	0.81	0.81	0.81	808
Weighted avg	0.81	0.81	0.81	808
Samples avg	0.81	0.81	0.81	808

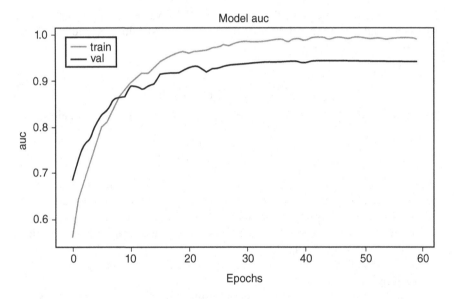

FIGURE 4.5   Accuracy of the proposed detection model.

MRI images. The present research also analyzed that an accurate diagnosis of AD plays a major role in a patient's health care at earlier stages which will help to prevent the disease before the brain gets damaged completely. In analyzing neurodegenerative disorders, neuroimaging plays an important role and it is widely accepted as a clinical tool in diagnosing subjects with AD, MCI, and CN. The efficacy of the CNN model was tested and validated using different measures. It can be inferred from the existing results that the CNN model achieved a phenomenal testing accuracy of 80.8%. Experimental evaluation validates the efficacy of the proposed model in detecting AD stages effectively with high accuracy and hence can be implemented for real-time applications. For future research, this

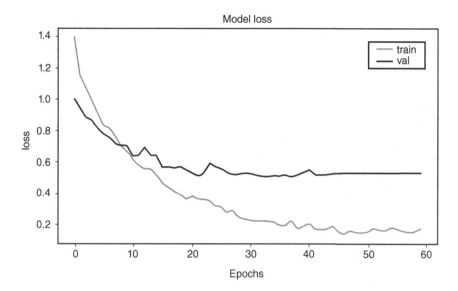

FIGURE 4.6   AUC of the proposed detection model.

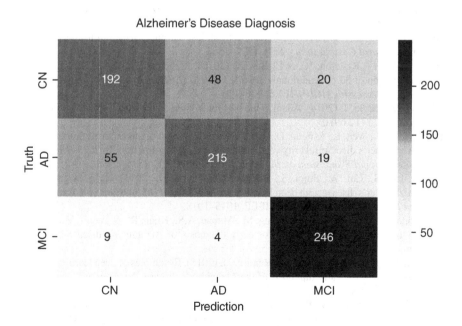

FIGURE 4.7   Training and validation loss of the proposed detection model.

work can implement a large-scale dataset for training the classifier to improve the performance and accuracy. Ensemble learning approaches can be implemented for verifying and validating the accuracy of the AD classification process with an aim of implementing it in a real-time environment, where the data is sparse.

REFERENCES

Aderghal, K., Khvostikov, A., Krylov, A., Benois-Pineau, J., Afdel, K., & Catheline, G. (2018). Classification of Alzheimer disease on imaging modalities with deep CNNS using cross-modal transfer learning. In *2018 IEEE 31st International Symposium on Computer-Based Medical Systems (CBMS)*, IEEE, 345–350.

Ahmed, O.B., Benois-Pineau, J., Allard, M., Catheline, G., Amar, C.B., & Initiative, A.D.N. (2017). Recognition of Alzheimer's disease and mild cognitive impairment with multimodal image-derived biomarkers and multiple kernel learning. *Neurocomputing, 220*, 98–110.

Bi, X., Li, S., Xiao, B., Li, Y., Wang, G., & Ma, X. (2019). Computer aided Alzheimer's disease diagnosis by an unsupervised deep learning technology. *Neurocomputing, 21*, 1232–1245.

Brookmeyer, R., Johnson, E., Ziegler-Graham, K., & Arrighi, H.M. (2007). Forecasting the global burden of Alzheimer's disease. *Alzheimer's & Dementia, 3*(3), 186–191.

Chaddad, A., Desrosiers, C., & Niazi, T. (2018). Deep radiomic analysis of MRI related to Alzheimer's disease. *IEEE Access, 6*, 58213–58221.

Çinar, A. & Yıldırım, M. (2020). Detection of tumors on brain MRI images using the hybrid convolutional neural network architecture. *Medical Hypotheses, 139*, 109684.

Gauthier, S., Reisberg, B., Zaudig, M., Petersen, R.C., Ritchie, K., Broich, K., & Winblad, B. (2006). Mild cognitive impairment. *The Lancet, 367*(9518), 1262–1270.

Hinton, G.E. (2002). Training products of experts by minimizing contrastive divergence. *Neural Computation, 14*(8), 1771–1800.

Hinton, G.E., Osindero, S., & Teh, Y.W. (2006). A fast learning algorithm for deep belief nets. *Neural Computation, 18*(7), 1527–1554.

Hosseini-Asl, E., Keynton, R., & El-Baz, A. (2016). Alzheimer's disease diagnostics by adaptation of 3d convolutional network. In *2016 IEEE International Conference on Image Processing (ICIP)*, IEEE, 126–130.

Kingma, D.P. & Ba, J. (2014). Adam: a method for stochastic optimization. *arXiv preprint arXiv, 9*, 1412.6980.

Liu, S., Cai, W., Wen, L., & Feng, D. (2013). Neuroimaging biomarker based prediction of Alzheimer's disease severity with optimized graph construction. In *2013 IEEE 10th International Symposium on Biomedical Imaging*, IEEE, 1336–1339.

Liu, S., Liu, S., Cai, W., Pujol, S., Kikinis, R., & Feng, D. (2014). Early diagnosis of Alzheimer's disease with deep learning. In *2014 IEEE 11th International Symposium on Biomedical Imaging (ISBI)*, IEEE, 1015–1018.

Mehmood, A., Yang, S., Feng, Z., Wang, M., Ahmad, A.S., Khan, R., & Yaqub, M. (2021). A transfer learning approach for early diagnosis of Alzheimer's disease on MRI images. *Neuroscience, 460*, 43–52.

Ortiz, A., Munilla, J., Gorriz, J.M., & Ramirez, J. (2016). Ensembles of deep learning architectures for the early diagnosis of the Alzheimer's disease. *International Journal of Neural Systems, 26*(07), 1650025.

Petersen, R.C., Aisen, P.S., Beckett, L.A., Donohue, M.C., Gamst, A.C., Harvey, D.J., & Weiner, M.W. (2010). Alzheimer's disease neuroimaging initiative (ADNI): clinical characterization. *Neurology, 74*(3), 201–209.

Roberson, E.D. & Mucke, L. (2006). 100 years and counting: prospects for defeating Alzheimer's disease. *Science, 314*(5800), 781–784.

Ruuska, S., Hämäläinen, W., Kajava, S., Mughal, M., Matilainen, P., & Mononen, J. (2018). Evaluation of the confusion matrix method in the validation of an automated system for measuring feeding behaviour of cattle. *Behavioural Processes, 148*, 56–62.

Yildirim, M. & Cinar, A.C. (2020). Classification of Alzheimer's disease MRI images with CNN based hybrid method. *Ingénierie des Systèmes d'Information, 25*(4), 413–418.

Zhang, D., Wang, Y., Zhou, L., Yuan, H., Shen, D., & Alzheimer's Disease Neuroimaging Initiative. (2011). Multimodal classification of Alzheimer's disease and mild cognitive impairment. *Neuroimage, 55*(3), 856–867.

5 Analysis on Detection of Alzheimer's using Deep Neural Network

Keerthika C and Anisha M. Lal
Vellore Institute of Technology

CONTENTS

DOI: 10.1201/9781003315452-5

5.1 INTRODUCTION

Alzheimer's disease is the sixth highest cause of death. It is grueling for a person to lose their close one's face or their memories. According to the "World Alzheimer Report," over 50 million individuals were affected in 2018, with the number expected to quadruple by 2050. In most cases, Alzheimer's disease symptoms appear after 65 years. Researchers built automated analysis tools after discovering that it is possible to read and scan photos on computers. We commonly use magnetic resonance imaging (MRI) of the brain of the person affected, and this system determines at which stage the AD is.

Deep learning has garnered a slice of interest in Alzheimer's disease detection research since 2013, with the count of papers circulated in this area increasing dramatically after 2017. Deep models ought to be demonstrated for more accurate decisions in detecting Alzheimer's disease than traditional machine learning procedures. Generally, the images are pre-processed, segmented, and then sent for classification. The detection of AD can be solved with the help of neural networks, mainly for feature extraction and classification. Practices of neurons are the totality of weighted synapses. Neurons sum the outputs from every synapse and pertain to an activation function.

The image scans will be pre-processed depending on the requirements of the network. The segmentation discovers the essential information of each specific data. Then, the process will extricate vital features from data to classify it conferring the user-provided conditions for the specified problem. Here, we provide a detailed review of diverse DNNs that have been employed for the treatment of Alzheimer's disease.

It benefits the doctors to detect AD earlier. It also decides the phase of AD in a patient with the spectrum and can guide the patient to the respective AD phase.

Deep neural networks (DNNs) contain the self-learning ability, are highly scalable, and are cost-effective. It also affords the greatest decision assistance system for clinicians and improved results in the categorization of benign and malignant MRI data.

DNN makes complex decisions and is applied in assorted applications of medical images. Very less models of DNN have been conducted for the detection of AD. It has the capability of acquiring significant information while categorizing an object accurately [1]. It also classifies the unstructured input data. It can produce parameters for accurate transformation although the input image has been changed. It contains fewer missing values. It is tested among LSTM, DNN, and NN in ADNI, MIRIAD, and OASIS datasets [2].

Fully connected stratums with DNN employed for categorization of two classes utilize cross-entropy as a deficit function. It executes validation of k-folds with diverse activation roles. It was constructed with the help of Keras library.

The activation roles do not apply null rates for negative values. This served as a benefit to resolve the perishing rectified linear unit setback. The prototype instructs the features connected with the output of conclusive classification to enhance the accuracy [3]. The HOG extractor utilizes to retrieve features and DNN, an unsupervised technique for classification accomplishes automated recognition of AD in images [4].

Researcher's [5] suggested unsupervised learning on raw images at binary phases for the diagnosis of AD. The first phase works on two-layer NN with scattered filtering to study features, and the next phase works on softmax regression to categorize the status of the features absorbed earlier. It adaptively absorbs features, shrinks manual work, moderates the local optimum risk, and implements beneficial diagnostic accuracy. It can analyze the features of NN for filling the gap in manual extraction with the assistance of feature learning and signal processing.

From Figure 5.1, the Scopus database (www.scopus.com) was examined with the strings "Alzheimer's disease" with the conjunction of each type of DNN. We can accomplish that CNN is the maximum applied technique in brain images for the detection of AD.

With the help of scans, Alzheimer's disease can be identified earlier and detected at what stage it is in the affected brain. It can be contributed to the doctors or physicians who work on this topic for detecting it in primary stage with classification of MR images.

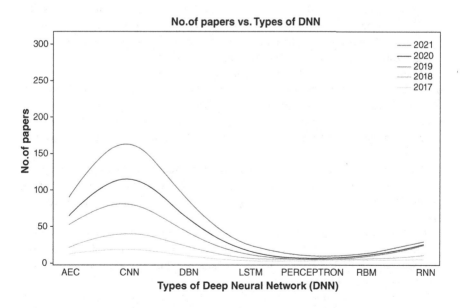

FIGURE 5.1 All types of papers published throughout the last 5 years represent the types of DNN.

The organization of this chapter includes:

- First, the introduction about Alzheimer's disease and DNN.
- Second, a study on types of DNNs used for the detection of AD is explained with the help of 40 papers from the recent 4 years.
- Third, the suitable methodology that can be applied to the problem and its architecture is investigated.
- Fourth, the results prove the method proposed is better than others and are discussed.
- Finally, the chapter concludes with the main points on AD detection.
- At last, it adds the references.

5.2   A STUDY ON ASSORTED DEEP NEURAL NETWORKS

This section deliberates the types of numerous DNNs utilized by the authors to detect AD. They are "convolutional neural network (CNN), long-term short memory (LSTM), recurrent neural network (RNN), autoencoder (AEC), perceptron, deep belief network (DBN), and restricted Boltzmann machine (RBM)."

5.2.1   CNN

CNN's models ResNet and AlexNet were applied to detect the disease in which AlexNet supplied high-accuracy results. It was instructed, verified, and authorized with an MRI dataset. It achieved exceptional metrics for performance. It increases the chance of CAD methods detecting AD in the investigation of medical images [6].

CNN can be operated in a retrieval system of steps in processing the images [7]. The CNN has been employed to extricate the discriminative features for the categorization of the area affected by Alzheimer's disease [8].

It detects seven morphological features that achieve greater than other methods. SegNet segments the image to retrieve seven features. The seven features of ROI instruct RNN, an architecture of CNN for the task of classification. It studies the features of image examining by itself. Segmentation in the DL categorizer enhances the functioning of the method. It requires a huge sample size for analysis [9].

A ready-to-use and open-source deep learning segmentation of hippocampus regions was tested on the HarP dataset. U-Net CNN activations combine to consensus for post-processing to mask segmentation in 3D images. It achieves less error [10].

CNN explores segmentation effects on MR images from patients for nursing and diagnosis of AD. It presents great precision with superior CDR and less MMSE. Hippocampus of neuronal composition damaged; the nursing method has been discovered [11].

AD was discovered with CNN and local binary pattern. The pre-processing was considered a fundamental step utilized for distinguishing the boundaries of a skull in images. The vital and basic images were required for the detection of points, and the procedures were accomplished on image voxels. Various thresholding techniques assist in the decision of vital points. The LBP and Fast Hessian matrix were combined for the discovery of descriptions and vital points [12].

Although LeNet is an old model, it consumes less time for implementation and eradicates the element information of minimum values [1].

CNN compacts with 2D and 3D scans of the brain with convolution. It also applies transfer learning with the model of VGG19. It has appropriate basic structures with values that have memory requirements, the ability to save time, overfitting, and less complexity for computation of the system [13].

Hippocampus segmentation can be sourced as the main element for the detection of AD. The augmentation of the dataset was with the help of convolutional GAN. Employing methods such as zooms, flips, crops, or supplementary basic transformations on the training dataset's prevailing images was mentioned as sophisticated augmentation methods. U-Net tunes the parameters accomplishes the task required with limited images of the training set and provides great exact results of segmentation in GPU. ResNet blocks built on the architecture of CNN utilize the transfer learning method and employ encoder–decoder layers in U-Net. It vanishes the problem of overfitting and enlarges the size of the dataset. It has a higher dice coefficient and accuracy [14].

The deep separable CNN with GoogLeNet and AlexNet enhances the efficiency and increases the model's performance. It was beneficial for feature retrieval. It lessens the complexity, cost of computation, and parameters [15].

ResNet evaluates the performance of the network and diminishes the complexity. It considers pre-processed MRI as key and builds manifold initial blocks with suppressed representation to uphold the accuracy for classification. It automatically extracts the features that ignore the limits of less processing information. According to the proficiency in signifying universal context and combining features, it can be profitable for the detection of AD-similar diseases such as hypothyroidism and depression [16].

Scale and move invariants' low-to-high intensity features were retrieved from an improved amount of organizing images utilizing CNN. It brought a great accurate and prescient repeatable model. The achieved exactness for two modalities of MRI such as designs of GoogLeNet and LeNet cutting edges performs greater than all previous strategies. ROC curve was drawn to confirm joined classifiers [17].

If the 3D MRI is exhausted with more slices in the last dimension, spatial information has been studied by filters that do not apply to 2D CNN. The 3D CNN procures structural, complicated, and distinguishing dependences according to the enclosure in classes of images [18].

CAD process with numerous algorithms can be utilized to predict AD. DCNN derived from CNN extracts the image attributes vigorously and globally. It mends the retrieval features of the object that enhances the reliability of the network. A novel method with a DCNN cluster analysis mixture for the disintegration of features enriches the accuracy of the network. This inventive design of DCNN blows the performance of the cutting edge scheme and generates ideal efficiency [19].

Training of spiking NN with pre-processed images retrieves important AD features. The spikes were sent to CNN for the task of classification. It increased the performance gain and validated the objective of integrating deep models from the initial stage for studying different features with neuroimage and medical processing. They are dependable and stable along with fault-free [20].

CNN with the adoption of the U-Net model segments the images to detect AD. Public database images support this method to be effective and reliable. It boosts the consistency for diagnosis of and detection of AD with less determination of the segmentation in brain images. It entails a bulky dataset for examining the method [21].

VGG-16 and ResNet, two base models of CNN, generate a diagnosis of images with higher accuracy. It affords decision-making accurately and has a respectable feature description that strengthens the stability and accuracy for improvement of 4%for classification. Optimization and experimental dimension were inadequate [22].

CNN can consider subregions of the brain for diagnosis of AD with the help of optimization techniques such as GWO, CS, PSO, and GA. AlexNet, the architecture of CNN retrieves features and categorizes the classes of AD. It diagnoses the changes in the brain through the hippocampus area. It confirms to be a tool for AD study and useful for screening systems clinically. The validation rate becomes low for missing data and generates reduced performance for the dataset of minor dimensions [23].

When there was a lack of adequate data, it was advisable to lessen the cost of computation with selective learning of slices. The network was guided for superfluous information from two coronal segments. It can be applied to distinguish the CNN method to categorize classes of AD and to study specific characteristics from PET images. ImageNet was recommended for the process of transfer learning. It trained the layers excluding the first three convolutional layers of the network [24].

It detects the initial stage of AD with CNN, and SVM classified three degrees of disease by a similar algorithm. It studies the necessary and distinguishing features that mark extreme accuracy in classification. It ignores the frantic and saves time in the segmentation process and generic extraction of features. The levels of performance enlarge by adding further subjects and working with CSF and PET multimodal data [25].

3D CNN with dual function in an end-to-end manner employs for the segmentation of the hippocampus bilaterally from MRI scans and simultaneously for detection of AD stages progression. It executes a loss function that balances diagnosis of disease and segmentation and cross-validation in a fivefold manner. It has been tested with segmentation functioning metrics such as dice coefficient and intersection over union, and with diagnosis implementation metrics such as accuracy, F1 score, precision, sensitivity, recall, and specificity. It can be utilized for other disease diagnoses and can check the correlation between ROI and particular attributes [26].

The process involves two base methods of CNN, ResNet and Inception-v4, to classify the analysis of 3D MRI brain images. It requires a large dataset for the process of training. The model depth was less, and layers were associated with prior layers. It abolishes the problem of "vanishing gradient" and supplies a better process of classification and propagation of features [27].

The neural network of multilayers is CNN in the investigation of images. It acquires feature maps from the model. The estimated volume is calculated by CNN for measuring the count of voxels that assists in the construction of the hippocampus. Although many layers have been proposed for the network, it recognizes the output layer in CNN for detection [28].

CNN lifts the process of classification with the use of trained weights in an autoencoder. The fusion of MRI and PET can apprehend significant patterns of 3D amyloid with the absence of noisy and unnecessary information on white matter. It improves the correctness of the combination of images [29].

5.2.2 LSTM

LSTM retrieves the features of images and captures information on time-invariant data. It prevents imbalance of classes, takes lesser time for training, and reduces information loss. But LSTM has limited graphic memory [30]. LSTM built the relation of features and predicts AD by the most important feature, i.e., average cortical thickness. It receives inadequate temporal information from images [31].

LSTM assists to retrieve spatial data for the feature maps. It familiarizes the idea of cell and gate state [32]. It predicts progression from MCI to AD by learning informative and condensed representations from perceptive data. They built models for projection on hippocampus measures. A recurrent neural network with LSTM has accomplished notable developments in MRI modeling, specifying RNN to be enhanced tools exemplifying longitudinal data [33].

5.2.3 RNN

It predicts and encodes with multiobjective function in optimization of end-to-end manner. It accomplishes advanced performance in classification, imputation, and regression. It handles the missing values, forecasts phenotypic measurements, estimates cognitive score, and predicts the clinical stage of AD. It does not consider feature relations [34]. RNN predicts the progress of AD from images. If there are missing values in the dataset, methods input the data by linear or forward filing and can utilize RNN to fill in both training and testing in comparison with base models. It affords improved execution than the base models in longitudinal images. It bestows superior in one-time points and can fill in the missing data [35].

5.2.4 AUTOENCODER

A convolutional autoencoder (CAEC) in an ensemble manner is used for feature extraction to diagnose AD. It has been applied to an ensemble of 11 CAE to extract features of images with an accuracy of above 90%. An ensemble of CAEs was employed for reconstruction and denoising the input images. It discovers the disease in an earlier stage for specificity and sensitivity rates. It also delivers less error rate with less complexity and time in training the network. It decreases the cost of computation [36].

5.2.5 PERCEPTRON

Frank Rosenblatt introduced Perceptron in 1957. Based on the original MCP neuron, he created a perceptron learning rule. A perceptron is a supervised learning technique for binary classifiers. This approach allows neurons to study and interpret individual components in the training set. The respiratory problems caused by Alzheimer's can be detected by a multilayer perceptron algorithm for classification [37].

5.2.6 DBN

It solves the problem of multitask learning with DBN. It lengthens the depth of the network, boosts the generalization, enriches the performance by listing the frequent points amid numerous tasks, and delivers satisfactory results with six classes [38].

5.2.7 RBM

A restricted Boltzmann machine was employed for the diagnosis of AD for MRI. RBM extracts time courses and spatial maps of intrinsic networks and provides more features than ICA. RBM increases the individuals' performance with SVM in classification and accuracy by 75%, as ICA produces an accuracy of 7.5% less than RBM. It requires more input size for training in RBM. It can use other non-constrained models for classification and can focus on fusion analysis [39].

5.3 METHODOLOGY

CNN, also identified as ConvNet typically, captures a key image and allocates absorbable weights with biases to an image of numerous aspects, successively distinguishing one image from another. In a minimum of one layer, CNN employs the operation of convolution in preference to matrix multiplication. It is majorly utilized in an amorphous dataset. 2D CNN controls features from width and height information, but 3D CNN recognizes the patches of volume that conserve temporal dimension in neuroimaging data. It produces enhanced performance but with more parameters that lead to enlargement of computational cost. Among them, the most diverse architectures of CNN (e.g., ResNet, GoogLeNet, VGGNet, AlexNet, LeNet) were employed to construct models for the classification and analysis of brain images [40]. It can be represented in multiple ways. It achieves by lessening parameters, reuse of features, and deciphering the "vanishing-gradients" problem [41].

The deep CNN (DCNN) design is made up of three convolutional layers, with max-pooling applied after each one. The sample size, learning rate, optimization function, loss function, and activation function influence the model. In the experiments, different parameter values can be employed. The goal of the optimization function is to reduce the loss function to the smallest possible value. It accomplishes this by altering the model's parameters (weights) throughout the training phase. In neural networks, the loss function acts as an important part of the process of training. It is utilized to determine the discrepancy between the predicted and actual values. By applying nonlinear transformations to the input, the activation function aids in the solution of difficult problems [42].

5.3.1 Types of CNN

Starting from the unique five-layer convolutional assembly of LeNet through the eight-layer network assembly of AlexNet, and finally, to the nineteenth-layer network assembly of VGG-19, CNN has developed considerably. As the number of network layers increases, the number of existing features expands, and it enhances the network's performance [43].

5.3.2 ResNet

ResNet permits to reveal of the concealed patterns of the brain, discovering the relations of the region and recognizing patterns of AD in MRI scans of the brain. The vanishing gradient problem creates trouble in training a deep network. When the gradient is backpropagated to preceding layers in the period of training, iterated multiplication would make it substantially small. As a result, the network's performance may suffer. ResNet's core concept is to present a "shortcut connection" that hops certain layers. It was studied to attain illuminating features; hence, it could be comprehensively used for the task of AD detection. The fully connected layer was adjusted to require two outputs including a factor of learning rate with the weight of ten epochs greater than the preceding layers to adapt ResNet-18 to AD challenges. It trains the novel fully connected layer faster by amending the learning rate [44].

From Figure 5.2, this model considers an input image of 28×28. It is passed through the first convolutional layer. Then, an activation function of ReLu is activated in all convolutional layers to enhance the performance. A layer of 1×1 is finally distributed to convolution layers of 3×3 and a pooling layer of dimension $23 \times 23 \times 128$. The fully connected layer and output layer produce 10 neurons.

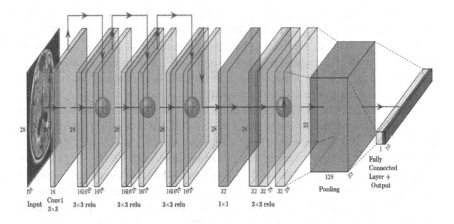

FIGURE 5.2   Visualizes the architecture for ResNet.

5.3.2.1   ResNet's Features

- Utilizes batch normalization as the main part of a network. It controls the input layer that enhances the network's performance.
- Solves the hindrance of covariate shift.
- Employs identity connection, which assists to defend the vanishing-gradients setback.
- Enriches the network's functioning by the design of residual blocks in a bottleneck manner [45].

5.3.3   GooGLeNet

Each of the nine modules in the GoogLeNet network is called inception. The layers of convolution and max-pooling in each inception are of dissimilar sizes. GoogLeNet contains 22 layers, showing good picture classification performance. Multiple convolution filters are applied to comparable inputs by the inception modules. The outputs will then be linked, permitting the network to benefit from multilevel feature extraction while also covering a large region by preserving a high resolution for little information on the images [46].

Figure 5.3 uses a different architecture than a standard CNN design, such as the LeNet-5 model. Inception modules were employed, which run several convolution procedures and max-pooling subsequently. As a result, selecting a specific size for the convolution kernel of a particular layer is not required. This method is effective not just in terms of classification results but also in terms of processing efficiency. It has the advantage that the inception module does a 1×1 convolution operation before each 3×3 or 5×5 convolution, resulting in dimensionality reduction. It considers a 256×256 grayscale image as input. Batch normalization is employed for all convolutional and interconnected layers to avoid internal covariate shift [47].

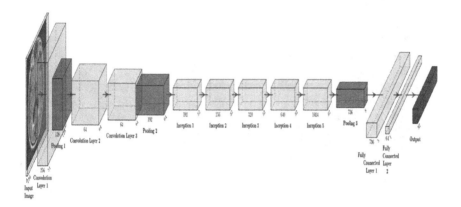

FIGURE 5.3   Envisions the model for GoogLeNet.

5.3.3.1   Features of GoogLeNet

- 1×1 convolution for expansion of depth by lessening the parameters.
- The global average pooling layer, the closing stage of the network, for example, considers a feature map with a value of 77% and averages it to a value of 11%. This also reduces the count of expanding parameters to zero and boosts top-1 accuracy by 0.6%.
- The inception module controls multiscale objects with diverse sizes of convolutional filters.
- Utilizes auxiliary classifier at training stage that offers regularization and resists against "vanishing gradient" problem [48].

5.3.4   VGGNet-16 AND VGGNet-19

VGGNet-16 is the standard feature extractor used by many well-known object identification systems. The architecture of VGGNet is fairly consistent. As a result, many developers have embraced this as their primary predictive model. The VGGNet's pre-accomplished model and weights settings are freely available in ImageNet. It is made up of five pooling and convolutional layer blocks. The initial two blocks have a max-pooling layer and two convolutional layers each, whereas the following three blocks each ensure three convolutional layers and then a max-pooling layer. This offers VGG-Net16 13 convolutional layers and a count of 16 hidden layers in comparison with 19 hidden layers in VGGNet-19.

VGGNet-16 and VGGNet-19 can be pre-trained on the images to utilize transfer learning to shrink the amount of time required for training. After that, the completely linked network was peeled away and substituted with a considerably shallower fully connected layer. It can be implemented to reduce overfitting, which had previously been identified as an issue in a deeper completely linked network. The fully connected network's topology includes a 40% dropout, followed by 256 nodes fully connected layer, a 50% dropout layer, and lastly a binary output [49].

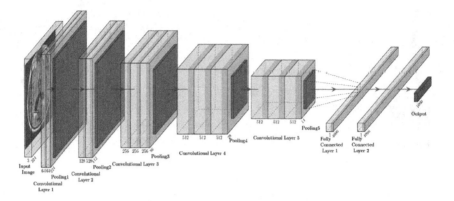

FIGURE 5.4   Pictures the model for VGGNet.

From Figure 5.4, VGGNet model summarizes the network key points.

5.3.4.1   Summary of VGGNet model

A fixed-size 224×224×3 RGB image is used as input to the model.

- Each pixel is pre-processed by removing the mean value of the RGB group in the training set.
- Layers of convolutional neural networks remain to be 17.
  - The stride has been set to one pixel.
  - Padding for 3×33×3 is one pixel.
- Spatial pooling layers
  - By convention, this part of a layer is not included in the network's depth.
  - Max-pooling layers are used for spatial pooling.
  - The size of the window is 2×22×2
  - The stride length is set at two.
  - Convolutional nets used a total of five max-pooling layers.
- Layers that are completely interconnected:
  - First: 4,096
  - Second: 4,096 (ReLU).
  - Third place: 1,000 (Softmax) [50].

5.3.5   ALEXNET

AlexNet has neurons of roughly 650,000 with a count of 60million parameters, which is a substantial upgrade over Lenet-5 in requisite of network scale. AlexNet is an eight-layer CNN with five convolutional and three fully connected layers, plus the operation of maximum pooling appearing after an initial stage of three convolutional levels. AlexNet, unlike prior neural networks, utilizes ReLU instead of the standard sigmoid and tan$h$ functions as the activation function. ReLU is a non-packed activation function that not barely enhances the model's

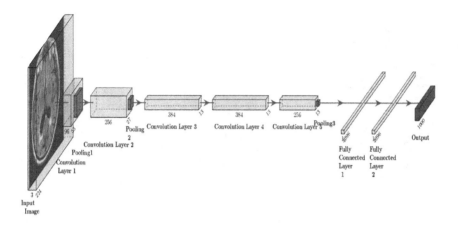

FIGURE 5.5   Scrutinizes the model for AlexNet.

training speed but additionally manages better in gradient loss and gradient eruption, making it simple to instruct a deeper network [51].

From Figure 5.5, the initial convolutional layer processes the 224×224×3 user-provided image using 96 kernels with the dimension of 11×11×3 and a 4-pixel stride. The (response-normalized and pooled) output of the initial convolutional layer is delivered into the second convolutional layer, which sieves it utilizing 256 kernels of dimension 5×5×48. The third, fourth, and fifth convolutional layers are associated, deprived of any pooling or normalizing layers in between. The outputs of the second convolutional layers are connected to 384 kernels of dimension 3×3×256 in the third convolutional layer. The previous to last convolutional layer contains the dimension of 3×3×192 of 384 kernels, while the last convolutional layer contains 256 kernels of dimension 3×3×192. Each of the completely connected layers has 4,096 neurons [52].

5.3.5.1   Details of the model

- ReLU is a function that activates other functions.
- Normalization layers were used, which is no longer prevalent.
- 128 as batch size.
- The SGD momentum algorithm has been utilized as a learning method.
- Extensive data augmentation, including color correction, flipping, cropping, jittering, and other techniques.

This helps in achieving the best outcomes by assembling models [53].

5.3.6   LeNet

LeNet consists of seven layers plus an output layer. The composition of layers includes three layers for convolution, two layers for subsampling, and the

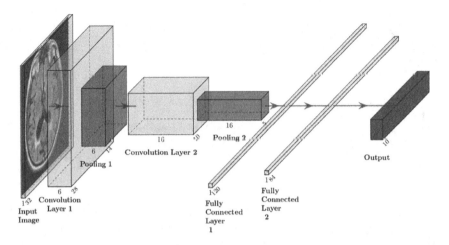

FIGURE 5.6   Regards the model for LeNet.

remaining fully connected layers. The network's input layer receives the photos as inputs and, after size-normalization, forwards them to the next layer. The convolutional layer is the second layer, which contains feature maps/kernel sets that are employed to retrieve key feature information such as edges, corners, and so on. Kernels, also known as feature maps, are a series of squared matrices with the same weights. The convolution operation is the process of overlapping and sliding kernels across the full image pixels. The usual convolutional procedures use additional time and memory space since it concatenates max- and min-pooling layers together. Depth-wise convolution is an eminent technique for reducing execution time, while representational convolution is another [1].

From Figure 5.6, the first layer is the input layer, which has a $32 \times 32 \times 1$ feature map. Then there is the convolution layer of the initial stage, which has six 5×5 filters with a stride of 1. tan$h$ is the activation function employed at this layer. The final feature map is $28 \times 28 \times 6$ in size. The average pooling layer follows, with a filter size of 2×2 and a stride of 1. The feature map that results is $14 \times 14 \times 6$. The number of channels is unaffected by the pooling layer.

The second convolution layer follows, with 16 5×5 filters and stride 1. tan$h$ is the activation function. The output size has been changed to $10 \times 10 \times 16$. The other average pooling layer of 2×2 with stride 2 appears once again. As a consequence, the feature map's size was decreased to $5 \times 5 \times 16$.

The final pooling layer comprises 120 5×5 filters with stride 1 and tan$h$ as the activation function. The output size has now increased to 120. The following layer is a completely linked layer with 84 neurons that outputs 84 values, and the activation function is tan$h$ once more.

The output layer, which has ten neurons and uses the Softmax function, is the final layer. The Softmax determines the likelihood that a data point belongs to a specific class. After then, the maximum value is anticipated. This design has a total of roughly 60,000 trainable parameters [54].

5.3.6.1 LeNet's Features

- Convolution, pooling, and activation functions in a nonlinear manner are all included in every convolutional layer.
- CNNs are used to extract spatial characteristics.
- Average pooling layer subsampling.
- Role of tanh activation.
- As the final classifier, MLP was used.
- To lower the complexity of computing, use sparse connections between layers.

The convolution layer followed by the subsampling layer produces function maps after reducing the dimensions of the previous layer. If the shape becomes unchanged and the input is large, the output is larger than one dimension. The benefits of the seventh layer, i.e., fully connected are in lessening the amount of training time [55].

From Figures 5.2–5.6, the input MR image is taken from the Kaggle dataset. The architecture is required for learning the features of every model effortlessly; the images were signified in GitHub and employed new accumulation in each model.

5.4 RESULTS AND DISCUSSION

CNN identifies the images with AEC by retrieval of features. When many models were used instead of one model, accuracy, recall, and precision was improved. Hippocampus, brain areas, and verbal tests were all identified [56]. 2D CNN reduces the time of computation and extricates features of classification by the AlexNet-SVM method. It increases efficiency and accuracy. This can be utilized in CAD systems for the detection of other diseases also [57]. Images can be converted from 3D to 2D that obtains features with VGG16, the architecture of CNN. The average accuracy for the classification of MRI scans was proved to be greater than PET images. It has no loss of information from significant images [58]. It brought ease in implementation for tuning the network. It deteriorates the semantic gap by learning discriminative features precisely from the images. It requires parameters on the count of iterations and regularization [59].

5.4.1 Experimental Analysis and Discussion of Datasets

5.4.1.1 ADNI

Dr. Michael W. Weiner founded the Alzheimer Disease Neuroimaging Initiative (ADNI) in 2004. The ADNI dataset includes 2,636 people, the majority of whom are between the ages of 70 and 79. For 18 months, the transition to AD was to be monitored. Many researchers are now using ADNI to classify Alzheimer's disease and track its progression. ADNI's main purpose is to see if serial MRI, PET, and other biological markers, as well as clinical and neuropsychological estimations, can be used to track MCI and early AD progression [60].

5.4.1.2 OASIS

Dr. Randy Buckner (Howard Hughes Medical Institute) created datasets for the Open Access Series of Imaging Studies at Harvard University, the Neuroinformatics Research Group at Washington University School of Medicine, and the Biomedical Informatics Research Network. It includes 416 cross-sectional participants, 150 longitudinal subjects, and 1,098 people in cognitive, neuroimaging, and clinical datasets. It also includes information on patients' demographics, such as age, gender, education, number of patients, MMSE score, socioeconomic status, and clinical dementia rating (CDR) [60]. The MMSE is a questionnaire-based test for assessing MCI and AD symptoms. Memory, hobbies, orientation, location, community affairs, and individual care are all used by CDR to calculate the rigidity of AD [61].

5.4.2 ANALYSIS OF TYPES OF DNN

5.4.2.1 ADNI Dataset

Table 5.1 represents some of the papers with their types of DNNs utilized and accuracies applied to the ADNI dataset for the detection of AD.

DNN+Adam [4] produces 99.5 accuracy followed by VGG-19 [13] and ResNet [14] with an accuracy of 97%.

DCNN [59] presents 99.77 accuracy and 99.02% [41] with the DNN method. From both Figures 5.7 and 5.8, DCNN presents higher accuracy than other types of DNN applied to the ADNI dataset.

5.4.2.2 OASIS Dataset

Table 5.2 represents some of the papers with their types of DNNs utilized and accuracies applied to the ADNI dataset for the recognition of AD.

First is ensemble of DCNNs with 93.18% accuracy [27], and second is 93.02% accuracy by GoogLeNet [15].

From Figures 5.7–5.9, the results show that CNN may be the correct technique for detecting AD. These results need to be considered when considering how to find specific areas of the brain that cause AD. The generalization of the results is limited by the fact that training takes a long time if the device does not have a gate processing unit (GPU) and requires a large amount of data to process. Further research is needed to identify detection results that are free of explosive gradients and class imbalances.

5.4.3 PERFORMANCE MEASURES

Patient care leaders and performance improvement professionals are constantly challenged to make decisions that have a wide range of impacts on patient care costs, productivity, and quality. With minimal time for multiple stakeholders to serve and consider options, and data overload, a new approach is needed to evaluate and monitor quality. This article describes the framework and

TABLE 5.1

Types of DNN vs. average accuracy (%) in the ADNI dataset

Papers	Types of DNN Utilized	Accuracy (%)
[4]	DNN	99.5
[9]	ResNet	95
[12]	CNN	88.73
[13]	VGGNet-19	97
[14]	ResNet	97
[16]	CNN	88.43
[18]	CNN+Perceptron	96.66
[20]	CNN	90.15
[22]	DCNN	95.03
[24]	CNN	91.02
[25]	CNN	97.77
[30]	LSTM	88
[31]	CNN+LSTM	82.17
[34]	RNN	85
[36]	CAEC	92.5
[38]	DBN	94.48
[39]	RBM	75
[41]	DNN	99.02
[42]	CNN	97.5
[43]	ResNet	93.58
[44]	CNN	96.88
[49]	VGGNet-16	70.4
[57]	AlexNet	97.94
[59]	CNN	99.77
[62]	LeNet	96.64

TABLE 5.2

Types of DNN vs. average accuracy (%) in the OASIS dataset

Papers	Types of DNN Utilized	Accuracy (%)
[7]	CNN	92.39
[15]	AlexNet	91.4
[15]	GoogLeNet	93.02
[27]	DCNN	93.18
[28]	CNN	80.25

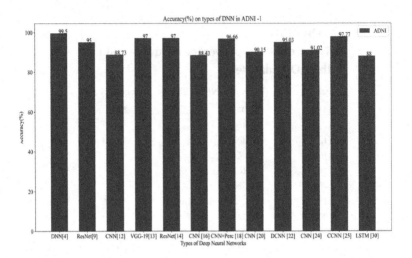

FIGURE 5.7   Visualizes the average accuracy for types of DNN applied to the ADNI dataset-1.

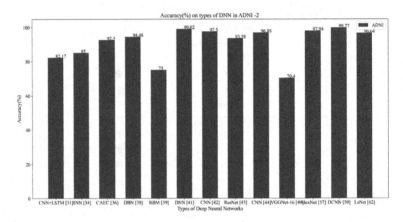

FIGURE 5.8   Visualizes the average accuracy for types of DNN applied to the ADNI dataset-2.

processes for healthcare leaders to make informed and timely decisions. Six aspects of healthcare (patient, caregiver, organization, quality, efficiency, and cost) are assessed in the context of the organization for their overall impact on performance. In this chapter, patients' MR images can be taken from publicly available datasets. Caregiver and organization are ADNI and OASIS. CNN produces higher efficiency, images are of good quality, and it provides cost for the requirement of GPU.

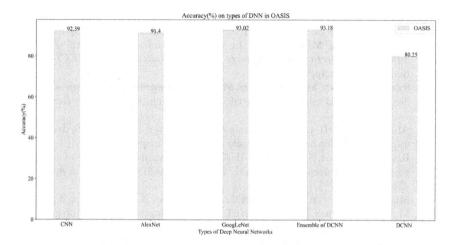

FIGURE 5.9 Visualizes the average accuracy for types of DNN applied to the OASIS dataset.

5.5 CONCLUSION

In this chapter, the papers were scrutinized on AD with images to detect the with help of numerous types of DNN. This study mainly focuses on each stage in diagnosing and predicting AD. It also competes for accuracy with all methods. It assists to select the finest method for diagnosis. Mostly, from the last 5 years in the Scopus database related to the keyword "AD," the recognized method was CNN, a type of DNN with the highest accuracy. It can be utilized for the prediction or recognition of AD from brain scans. This review discusses the networks of CNN with their architectures and working of it. This chapter will guide in determining techniques to be employed for early detection and checking for AD progression in images. The accuracy of every technique and comparison of methods by graphs for ADNI and OASIS datasets can be supportive for presenting techniques for earlier detection of AD in the future.

REFERENCES

1. Hazarika, R. A., Abraham, A., Kandar, D., & Maji, A. K. (2021). An improved LeNet-deep neural network model for alzheimer's disease classification using brain magnetic resonance images. *IEEE Access*, *9*, 161194–161207.
2. Suresha, H. S., & Parthasarathy, S. S. (2021). Detection of Alzheimer's disease using grey wolf optimization based clustering algorithm and deep neural network from magnetic resonance images. *Distributed and Parallel Databases*, *40*(4), 627–655.
3. Prajapati, R., Khatri, U., & Kwon, G. R. (2021, April). An Efficient Deep Neural Network Binary Classifier for Alzheimer's Disease Classification. In *2021 International Conference on Artificial Intelligence in Information and Communication (ICAIIC)*, IEEE, Jeju Island, Korea(South), (pp. 231–234).

4. Suresha, H. S., & Parthasarathy, S. S. (2020, December). Alzheimer Disease Detection Based on Deep Neural Network with Rectified Adam Optimization Technique using MRI Analysis. In *2020 Third International Conference on Advances in Electronics, Computers and Communications (ICAECC)*, IEEE, Bengaluru, India, (pp. 1–6).

5. Razavi, F., Tarokh, M. J., & Alborzi, M. (2019). An intelligent Alzheimer's disease diagnosis method using unsupervised feature learning. *Journal of Big Data*, *6*(1), 1–16.

6. Al-Adhaileh, M. H. (2022). Diagnosis and classification of Alzheimer's disease by using a convolution neural network algorithm. *Soft Computing*, 1–12.

7. Basheer, S., Bhatia, S., & Sakri, S. B. (2021). Computational modeling of dementia prediction using deep neural network: analysis on OASIS dataset. *IEEE Access*, *9*, 42449–42462.

8. Murugan, S., Venkatesan, C., Sumithra, M. G., Gao, X. Z., Elakkiya, B., Akila, M., & Manoharan, S. (2021). DEMNET: a deep learning model for early diagnosis of Alzheimer diseases and dementia from MR images. *IEEE Access*, *9*, 90319–90329.

9. Buvaneswari, P. R., & Gayathri, R. (2021). Deep learning-based segmentation in classification of Alzheimer's Disease. *Arabian Journal for Science and Engineering*, *46*(6), 5373–5383.

10. Carmo, D., Silva, B., Yasuda, C., Rittner, L., Lotufo, R., & Alzheimer's Disease Neuroimaging Initiative. (2021). Hippocampus segmentation on epilepsy and Alzheimer's disease studies with multiple convolutional neural networks. *Heliyon*, *7*(2), e06226.

11. Chen, X., Li, L., Sharma, A., Dhiman, G., & Vimal, S. (2021). The application of convolutional neural network model in diagnosis and nursing of MR imaging in Alzheimer's disease. *Interdisciplinary Sciences: Computational Life Sciences*, *14*(-1), 34–44.

12. Francis, A., & Pandian, I. A. (2021). Early detection of Alzheimer's disease using local binary pattern and convolutional neural network. *Multimedia Tools and Applications*, *80*(19), 29585–29600.

13. Helaly, H. A., Badawy, M., & Haikal, A. Y. (2021). Deep learning approach for early detection of Alzheimer's disease. *Cognitive Computation*, *14*, 1711–1727.

14. Helaly, H. A., Badawy, M., & Haikal, A. Y. (2021). Toward deep mri segmentation for Alzheimer's disease detection. *Neural Computing and Applications*, *34*(2), 1047–1063.

15. Liu, J., Li, M., Luo, Y., Yang, S., Li, W., & Bi, Y. (2021). Alzheimer's disease detection using depthwise separable convolutional neural networks. *Computer Methods and Programs in Biomedicine*, *203*, 106032.

16. Pei, Z., Gou, Y., Ma, M., Guo, M., Leng, C., Chen, Y., & Li, J. (2021). Alzheimer's disease diagnosis based on long-range dependency mechanism using convolutional neural network. *Multimedia Tools and Applications*, *81*(25), 36053–36068.

17. Raghavaiah, P., & Varadarajan, S. (2021). Novel deep learning convolution technique for recognition of Alzheimer's disease. *Materials Today: Proceedings*, *46*, 4095–4098.

18. Raju, M., Gopi, V. P., & Anitha, V. S. (2021, March). Multi-class Classification of Alzheimer's Disease using 3DCNN Features and Multilayer Perceptron. In *2021 Sixth International Conference on Wireless Communications, Signal Processing and Networking (WiSPNET)*, IEEE, Chennai, India, (pp. 368–373).

19. Sathiyamoorthi, V., Ilavarasi, A. K., Murugeswari, K., Ahmed, S. T., Devi, B. A., & Kalipindi, M. (2021). A deep convolutional neural network based computer aided diagnosis system for the prediction of Alzheimer's disease in MRI images. *Measurement*, *171*, 108838.

20. Turkson, R. E., Qu, H., Mawuli, C. B., & Eghan, M. J. (2021). Classification of Alzheimer's disease using deep convolutional spiking neural network. *Neural Processing Letters, 53*(4), 2649–2663.
21. Allioui, H., Sadgal, M., & Elfazziki, A. (2020). Utilization of a convolutional method for Alzheimer disease diagnosis. *Machine Vision and Applications, 31*(4), 1–19.
22. Chen, C. Z., Wu, Q., Li, Z. Y., Xiao, L., & Hu, Z. Y. (2021). Diagnosis of Alzheimer's disease based on deeply-fused nets. *Combinatorial Chemistry & High Throughput Screening, 24*(6), 781–789
23. Chitradevi, D., & Prabha, S. (2020). Analysis of brain sub regions using optimization techniques and deep learning method in Alzheimer disease. *Applied Soft Computing, 86*, 105857.
24. Kim, H. W., Lee, H. E., Oh, K., Lee, S., Yun, M., & Yoo, S. K. (2020). Multislice representational learning of convolutional neural network for Alzheimer's disease classification using positron emission tomography. *BioMedical Engineering OnLine, 19*(1), 1–15.
25. Raju, M., Gopi, V. P., Anitha, V. S., & Wahid, K. A. (2020). Multi-class diagnosis of Alzheimer's disease using cascaded three dimensional-convolutional neural network. *Physical and Engineering Sciences in Medicine, 43*(4), 1219–1228.
26. Sun, J., Yan, S., Song, C., & Han, B. (2020). Dual-functional neural network for bilateral hippocampi segmentation and diagnosis of Alzheimer's disease. *International Journal of Computer Assisted Radiology and Surgery, 15*(3), 445–455.
27. Islam, J., & Zhang, Y. (2018). Brain MRI analysis for Alzheimer's disease diagnosis using an ensemble system of deep convolutional neural networks. *Brain Informatics, 5*(2), 1–14.
28. Ullah, H. T., Onik, Z., Islam, R., & Nandi, D. (2018, April). Alzheimer's Disease and Dementia Detection from 3D Brain MRI Data using Deep Convolutional Neural Networks. In *2018 3rd International Conference for Convergence in Technology (I2CT)*, IEEE, Pune, India, (pp. 1–3).
29. Vu, T. D., Ho, N. H., Yang, H. J., Kim, J., & Song, H. C. (2018). Non-white matter tissue extraction and deep convolutional neural network for Alzheimer's disease detection. *Soft Computing, 22*(20), 6825–6833.
30. Li, W., Lin, X., & Chen, X. (2020). Detecting Alzheimer's disease based on 4D fMRI: an exploration under deep learning framework. *Neurocomputing, 388*, 280–287.
31. Hong, X., Lin, R., Yang, C., Zeng, N., Cai, C., Gou, J., & Yang, J. (2019). Predicting Alzheimer's disease using LSTM. *IEEE Access, 7*, 80893–80901.
32. Feng, C., Elazab, A., Yang, P., Wang, T., Zhou, F., Hu, H., & Lei, B. (2019). Deep learning framework for Alzheimer's disease diagnosis via 3D-CNN and FSBi-LSTM. *IEEE Access, 7*, 63605–63618.
33. Li, H., & Fan, Y. (2019, April). Early Prediction of Alzheimer's Disease Dementia Based on Baseline Hippocampal MRI and 1-year Follow-up Cognitive Measures Using Deep Recurrent Neural Networks. In *2019 IEEE 16th International Symposium on Biomedical Imaging (ISBI 2019)*, Early Prediction of Alzheimer's Disease Dementia Based on Baseline Hippocampal MRI and 1-year Follow-up Cognitive Measures Using Deep Recurrent Neural Networks. In *2019 IEEE 16th International Symposium on Biomedical Imaging (ISBI 2019)*, IEEE, Venice, Italy, (pp. 368–371).
34. Jung, W., Jun, E., Suk, H. I., & Alzheimer's Disease Neuroimaging Initiative. (2021). Deep recurrent model for individualized prediction of Alzheimer's disease progression. *NeuroImage, 237*, 118143.
35. Nguyen, M., He, T., An, L., Alexander, D. C., Feng, J., Yeo, B. T., & Alzheimer's Disease Neuroimaging Initiative. (2020). Predicting Alzheimer's disease progression using deep recurrent neural networks. *NeuroImage, 222*, 117203.

36. Hedayati, R., Khedmati, M., & Taghipour-Gorjikolaie, M. (2021). Deep feature extraction method based on ensemble of convolutional auto encoders: application to Alzheimer's disease diagnosis. *Biomedical Signal Processing and Control, 66,* 102397.

37. Shubhangi, D. C., & Pratibha, A. K. (2021, September). Asthma, Alzheimer's and Dementia Disease Detection based on Voice Recognition using Multi-Layer Perceptron Algorithm. In *2021 International Conference on Innovative Computing, Intelligent Communication and Smart Electrical Systems (ICSES)*, IEEE, Chennai, India, (pp. 1–7).

38. Zeng, N., Li, H., & Peng, Y. (2021). A new deep belief network-based multi-task learning for diagnosis of Alzheimer's disease. *Neural Computing and Applications,* 1–12.

39. Pei, S., & Guan, J. (2021). Classifying cognitive normal and early mild cognitive impairment of Alzheimer's disease by applying restricted 30lzheimer machine to fMRI data. *Current BioInformatics, 16*(2), 252–260.

40. Noor, M. B. T., Zenia, N. Z., Kaiser, M. S., Mamun, S. A., & Mahmud, M. (2020). Application of deep learning in detecting neurological disorders from magnetic resonance images: a survey on the detection of Alzheimer's disease, Parkinson's disease and schizophrenia. *Brain Informatics, 7*(1), 1–21.

41. Ashraf, A., Naz, S., Shirazi, S. H., Razzak, I., & Parsad, M. (2021). Deep transfer learning for 30lzheimer neurological disorder detection. *Multimedia Tools and Applications, 80*(20), 30117–30142.

42. AbdulAzeem, Y., Bahgat, W. M., & Badawy, M. (2021). A CNN based framework for classification of Alzheimer's disease. *Neural Computing and Applications, 33*(-16), 10415–10428.

43. Xu, M., Liu, Z., Wang, Z., Sun, L., & Liang, Z. (2019, October). The Diagnosis of Alzheimer's Disease Based on Enhanced Residual Neutral Network. In *2019 International Conference on Cyber-Enabled Distributed Computing and Knowledge Discovery (CyberC)*, IEEE, Guilin, China, (pp. 405–411).

44. Ebrahimi, A., Luo, S., & Chiong, R. (2020, November). Introducing Transfer Learning to 3D ResNet-18 for Alzheimer's Disease Detection on MRI Images. In *2020 35th International Conference on Image and Vision Computing New Zealand (IVCNZ)*, IEEE, Wellington, New Zealand, (pp. 1–6).

45. Sachan, A. N. K. I. T., (2019) Detailed Guide to Understand and Implement ResNets, https://cv-tricks.com/keras/understand-implement-resnets/.

46. Zakaria, N., Mohamed, F., Abdelghani, R., & Sundaraj, K. (2021, November). VGG16, ResNet-50, and GoogLeNet Deep Learning Architecture for Breathing Sound Classification: A Comparative Study. In *2021 International Conference on Artificial Intelligence for Cyber Security Systems and Privacy (AI-CSP)*, IEEE, El Oued, Algeria, (pp. 1–6).

47. Siegmund, D., Tran, V. P., Wilmsdorff, J. V., Kirchbuchner, F., & Kuijper, A. (2019, October). Piggybacking Detection Based on Coupled Body-Feet Recognition at Entrance Control. In *Iberoamerican Congress on Pattern Recognition* (pp. 780–789). Springer, Cham, Havana.

48. Understanding GoogLeNet Model – CNN Architecture, 2021, https://www.geeksforgeeks.org/understanding-googlenet-model-cnn-architecture/.

49. Jonsson, T., & Tapper, I. (2020). Evaluation of two CNN models, VGGNet-16 & VGGNet-19, for classification of Alzheimer's disease in brain MRI scans, Stockholm, Sweden.

50. Build VGG Net from Scratch with Python!, 2021, https://www.analyticsvidhya.com/blog/2021/06/build-vgg-net-from-scratch-with-python/.Journal.

51. Li, S., Wang, L., Li, J., & Yao, Y. (2021, February). Image Classification Algorithm Based on Improved AlexNet. In *Journal of Physics: Conference Series*, Xiamen,China (Vol. 1813, No. 1, p. 012051). IOP Publishing.

52. Krizhevsky, A., Sutskever, I., & Hinton, G. E. (2012). Imagenet classification with deep convolutional neural networks. *Advances in Neural Information Processing Systems, 25*, 1097–1105.

53. AlexNet: The first CNN to win ImageNet, Great Learning Team, https://www. mygreatlearning.com/blog/alexnet-the-first-cnn-to-win-image-net/. Accessed on 15 Jan 2022.

54. The Architecture of Lenet-5, https://www.analyticsvidhya.com/blog/2021/03/the-architecture-of-lenet-5/. Accessed on 15 Jan 2022.

55. LeNet-5 Tutorial: Architecture, Features and Importance, Ayush Singh Rawat 2021,https://www.analyticssteps.com/blogs/lenet-5-tutorial-architecture-features-and-importance.

56. Venugopalan, J., Tong, L., Hassanzadeh, H. R., & Wang, M. D. (2021). Multimodal deep learning models for early detection of Alzheimer's disease stage. *Scientific Reports, 11*(1), 1–13.

57. Shakarami, A., Tarrah, H., & Mahdavi-Hormat, A. (2020). A CAD system for diagnosing Alzheimer's disease using 2D slices and an improved AlexNet-SVM method. *Optik, 212*, 164237.

58. Janghel, R. R., & Rathore, Y. K. (2020). Deep convolution neural network based system for early diagnosis of Alzheimer's disease. *IRBM, 42*(4), 258–267.

59. Qayyum, A., et al. (2017). Medical image retrieval using deep convolutional neural network. *Neurocomputing, 266*, 8–20.

60. Al-Shoukry, S., Rassem, T. H., & Makbol, N. M. (2020). Alzheimer's diseases detection by using deep learning algorithms: a mini-review. *IEEE Access, 8*, 77131–77141.

61. Suresha, H. S., & Parthasarathy, S. S. (2021). Probabilistic principal component analysis, and long short-term memory classifier for automatic detection of Alzheimer's disease using MRI the brain images. *Journal of The Institution of Engineers (India): Series B, 26*(1), 53–64.

62. Hazarika, R. A., Abraham, A., Kandar, D., & Maji, A. K. (2021). An improved LeNet-deep neural network model for Alzheimer's disease classification using brain magnetic resonance images. *IEEE Access, 9*, 161194–161207.

6 Detection and Classification of Alzheimer's Disease
A Deep Learning Approach with Predictor Variables

Deepthi K. Oommen and J. Arunnehru
SRM Institute of Science and Technology

CONTENTS

6.1 INTRODUCTION

Alzheimer's disease (AD) is a devastating ailment and difficult to rehabilitate; it is also known as senile dementia. AD is an accelerating neurological illness that is source to gradual memory and cognition loss. After cardiovascular disease, cancer, and stroke, AD is the fourth-largest cause of mortality [1]. Mild cognitive impairment (MCI), a precursor to Alzheimer's disease, affects 10%–20% of adults aged 45 and over, according to Alzheimer's Association research. The symptoms of Alzheimer's disease normally appear gently and worsen as the disease progresses. Compared with other neurodevelopmental disorders, Alzheimer's disease has been a significant cost strain in Asia, North America, and worldwide [2]. According to study investigations, the number of persons who would be affected by 2,050 might reach $64 billion [3]. The rise in AD cases can lead to a variety of causes, including population growth, aging, and shifting social and economic development patterns. There is presently no treatment available to slow or halt the progression of this disease. The illness can, however, be managed if diagnosed early enough. Individuals with Alzheimer's disease are often diagnosed using cerebral scanning technology such as MRI scans in combination with clinical evaluations that look for signs of memory loss [4]. Various variables, including population growth, aging, and changing social and economic development practices, are all contributing to the rise in AD cases. In the field of neurodegenerative diseases such as Alzheimer's and Parkinson's, many studies have examined the potential of deep learning (DL) approaches. The use of data collected by magnetic resonance imaging (MRI) or positron emission tomography (PET) for this purpose has been widely researched [5]. The deterioration of cognitive capacity involved with Alzheimer's disease is shown by brain shrinkage, notably in the hippocampal section. The major focus of research is to build a deep neural network model to detect Alzheimer's disease using brain imaging and clinical evaluation.

The hippocampus and cortical thickness are the two most important sections in the brain for detecting disease. The hippocampal region of someone with Alzheimer's disease shrinks, and cortical thickness of ventricles expand [6]. These parts are thought to be the link between the body's central nervous system. The demise of cells and impairment of neurons and synapses occurs when the hippocampus region shrinks. It brings a halt to communication across neurons and synapses since they can no longer engage. As a result, brain regions involved in memory, organizing, reasoning, and judgment suffer. The deteriorated brain cell has a lower frequency on MRI [7,8]. Figure 6.1 depicts the MRI image of a healthy and AD-affected brain.

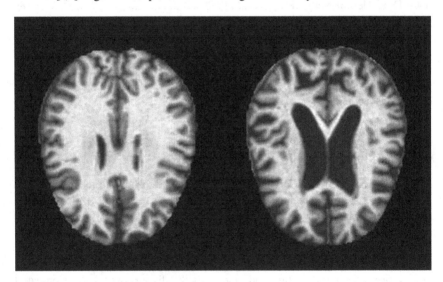

FIGURE 6.1   MRI of healthy brain and AD brain.

The mini-mental state examination (MMSE), clinical dementia rating (CDR), and Alzheimer's disease assessment scale (ADAS) are all longitudinal clinical examinations test that has a strong connection to the course of Alzheimer's disease [9]. The charting of this connection is helpful since it allows practitioners to intervene while the condition is still unidentified. While there is no cure for Alzheimer's disease, it can be slowed down if symptoms are addressed early enough. Memory drugs, behavior mediation, sleep, and occupation rehabilitation, as well as supported living, are all options for treatment [10,11]. As an outcome, detecting the disease early is indispensable for reducing the rate of illness advancement. The work utilized the OASIS dataset to conduct a hierarchical analysis of all available data points to predict AD.

The following is a breakdown of the paper's structure: Section 6.2 describes related works, Section 6.3 conveys an in-depth overview of the proposed methodology and an elaboration of the deep neural network, and Section 6.4 uncovers the experimental outcomes, which defines the dataset and predictor variables, as well as experimental work performed with the deep neural network on the given dataset and results. It describes the performance measure of the classifier and accuracy results with confusion matrix and ROC curve inculcated to depict the system performance. Finally, Section 6.5 concludes with a list of upcoming projects.

6.2   RELATED WORK

This section will look at some of the most modern methods for predicting and diagnosing Alzheimer's disease utilizing predictor variables and various types of computational models. Papers [12,13] detect dementia, so electronic health record scores were used. For dementia prediction, the researchers additionally employed cross-sectional preliminary data, ADNI registry datasets, MRI measures, and an artificial neural network. Another study used MRI brain images to construct selective maps that were used to apply a vascular approach to the brain tissues, and the results were used to correctly detect Alzheimer's disease and its phases. Paper [14] describes a distributed multitask multimodal (DMM) strategy proposed in this research to address the difficult challenge of learning relevant features from disparate but connected input. However, they overlook important baseline cognitive data that might be useful in predicting the advancement of such ratings at a later time point which could be a predictor factor in identifying the disease.

A part of the OASIS data was utilized to create methods for detecting binary-coded AD using Eigenbrain imaging. It ruled out people under the age of 60 and data that was missing, defined Alzheimer's disease, limited its study to a restricted number of coronal slice pictures, and ran 50 10-fold cross-validations.

The MMSE scores and the ADAS scale were the variables used to predict the symptom progress stages over 6 years for 1,000 individuals. The researchers used MR imaging, genetic proteins, clinical data, and a Siamese neural network with two identical equally weighted subnetworks to predict AD development [15,16].

Paper [17] employed SVM with 10-fold cross-validation to automatically categorize Alzheimer's disease using a tiny sample set of test images and controls and achieved outstanding accuracy. The OASIS datasets are open source, which makes them simple to use and test new approaches. OASIS-1 is cross-sectional research with 416 people, 100 of whom are over 60 and have been diagnosed with extremely mild or severe Alzheimer's disease (as measured by the clinical dementia rate) [18].

A decision tree strategy partitions information into subgroups in an ML framework. The objective of a choice tree is to consolidate the preparation information into the smallest tree conceivable [19,20]. Decision tree approaches are used to identify the qualities to be evaluated at each node in order to obtain the "best" division. Because of their adaptability and stability, decision trees are frequently utilized in categorization challenges of AD classification [21].

In clinical findings, machine learning is turning out to be regularly used to learn models. This exploration examines the consequences of different AI calculations for diagnosing the disorder. The machine learning models with tuned hyper-parameters can perform well in the classification and detection of AD [22–24].

The current strategy relied on the SVM algorithm to forecast Alzheimer's details. The SVM algorithm merely performs a clustering procedure and isolates those who are most likely suffering from Alzheimer's disease. The SVM algorithm is a time-consuming procedure for classifying all of the information provided [25,26].

In Alzheimer's sickness, an enormous number of neurons stop it are lost to fire and synaptic associations. Alzheimer's illness is exceptional in grown-ups between the ages of 30 and 60 [27]. Alzheimer's illness can cause changes in rest designs, misery, uneasiness, and inconvenience doing basic abilities like perusing or composing, as well as forceful way of behaving and unfortunate direction. Alzheimer's sickness and the principal adjustments in the mind happen 10–20 years before side effects show up. It continuously falls apart memory and lessens thinking capacities [28].

6.3 MOTIVATION AND OBJECTIVE

Memory loss is a common symptom of Alzheimer's disease (AD), which is an incurable condition that cannot be cured. The pathogenesis of Alzheimer's disease is connected to the damage and death of neurons, which begins in the area of the brain known as the hippocampus. If the condition is recognized in its earliest stages, the patient has a better chance of receiving the appropriate therapy and avoiding additional irreparable brain damage. The ability to forecast and classify a patient's condition early on can, to some extent, enhance that patient's life expectancy. This work presents an automated AD recognition approach based on deep neural networks. The objective is to use deep learning techniques paired with clinical assessments and brain atrophy volume to construct deep neural network models that can effectively diagnose the presence of Alzheimer's disease.

6.4 DEEP NEURAL NETWORK

Deep neural networks (DNNs) are multilayer variants of traditional artificial neural networks (ANNs). DNN models have lately become popular in demand, on account of their superior performance in learning not only the non-linear input–output mapping but also the underlying structure of the input data vectors. The network is made up of nodes, which are linked units. This is the tiniest component of the neural network. Whenever a neuron accepts a signal, it initiates a sequence of events. Based on the input obtained, the signal is transmitted from one neuron to the next. The result is a complicated network that adapts from feedback. Layers are used to organize the nodes. The different levels between the input and output layers are processed to solve a problem. The deeper the network, the larger the number of layers to be analyzed, therefore the name deep learning. Since each unit in a DNN is eventually connected, it gains connections from all units in the previous layers. The unit has its weight and bias for every pair of consecutive layers. Multiplying each input by its weights and adding results computes the input. An activation function also applies to the net input layer as it helps in understanding the complex data patterns. Figure. 6.2 represents a sample diagram of a DNN with three hidden layers.

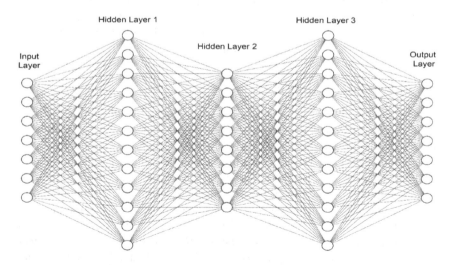

FIGURE 6.2   Sample DNN with three hidden layers.

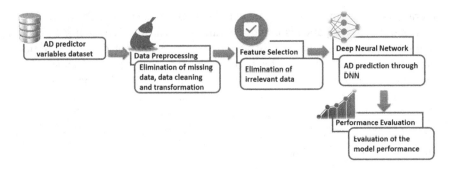

FIGURE 6.3   Proposed model architecture.

6.5   PROPOSED METHOD

To distinguish between demented and non-demented AD people, we used a DNN model for training and testing, with the prediction criteria termed predictor variables. The categories are learned incrementally by the hidden layers of the network model. The AD predictor variables dataset took into account a set of seven parameters for disease identification. The selected parameters are mainly based on analyzing cognitive stability and brain volume statistics; these factors depicted a major contribution to identifying AD. Dataset is acquainted with OASIS, and the selected set of parameters was undergone preprocessing to remove the improper inconsistent data. The rows with missing values can either drop it or can replace with some corresponding values, and the process is called imputation. Our dataset has only 400 data points, and the consideration of data points can help in increasing the model performance. The current method has used a DNN-based detection model, to classify the demented control and non-demented controls. The particular approach utilized a set of 400 data and portioned it into a 70:30 ratio for training and testing. The DNN has considered five hidden layers to achieve an accurate classification and performance. Figure 6.3 depicts the DNN models for detecting AD through risk variables.

6.6   EXPERIMENTAL SETUP

The section focuses on the parameters and experimental working of the current method. The experimental setup was carried out on Windows 10 with an Intel i7 processor with 2.10 GHz and 8 GB RAM. Python (3.7.6), Keras (2.4.3) framework, and Tensor flow (2.3.1) backend with libraries are the software requirements for the proposed deep learning model. Choosing hyper-parameter combinations using cross-fold validation and the grid search technique to improve the model's accuracy and efficiency is one of the most difficult components of constructing deep neural networks models. The suggested network has investigated several hidden layer ranges with a variety of nodes, learning rates, optimizers, activation functions, batch size, epochs, dropouts, and output functions to develop a network with fine-tuned parameters. Table 6.1 shows the model with distinct parameter ranges.

TABLE 6.1

Proposed network's hyper-parameter setup

Network Hyper-Parameters	Range Distribution
Batch size	16, 32, 64, 128
Training epochs	100, 150, 200, 250, 300
Learning rates	0.0001–0.01
Hidden layers	3, 5, 7
optimization method	SGD, Adam, Adamax, Adagrad
Output function	Softmax
Activation function	Sigmoid, ReLU, Leaky ReLU, tanh

6.7   DATASET

Data from the Open Access Series of Imaging Studies (OASIS) [29] is used to test the suggested model. Four hundred observations of 142 people of age from 58 to 96 are the considered dataset for the current work. The dataset includes 400 samples from 142 people ranging in age from 58 to 96 years old. Both genders are considered in the dataset, and all are right-handed. The considered parameters analyze the cognitive stability and statistical measurement of brain volume, as it plays a major in the identification of disease [30]. The disease impacts the brain volume as it progresses, its size starts to decrease, and instability occurs in the cognitive ability of a person. The following describes in detail the selected predictor variables of the proposed work, and Figure 6.3 depicts a total intracranial volume of brain.

- **Subject Id**: A unique value has been given to each subject. The values vary from 1 to 142 for the current work.
- **Age and Gender**: It specifies the age of the selected individuals (male and female) for the proposed work.
- **MRI Id**: Each MRI test is represented by a unique identifier. As it can be many MRIs ids for a single person.
- **Group**: The class is divided into two stages: demented and non-demented.
- **Mini-Mental State Examination (MMSE)**: AD and other dementing diseases are common targets for the MMSE, which is a widely used assessment tool for finding brain abnormalities. There are 21 distinct items throughout 11 separate assessments, with a score scale from 0 to 30. Psychological resistance and the evolution of a person's subjective changes over time may be assessed using this technique, making it an effective tool for tracking a patient's reaction to therapy [12,13].
- **Clinical Dementia Rate (CDR)**: The CDR is based on a structured and systematic diagnostic method with the patient and an eligible source, and it assigns a score to each of the five scales of impairment. On a five-point scale, the primary areas are: recollection, awareness, reasoning, and perception; volunteerism; lifestyle and pastimes; and problem-solving. The

scaling rate as none=0, questionable=0.5, mild=1, moderate=2, and severe=3. As a result, the CDR appears to be a robust and considerable strategy for assessing and analyzing dementia [14].

- **Estimated Total Intracranial Volume (eTIV)**: The capacity of cavities contained in a brain is measured by estimated total intracranial volume (eTIV). If eTIV is not one-sided, its difference should be abnormal beyond what the true intracranial volume can explain. While adjusting for completely specified intracranial capacity, we believe there will be no link between eTIV and total brain volume. Total intracranial volume is an essential covariate in volumetric brain and brain region analysis, particularly in the study of neurodegenerative illnesses, where it can serve as a substitute for optimum pre-morbid brain volume. Its values are from 1,488±176.13 [17,18].

- **Normalized Whole Brain Volume (nWBV)**: Normalized whole brain volume (nWBV) is the whole capacity of the brain excluding vacant volumes. Adults with no history of mental illness had a clear, substantial quadratic drop in nWBV levels, which could be traced back to a leveling-off of nWBV occurrences over time. This variable measures the entire brain's volume. The range of nWBV is considered from 0.730±0.037.

- **Atlas Scaling Factor (ASF)**: The eTIV and nWBV are related to (ASF). To keep everyone aligned with the chart book purpose, the ASF is the density factor that everyone needs. Because chart book standardization compares head size, the ASF should be proportional to TIV. Its value ranges from 1.195±0.138.

6.8   PERFORMANCE METRICS

Accuracy, precision, sensitivity or recall, and F1-score are the four metrics used for quantitative evaluation. The True Positive (TP), False Positive (FP), True Negative (TN), and False Negative (FN) are the values for the quantitative analyses, assessment, and comparison of the competing methods. Table 6.2 describes

TABLE 6.2

Performance metrics

Performance Measures

$$Accuracy = \frac{TP + TN}{TP + TN + FP + FN}$$

$$Precision = \frac{TP}{TP + FP}$$

$$Recall = \frac{TP}{TP + FN}$$

$$F1\text{-}Score = \frac{2TP}{2TP + FP + FN}$$

the performance metrics. In the current work, the True Positive displays the range of subjects that have been correctly classified. The number of individuals classified erroneously is represented by True Negatives. False Positives misdiagnose a person as demented control, while False Negatives miss the person who has it.

6.9 RESULTS AND DISCUSSION

DNN model comprising five hidden layers and distinctive neurons was used to train the features using the OASIS dataset's model parameters. The network optimizes its weight to reduce the loss function using a learning rate of 0.001 and a batch size of 32. For constructing the Keras framework, the categorical cross-entropy and Adam optimizer are used to iterate the model parameters for 350 epochs. To maximize the performance of the network, the system utilizes sigmoid as the activation function for all units in the hidden layer and the softmax as the output function. The model has experimented with different hyper-parameters to ensure the proposed model will be to work at its maximum efficiency. Table 6.3 shows the description of the proposed DNN for enhanced hyper-parameters in AD. The efficiency of our model is evaluated by training the network with 10–25 layers, and it has shown a significant drop in accuracy as the size of the layer increases. As a result, we chose an architecture with few layers that responded with a 94% accuracy. In identifying demented and non-demented controls, the suggested model has shown significant inference.

Table 6.4 shows the performance characteristics of the deep neural network model for binary classification of AD detection. The researchers used a 400 data points from the OASIS dataset with seven parameters to find demented and non-demented patients, with a 70:30 training/test ratio. With the suggested network model, the chosen parameters were optimal enough to perform binary classification. The model acquired an accuracy 94%, precision 91.5%, recall 90.5%, and F1-score 89.5%.

TABLE 6.3
DNN model with optimized hyper-parameter

Hyper-Parameter	Optimized Value
Hidden layers	5
Activation function	Sigmoid
Learning rate	0.001
Maximum iteration	350
Optimization algorithm	Adam
Batch size	32
Output function	Softmax

TABLE 6.4

Model performance obtained for OASIS dataset

Class	Accuracy	Precision	Recall	F1 Score
Non-demented	0.96	0.92	0.90	0.89
Demented	0.92	0.91	0.91	0.90

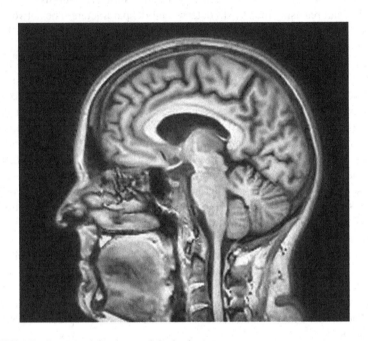

FIGURE 6.4 Intracranial volume of the brain.

Figure 6.4 shows the whole confusion matrix (CM) for the OASIS dataset comparable to the model execution. It can make a determination with respect to classification algorithm performance. The proposed model is entrusted with obtaining better results for analyzing the demented to the non-demented subjects. The CM of the current model depicts the True Negative and Positive as 96% and 92%, respectively. The model performed well in predicting non-demented classes compared with demented subjects. The system failed with 4% in predicting incorrectly demented class, and it needs more focus in this area to accomplish the performance to its maximum. Figure 6.5 displays the ROC (Receiver Operating Characteristics) curve of AD classification. ROC explains the intercorrelation between the parameters specificity (False Positive rate) and sensitivity (True Positive rate). Its goal is to figure out how accurate certain classifiers are. The ROC curve illustrated an approach that relies on a TPR and FPR while taking AD factors into account to determine demented and non-demented controls

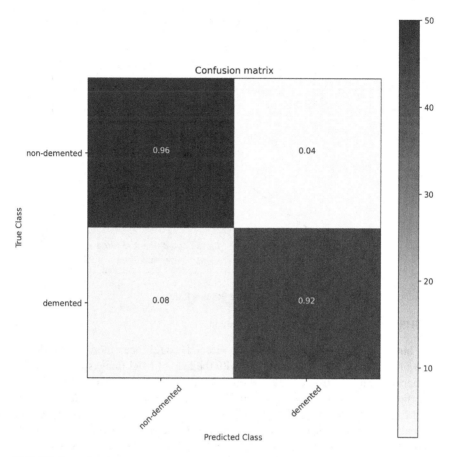

FIGURE 6.5   Confusion matrix: for demented and non-demented subjects.

in this methodology. The ROC curve is classified by the combination of the area under the curve (AUC = 1) exhibiting a high assurance of inappropriately organizing normal participants and afflicted subjects (Figure 6.6).

6.10   CONCLUSION

The proposed work has demonstrated a successful method of dealing with Alzheimer's disease detection by utilizing a number of clinically verified indicator criteria. The feasibility of the comprehensive DNN model in classifying AD and healthy participants was investigated in this work. The present DNN model has five hidden layers and fine-tuned hyper-parameters, with various iterations that could obtain 94% accuracy in classifying the demented with non-demented controls. The current study's risk variables were limited to cognitive stability and brain volume size. They are sufficient for distinguishing between AD-affected and healthy individuals, and the proposed model could locate it sufficiently for

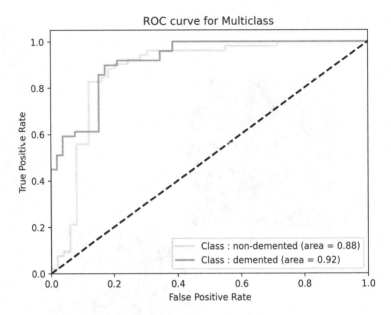

FIGURE 6.6   ROC curve for AD classification.

the binary classification. In future, the research could focus more on the detection of MCIs and their classification, with the help of MRI images in 2D and 3D dimensions and electronic health records. A multimodal technique with decreased overfitting can enhance the system, and it can also be used to anticipate the transition from stable AD to prolonged AD. As this process can build up a profound e-health system and help the AD patients to an extent, the model can be trained and work for various neurological diseases and also in the medical research field.

REFERENCES

1. R. Brookmeyer, E. Johnson, K. Ziegler-Graham, and H. M. Arrighi. "Forecasting the global burden of Alzheimers disease." *Alzheimer's & Dementia*, 3(3):186–191, 2007.
2. M. Sado, A. Ninomiya, R. Shikimoto, B. Ikeda, T. Baba, K. Yoshimura, and M. Mimura. "The estimated cost of dementia in Japan is the most aged society globally." *PloS One*, 13(11):e0206508, 2018.
3. J. Islam and Y. Zhang. "Brain MRI analysis for Alzheimer's disease diagnosis using an ensemble system of deep convolutional neural networks." *Brain Informatics*, 5(2):1–14, 2018.
4. C. Carlos, and M. Silveira. "Classification of Alzheimer's disease from FDG-PET images using favourite class ensembles." In *2013 35th Annual International Conference of the IEEE Engineering in Medicine and Biology Society (EMBC)*, IEEE, Osaka, Japan, 2013.

5. D. K. Oommen and J. Arunnehru, "A comprehensive study on early detection of Alzheimer disease using convolutional neural network." *International Conference on Advances in Materials, Computer and Communication Technologies*, Kanyakumari, India. 2385: 050012, 2022.

6. S. Sarraf, G. Tofighi et al. "Alzheimer's Disease Neuroimaging Initiative, DeepAD: Alzheimer's disease classification via deep convolutional neural networks using MRI and fMRI." *BioRxiv*, 070441, 2016.

7. J. Arunnehru and M. K. Geetha. "Automatic human emotion recognition in surveillance video." In *Intelligent Techniques in Signal Processing for Multimedia Security*, Springer, Cham, 321–342. 2017.

8. M. A. Warsi. *The fractal nature and functional connectivity of brain function as measured by BOLD MRI in Alzheimer's Disease*. PhD Thesis, 2012

9. N. Bhagwat, J. D. Viviano, A. N. Voineskos, M. M. Chakravarty, and A. D. N. Initiative, "Modeling and prediction of clinical symptom trajectories in Alzheimer's disease using longitudinal data," *PLoS Computational Biology* 14(9):e1006376, 2018

10. L. Huang, et al. "Soft-split sparse regression-based random forest for predicting future clinical scores of Alzheimer's disease." *International Workshop on Machine Learning in Medical Imaging*. Springer, Cham, 2015.

11. J. Arunnehru, and M. K. Geetha. "Motion intensity code for action recognition in video using PCA and SVM." *Mining Intelligence and Knowledge Exploration*, Springer, Cham, 70–81. 2013.

12. N. Bhagwat, et al. "An artificial neural network model for clinical score prediction in Alzheimer disease using structural neuroimaging measures." *Journal of Psychiatry & Neuroscience: JPN* 44(4):246, 2019.

13. J. Arunnehru, G. Chamundeeswari, and S. Prasanna Bharathi. "Human action recognition using 3D convolutional neural networks with 3D motion cuboids in surveillance videos." *Procedia Computer Science* 133 471–477, 2018.

14. S. Tabarestani and et al. "A distributed multitask multimodal approach for the prediction of Alzheimer's disease in a longitudinal study." *Neuroimage* 206 116317, 2019.

15. Y. Zhang, et al. "Three-dimensional eigenbrain for the detection of subjects and brain regions related with Alzheimer's disease." *Journal of Alzheimer's Disease* 50(4):1163–1179, 2016.

16. L. E. Collij, et al. "Application of machine learning to arterial spin labelling in mild cognitive impairment and Alzheimer disease." *Radiology* 281(3):865–875, 2016.

17. T. N. Duc et al. "3D-deep learning based automatic diagnosis of Alzheimer's disease with joint MMSE prediction using resting-state fMRI." *Neuro Informatics* 18 (1):71–86, 2020.

18. J. Venugopalan, et al. "Multimodal deep learning models for early detection of Alzheimer's disease stage." *Scientific Reports* 11(1):1–13, 2021.

19. L. M. Wang, X. L. Li, C. H. Cao, and S. M. Yuan "Combining decision tree and Naive Bayes for classification." *Knowledge-Based Systems* 19(7):511–515, 2006.

20. M. J. Aitkenhead, "A co-evolving decision tree classification method." *Expert Systems with Applications* 34(1):18–25, 2008.

21. H. H. Patel, and P. Prajapati. "Study and analysis of decision tree based classification algorithms." *International Journal of Computer Sciences and Engineering* 6(10):74–78, 2018.

22. A. Tayal, et al. "DL-CNN-based approach with image processing techniques for diagnosis of retinal diseases." *Multimedia Systems* 28(4):1417–1438, 2022.
23. M. Masud, N. Sikder, A.A. Nahid, A. K. Bairagi, and M. A. AlZain, "A machine learning approach to diagnosing lung and colon cancer using a deep learning-based classification framework," *Sensors* 21(3):748, 2021.
24. M. Masud, H. Alhumyani, S. S. Alshamrani et al., "Leveraging deep learning techniques for malaria parasite detection using mobile application," *Wireless Communications and Mobile Computing*, 2020, 15, Article ID: 8895429, 2020.
25. D. Zhang, D. Shen, "Predicting future clinical changes of MCI patients using longitudinal and multimodal biomarkers." *PLoS One* 7(3):1–5, 2012.
26. K.N. Batmanghelich, D.H. Ye, K.M. Pohl, B. Taskar, C. Davatzikos, "Disease classification and prediction via semi-supervised dimensionality reduction." *Biomedical Imaging: From Nano to Macro, 2011 IEEE International Symposium*, IEEE, Chicago, IL, USA, 1086–1090. 2011
27. S. Y. Ryu, et al. "Measurement of precuneal and hippocampal volumes using magnetic resonance volumetry in Alzheimer's disease." *Journal of Clinical Neurology* 6(4):196–203, 2010.
28. D. Oommen and J. Arunnehru. "Early diagnosis of Alzheimer's disease from MRI images using Scattering Wavelet Transforms (SWT)." *International Conference on Soft Computing and its Engineering Applications* 1572:249–263, 2022.
29. D. S. Marcus, T. H. Wang, J. Parker, J. G. Csernansky, J. C. Morris, and R. L. Buckner. "Open access series of imaging studies (oasis): cross-sectional mri data in young, middle aged, nondemented, and demented older adults." *Journal of Cognitive Neuroscience* 19:1498–1507, 2007.
30. V. Sekar, and A. Jawaharlalnehru. "Semantic-based visual emotion recognition in videos-a transfer learning approach." *International Journal of Electrical & Computer Engineering* 12(4):2088–8708, 2022.

7 Classification of Brain Tumor Using Optimized Deep Neural Network Models

P. Chitra
Dhanalakshmi Srinivasan University

CONTENTS

7.1 INTRODUCTION

A brain tumor is a mass of abnormal cells that inside the brain or relevant spinal canal. The skull protects our brain and may be very rigid. Assume that any increase internal this kind of restricted area will cause a slew of troubles for humans. Brain

DOI: 10.1201/9781003315452-7

tumors may be malignant (cancerous) or benign (noncancerous). This system has brought about damage to the brain, which could be life-threatening. Brain tumors are seen in numerous places with particular dimensions and shapes.

Brain tumor cells are often labeled as a primary stage or secondary stage. The preliminary location of a brain tumor is our brain; however, brain tumors are handled as benign in many numbers. A secondary phase of brain tumor, also called a metastatic brain tumor, occurs while most cancer cells unfold to our brains from any other organ, including the part of the lung or the breast.

Meanwhile, the early detection of tumor cells can save many human lives. Detecting the brain tumor and its degree undergoes a complicating and time-delaying system. The affected person refers to MRI, while a few associated signs of tumors have appeared. After analyzing the brain images, if a tumor lifestyle is suspected, the affected person's brain biopsy comes into action.

The organization of this chapter includes a recent literature review in related work and describes a methodology in the next section, the outcome of the research work is demonstrated in the results and discussion part, and the conclusion of this chapter discriminates the consequences of this chapter.

7.2　RELATED WORK

Tumors are out of control tissue growths in each part of the body. Tumors are available in many shapes and sizes, each with its own set of traits and remedy options. Because of the recent lifestyles inside the limited intracranial cavity area, thoughts tumors are intrinsically actual and life-threatening. Using wavelet transform, Chaplot et al. [1] used a technique to enter neural community self-organizing maps to categorize magnetic resonance (MR) images of the human brain. This approach classifies MR brain images accordingly. Advanced K-means and fuzzy C-means algorithms carry out photo segmentation to discover a mass or malignant MRI image [2]. In this approach, earlier than using the K-means set of rules, noise is eliminated after observing the noise-unfastened image entered into the rules. Kalaiselvi and Somasundaram [3] used fuzzy C-means to discover a tumor in the image dataset for brain tissue segmentation. The author described the brain region's information on MRI depth traits to initialize the use of random values to lessen the time for achieving the most excellent solution. Csaholczi et al. [4] describe a brain tumor detection framework that used fuzzy C-means for magnetic resonance images. Soltaninejad et al. [5] proposed a method for detecting brain tumor using Fluid-Attenuated Inversion Recovery (FLAIR) Magnetic Resonance Imaging (MRI). To enhance the brain tumor detection from the overall performance, Kamnitsas et al. in reference [6] used a convolution neural network, which includes 11 convolution layers in preference to a machine learning set of rules for bizarre tissue segmentation.

This scenario routinely extracts functions from detailed enter images and produces extra accuracy than older current systems. Excessive correct detection gadgets may be advanced quickly using a deep neural community. Hence, we've used

DNN methods to expand an excessive accuracy gadget for detecting brain tumors from MRI images.

7.3 DATASET USED FOR PROPOSED METHOD

7.3.1 IBSR DATASET

The Internet Brain Segmentation Repository (IBSR) is a guided expert system for segmentation results and magnetic resonance brain image data. The primary goal of choosing this repository is to encourage and evaluate and develop segmentation methods. The dataset includes 1.5 mm data which consists of 18 subjects aged 7–71. The dataset was classified into (i) T1-weighted volumetric images and (ii) general segmentation of 43 individually labeled principal gray and white matter structures of the brain.

7.3.2 MRI SCAN IMAGES

The MRI sequences are classified from scans into T1- and T2-weighted images. T1-weighted images are represented by using short TE or TR times. T1 properties of tissue predominately determine the contrast and brightness of the image issue. T2-weighted images are described by using long TE or TR times. These images have contrast, and tissue properties predominately determine brightness; T1- and T2-weighted images can be easily differentiated by looking at the CSF. CSF is dark on T1-weighted imaging and bright on T2-weighted imaging.

The Fluid-Attenuated Inversion Recovery (FLAIR) is a third commonly used sequence. The FLAIR sequence is similar to a T2-weighted image, except the TE and TR times are very long. By doing so, abnormalities remain bright, but normal CSF fluid is attenuated and made dark. This sequence is very sensitive to pathology and makes the differentiation between CSF and an exception much easier.

This research work used a total of 1,000 images from the dataset. The dataset is split into training and testing datasets to test the accuracy of this technique. Finally, the testing will be performed using 200 images out of 1,000 images. The rest of the images will be taken for training.

7.4 PERFORMANCE EVALUATION METHOD

The assessment metrics are crucial for the classifier version and overall performance assessment [7]. In Table 7.1, the confusion matrix demonstrates the outcomes of incorrectly and effectively labeled times of every magnificence within the three lessons of the problems.

The accuracy is mostly an accepted evaluation metric. Effective measures are being conducted to correct the rates of all classes. These measures are defined below.

TABLE 7.1

Metrics from the confusion matrix

Metric	Computation
Accuracy	(TP+TN)
Misclassification rate	(FP+FN)=Total
True-positive rate or recall	TP=Actual yes
False-positive rate	FP=Actual no
True-negative rate	TN=Actual no

7.4.1 ACCURACY

Accuracy is a quality metric that describes how the model performs across all data classes. It measures using the ratio between the numbers of correct predictions to the total number of predictions.

$$\text{Accuracy} = \frac{\text{True}_{positive} + \text{True}_{negative}}{\text{True}_{positive} + \text{True}_{negative} + \text{False}_{positive} + \text{False}_{negative}} \quad (7.1)$$

The calculation of prediction is based on a confusion matrix. The accuracy variable holds the result of dividing the sum of true positives and negatives of true values over the sum of all values in the matrix. The achieved result is 0.6312, which shows the model is 63.12% accurate in prediction.

7.4.2 PRECISION

The precision is usually calculated as the ratio between the numbers of positive samples. The samples are classified using the total number of samples classified as Positive. The precision measure is the model's accuracy in classifying a sample data as positive.

$$\text{Precision} = \frac{tp}{(tp + fp)} \quad (7.2)$$

7.4.3 RECALL

The recall measure is calculated using the ratio between the number of positive data samples classified as Positive and the total number of positive data samples. Also, it measures the model's ability to detect positive samples. The higher range of recall values means that more positive samples were detected.

$$\text{Recall} = \frac{tp}{(tp + fn)} \quad (7.3)$$

7.4.4   F-Measure

The F-measure is measured using the harmonic mean of precision and recall given in the same weighting terms. It allows a model to be evaluated using both the accuracy and recall into account using a single score.

$$F - \text{Measure} = \frac{(1+\beta)^2 * \text{Recall} * \text{Precision}}{\beta^2 * \text{Recall} * \text{Precision}} \tag{7.4}$$

where β is a co-efficient to adjust the importance of precision and recall (usually $\beta = 1$).

7.4.5   FP Rate

A false-positive rate (FPR) measures the accuracy of the samples. It considers a medical image diagnosis test, a machine learning model. In technical terms, we have used find the false-positive rate as the probability of rejecting the false entries in the null hypothesis.

$$\text{FP rate} = \frac{\text{FP}}{(\text{FP+TN})} \tag{7.5}$$

7.4.6   TP Rate

In machine learning, a performance scheme using the true-positive rate is referred to as sensitivity or recall. The term is used to measure the percentage of actual positives which are correctly identified.

$$\text{TP rate} = \frac{\text{TP}}{(\text{TP+FN})} \tag{7.6}$$

The terms of prediction included the following weighted accuracy.

Macro-Average: Macro-averaging is a straightforward method among other methods. Macro-averaged F1-score is computed using the arithmetic mean. The macro-method treats all classes of data in an equal manner regardless of their support values.

Micro-Average: Micro-average can be represented using the sum of true positives for all the classes divided by all positive predictions. The optimistic prediction is the sum of all true positives and false positives. Micro-average computes a global average F1-score by using true positives (TP), false negatives (FN), and false positives (FP).

Weighted Average: The weighted-average F1-score is calculated using the mean of all class F1-scores, which will consider each class support value. Support value refers to the number of occurrences performed in the class and the dataset.

Overall Average: It is the proportion of the correct predictions. In other words, it is the ratio between the number of correctly predicted samples and the total samples.

The performance metrics are used in this proposed work efficiently. The result of this work reveals a higher accuracy value compared with other existing techniques. The proposed work is an ideal choice for medical image processing as well.

7.5 METHODOLOGY OF PROPOSED DNN MODELS

Our research work aims to build a novel methodology and techniques to identify the brain tumor tissues in healthcare applications. This model can help to predict the disease by achieving high accuracy data with a prediction basis. This research work provides novel optimized deep learning models to achieve good-quality images with reduced time complexity. Convolution neural network is used to force a deep studying framework. It includes discrete factors known as neurons, which can be interconnected and organized as layers. The neural network (NN) is a device studying a set of rules constructed at the idea of logistics and organic neural community functions. The simple neural community structure is visualized in Figure 7.1.

7.5.1 VGG16

It has been found that the functions of a pre-skilled CNN in advance layers typically include area and coloration facts. The last layers inside the subsequent view

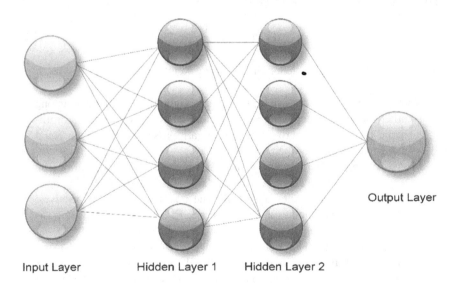

FIGURE 7.1   Structure of VGG16.

of the imaginative and prescient consist of attributes that might be extra precise to the specifics of the lessons. As a result, the parameters of the sooner layers want little to no fine-tuning.

The following is an outline of a way to extrude the layers. It can classify images into a thousand exclusive categories [8]. The VGG16's closing three layers are installed for those a thousand lessons. These want to be fine-tuned for a more recent category mission [9,10]. Fine-tuning is done via way of means of extracting all the community's layers besides the closing 3. Substitute the closing three layers determined for the cutting-edge category assignment, including the layer of FC, a softmax, and a category output. The scale of the FC layer has been set to the variety of lessons inside the new facts [9,10]. For the functions of this project, the scale fee is the same as the variety of lessons, i.e., every day and bizarre. The basic structure of VGG16 is visually represented in Figure 7.2.

7.5.2 ResNet50

ResNet50 is a community of 50 people. It corresponds to 50 layers of Kaiming He et al. Residual's Network at Microsoft Research [11]. The term "characteristic subtraction" has been utilized by Residual. It refers to the functions that layer has found from its feedback. Shortcut connections (without delay connecting the center of mth layer to any (m+x) layer) are utilized by ResNet. These networks are distinctly less challenging to teach than traditional deep CNN. These may

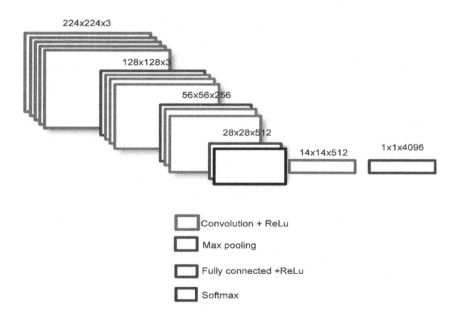

FIGURE 7.2 Architecture of ResNet 50.

additionally remedy the hassle of degrading accuracy. The structure of ResNet50 accommodates hidden connections in conjunction with extensive batch normalization. These bypass connections have stated gated devices or gated recurrent devices. It has a decreased complexity as compared with VGG. The simple ResNet50 architecture is offered in Figure 7.3.

7.5.3 Inception-V3

Inception-V3 is based on the convolutional neural network via the Google Brain Team, used in the ImageNet database. It contains a 48-layer network, which classifies images into a 1,000 items. The version can examine wealthy function representations for exclusive images.

The community calls for an entered image of length in a particular dimension. Inception-v3 uses batch normalization, distortion in images, RMSprop, and lots of small convolutions to lower the parameters significantly.

It is a modern deep-study method wherein pre-trained methods have been implemented to the initial state [12–16].

7.5.4 Develop a Model Approach

- **Select a Source Task**: An associated predictive modeling hassle needs to have decided on the importance of facts wherein there may be associated facts on entering points, output facts, and ideas found out in the mapping from entering to output facts.
- **Develop a Source Model**: This version has advanced for the task of the primary phase. We say that the performance should be higher than a naive version to ensure that a few function studies have been carried out correctly.
- **Reuse a Model**: The version can suit the supply mission then described because the place to begin for a performance on the second mission of

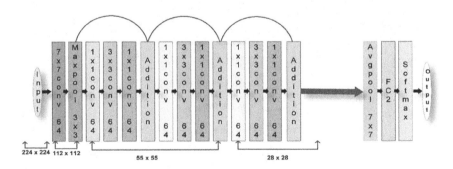

FIGURE 7.3 Proposed approach.

interest. This method can also contain the use of all or components of the version, relying on the modeling mechanics.

- **Tune a Model**: Significantly, the version can also want to be tailored or delicate at the enter–output pair facts for the mission of interest.

7.5.5 PRE-TRAINED MODEL APPROACH

- **Select a Source Model**: A pre-skilled supply version has been selected to have architectures. Many studies establishments launch approaches for vast and challenging datasets, bringing them to the pool of candidate methods.
- **Reuse a Model**: This mechanism can also contain the use of all or components of the version, relying on the modeling approach used.
- **Tune a Model**: Optionally, the performance is customized or fine-tuned at the enter–output pair facts to be had for interest. The proposed DNN architecture is depicted in Figure 7.4.

Figure 7.4 visualizes the structure of the proposed DNN structure. Also, it described the particular version of the proposed system. This diagram indicates the proposed work model and the process of each stage visually in Figure 7.5.

Figure 7.5 indicates the float of the proposed paintings. Also, it blanketed the connections among the numerous parameters and methods.

7.6 RESULTS AND DISCUSSION

This phase provides the outcomes and deserves of the proposed set of rules. Additionally, the comparative evaluation has been carried out with tabular facts. The tabular facts have blanketed precision, recall, FI-rating, and aid measures. These metrics have analyzed the energy of the proposed paintings (Table 7.2).

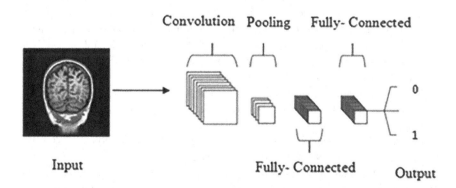

FIGURE 7.4 The working of the proposed model.

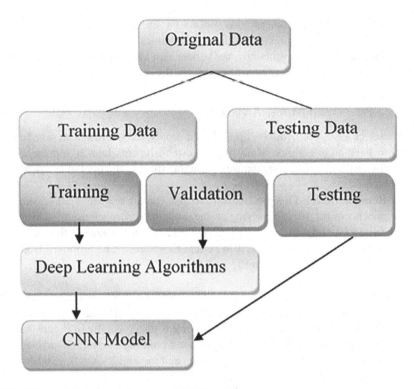

FIGURE 7.5   Training and testing of CNN model.

This evaluation proves that the four layer-CNN methods are the quality structure for brain tumor detection. These outcomes are visually annotated in Figures 7.6 and 7.7. The micro commonly denotes the accuracy of genuine positive (precision), the macro commonly is a degree of accuracy on fake positive (recall), and the weighted commonly is a degree of F1-score.

The aid is a quantitative metric that counts the variety of images taken into consideration via way of means of DNN in the category in opposition to the whole array of images depending on the experimental dataset. In the IBSR dataset with 224 images, 112 images are standard, and 112 are tumor-affected. The DNN version is correctly supported via way of means of all of the dataset images, as depicted via the found aid values.

The above visualization of Figure 7.6 indicates the category report's overall performance evaluation of the DNN version. It can visualize a clean photo of approximately the accuracy factors.

Figure 7.7 describes the proposed optimized DNN version on VGG16, Inception-V3, and ResNet50 for the tumor category.

DNN profits interest for robust function extraction and facts mining for several programs, including item reputation, photo super-resolution, and semantic segmentation. The VGG16, Inception-V3, and ResNet50 are the well-known DNN

TABLE 7.2

Performance measures of DNN models

Group	Precision	Recall	F1-Score	Support
		VGG16		
Normal (0)	0.00	0.30	0.47	112
Brain tumor(1)	0.59	1.00	0.74	112
		ResNet50 (Proposed)		
Normal (0)	0.87	0.73	0.79	112
Brain tumor(1)	0.76	0.89	0.82	112
		Inception (Proposed)		
Normal (0)	1.00	0.21	0.34	112
Brain tumor(1)	0.56	1.00	0.72	112
		Classification Report		
VGG16 (Accuracy: 0.65)				
Micro-average	0.65	0.65	0.65	224
Macro-average	0.79	0.65	0.60	224
Weighted average	0.79	0.65	0.60	224
ResNet50 (Accuracy: 0. 81)				
Micro-average	0.81	0.81	0.81	224
Macro-average	0.82	0.81	0.81	224
Weighted average	0.82	0.81	0.81	224
Inception (Accuracy: 0. 60)				
Micro-average	0.60	0.60	0.60	224
Macro-average	0.78	0.60	0.53	224
Weighted average	0.78	0.60	0.53	224

architectures added for the item reputation mission. In this bankruptcy, optimized switch studying fine-tunes the pre-skilled community (ResNet50) parameters for the photo category mission. Performance assessment performed the use of joint recall, precision, and F-rating. Performance evaluation indicates that fine-tuned ResNet50 structure outperforms the opposite DNN and hybrid studying methods for the photo category mission.

Overall, the performance of the proposed work reveals higher accuracy using for evaluating measures. All the results show the quality of the techniques and prove the efficiency of the proposed work.

7.7 CONCLUSION

In this chapter, a novel approach to the deep learning model is proposed efficiently. This study's observation reports that ResNet50 reveals higher accuracy (81%)

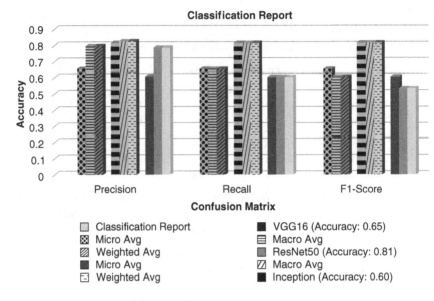

FIGURE 7.6 Classification report of the model.

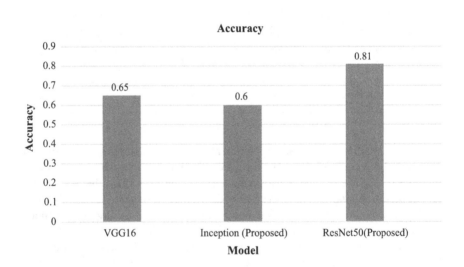

FIGURE 7.7 Accuracy comparison of the model.

than the other approaches such as Inception-V3 and VGG16 accuracy (60%–65%). Overall performance could be measured by using the individual results of precision, recall, F1-score, support, micro-average, macro-average, weighted-average, and overall-average endorse the optimized DNN OTL-DNN and have shown an appreciable increase in the accuracy of classification. Further, these experimental results show the subjective augmentation of layers may result in overfitting. The principle of transfer learning has substantially impacted the accuracy of classification. The future enhancement of this research work is to process the proposed algorithm with some popular techniques to increase the accuracy score.

REFERENCES

1. Chaplot, S., Patnaik, L.M. and Jagannathan, N.R., 2006. Classification of magnetic resonance brain images using wavelets as input to support vector machine and neural network. *Biomedical Signal Processing and Control, 1*(1), pp. 86–92.
2. IlaVennila, S.M.P.D., 2010. Optimization fusion approach for image segmentation using k-means algorithm. *International Journal of Computer Applications, 975*, p. 8887.
3. Kalaiselvi, T. and Somasundaram, K., 2011. Fuzzy c-means technique with histogram based centroid initialization for brain tissue segmentation in MRI of head scans. In: *2011 International Symposium on Humanities, Science and Engineering Research* (pp. 149–154). IEEE.
4. Csaholczi, S., Kovács, L. and Szilágyi, L., 2021. Automatic segmentation of brain tumor parts from MRI data using a random forest classifier. In: *2021 IEEE 19th World Symposium on Applied Machine Intelligence and Informatics (SAMI)* (pp. 000471–000476). IEEE.
5. Soltaninejad, M., Yang, G., Lambrou, T., Allinson, N., Jones, T.L., Barrick, T.R., Howe, F.A. and Ye, X., 2017. Automated brain tumour detection and segmentation using superpixel-based extremely randomized trees in FLAIR MRI. *International Journal of Computer Assisted Radiology and Surgery, 12*(2), pp. 183–203.
6. Kamnitsas, K., Ledig, C., Newcombe, V.F., Simpson, J.P., Kane, A.D., Menon, D.K., Rueckert, D. and Glocker, B., 2017. Efficient multi-scale 3D CNN with fully connected CRF for accurate brain lesion segmentation. *Medical Image Analysis, 36*, pp. 61–78.
7. Precision. https://en.wikipedia.org/wiki/Precision_and_recall. F1 Score. https://en.wikipedia.org/wiki/ F1-Score. Accessed on 01 April 2019.
8. Simonyan, K. and Zisserman, A., 2014. Very deep convolutional networks for large-scale image recognition. *arXiv preprint arXiv:1409.1556*.
9. Sonawane, P.K. and Shelke, S., 2018. Handwritten Devanagari character classification using deep learning. In: *2018 International Conference on Information, Communication, Engineering and Technology (ICICET)* (pp. 1–4). IEEE.
10. Lu, S., Lu, Z. and Zhang, Y.D., 2019. Pathological brain detection based on AlexNet and transfer learning. *Journal of Computational Science, 30*, pp. 41–47.
11. He, K., Zhang, X., Ren, S., & Sun, J. (2016). Deep residual learning for image recognition. In *Proceedings of the IEEE Conference on Computer Vision and Pattern Recognition* (pp. 770–778). USA.
12. Chitra, P. and Mary Shanthi Rani, M., 2019. Differential coding-based medical image compression. In: *Computer Aided Intervention and Diagnostics in Clinical and Medical Images* (pp. 11–19). Springer, Cham.

13. Mary Shanthi Rani, M., Chitra, P., Lakshmanan, S., Kalpana Devi, M., Sangeetha, R., & Nithya, S. (2022). DeepCompNet: A Novel Neural Net Model Compression Architecture. *Computational Intelligence and Neuroscience*, 2022.

14. Chitra, P. and Rani, M., 2018. Modified scheme of embedded zero-tree wavelet (EZW) using vector quantization and run length encoding for compressing medical images. *Journal of Computational and Theoretical Nanoscience*, *15*(6–7), pp. 2415–2419.

15. Chitra, P. and Rani, M.M.S., 2021. A hybrid medical image coding based on block truncation coding and residual vector quantisation. *International Journal of Intelligent Enterprise*, 8(2–3), pp. 278–287.

16. Chitra, P., Rani, M.M.S. and Sivakumar, V., 2019. Adaptive fractal image coding using differential scheme for compressing medical images. In: *Advances in Computerized Analysis in Clinical and Medical Imaging* (pp. 243–252). Chapman and Hall/CRC.

8 Fully Automated Segmentation of Brain Stroke Lesions Using Mask Region-Based Convolutional Neural Network

Emre Dandıl and Mehmet Süleyman Yıldırım
Bilecik Seyh Edebali University

CONTENTS

8.1 INTRODUCTION

Cerebro-cardiovascular diseases are dangerous to human life and are a major cause of disability for adults worldwide (Zhang et al., 2021). Stroke, which is the most common of the cerebrovascular diseases, occurs when there is an abnormal condition (reduction or interruption) in the blood flow in the brain and can cause some damage to the nervous system. Major symptoms of stroke disease include lack of focus, seizures, language disorders, and loss of emotion (Zhou et al., 2021). Stroke is also the most common disease condition worldwide, after cancer and cardiovascular disease (Clèrigues et al., 2020). If stroke is not treated

DOI: 10.1201/9781003315452-8

at an early stage, death of brain cells and disability and death can occur. Stroke is one of the leading causes of death worldwide, and according to the latest data of the World Stroke Organization (WSO, 2022), more than 13 million people suffer from stroke every year, and approximately 5.5 million people die from this disease. In addition, it can be seen that two-thirds of people who have had a stroke have difficulty in doing their daily activities in the long term (Feigin et al., 2014). In addition, according to the Global Burden of Disease Study 2019 report, stroke was top-ranked cause of disability-adjusted life-years in people over 50 (Vos et al., 2020).

Stroke is an acute cerebrovascular disease with a high prevalence. While the disability and death rate is high in stroke, the cure rate is low. Stroke disease can be classified into two main categories as ischemic and hemorrhagic stroke (Wang et al., 2014; Wu et al., 2015). Ischemic stroke, which happens when blood flow to the brain is interrupted by an obstruction (blockage), is the most common type and accounts for almost 87% of all stroke cases (Karthik et al., 2020; Wajngarten and Silva, 2019). A hemorrhagic stroke occurs when there is bleeding in or around the brain, especially in weak blood vessels (Unnithan and Mehta, 2020). In addition, transient ischemic attack (TIA), known as "mini-stroke," is sometimes considered another type of stroke (Kanchana and Menaka, 2020). In TIA, the attack is usually quite short, as blood flow to the brain is slowed/cut off for a short time (Coutts, 2017). In addition, the processes after stroke are evaluated in three different stages. The first 2 weeks after the stroke (onset) lesion begins to form is called the acute stage. In contrast, the second stage is known as subacute and covers the last 6 months of stroke. Finally, the chronic stage begins many years after the stroke and continues throughout a person's life (Kiran, 2012).

Segmentation of stroke lesions on medical images plays a key role in subsequent diagnosis and treatment planning. Low-resolution computerized tomography (CT) scans and structural MR imaging are generally preferred for clinical evaluations in the acute phase of stroke disease (Liew et al., 2018; Liu et al., 2019). However, for chronic stroke, T1-weighted (T1-w) magnetic resonance imaging (MRI), high-resolution, is preferred for imaging and follow-up stroke lesions in the brain (Allen et al., 2012). Traditionally, stroke diagnosis is performed by evaluating MR scans by a slice-to-slice specialist and manually delineating strokes. Here, in the diagnosis of the disease, the location, precise boundaries, size, and number of the lesion have to be determined accurately. Strokes can occur in different locations in the brain, in different sizes, in different shapes, and with unclear boundaries. In Figure 8.1a–c, some T1-w MR scans from the open-source public ATLAS v2.0 dataset used in this study show some stroke lesions developing in different locations, shapes, and sizes, and roughly delineated boundaries.

Detection and segmentation of stroke lesions can be performed both automatically and manually. Manual assessment of stroke is time consuming, expensive, and the process can be prone to errors. In addition, this process may include subjective evaluations of different experts in the same case. While lesions can be segmented in roughly 1 minute in automated methods, this time

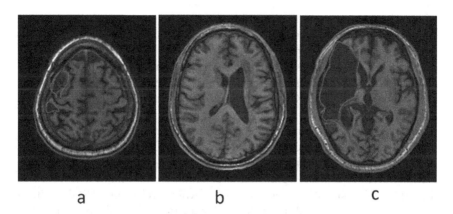

a   b   c

FIGURE 8.1 Several T1-w MR scans from the ATLAS v2.0 dataset, some stroke lesions developing in different locations, shapes, and sizes and their boundaries roughly delineated. (a) Small-sized stroke. (b) Different-shaped stroke. (c) Large-sized stroke.

is higher and generally less accurate in manual segmentation (Wilke et al., 2011). Moreover, since experts perform segmentation at intense efforts, errors can occur. For this reason, it is very important to develop methods that allow the automatic segmentation of stroke lesions and facilitate the decision-making process of physicians.

In previous studies, a number of studies have been proposed for segmentation of stroke lesions using machine learning methods and traditional methods. While some of these studies offer semi-automatic solutions (De Haan et al., 2015; Wilke et al., 2011), some studies are proposed as fully automatic methods (Griffis et al., 2016; Pustina et al., 2016). While there are methods such as traditional thresholding and region growing in semi-automatic methods, machine learning methods such as random forest (RF), artificial neural networks (ANN), support vector machines (SVM), and evolutionary algorithms are generally used in fully automatic methods. With a proposed approach for automatic detection of ischemic stroke lesions (Rajini and Bhavani, 2013), they proposed a computer-assisted method by classifying ischemic stroke using decision tree, SVM, k-NN, and ANN by aid of textural features. However, Nabizadeh et al. (2014) proposed a histogram-based gravitational optimization algorithm for automatic lesion detection and segmentation from a single anatomical MR modality. In another study (Subudhi et al., 2018), Darwinian particle swarm optimization and Delaunay triangulation methods were combined. In the study, classification was also applied by using statistical and morphological features with SVM and RF classifiers. In another study (Bharathi et al., 2019) proposed for the detection of ischemic stroke lesions from MR images, textural features with gray level co-occurrence matrix and unsupervised learned features with k-means clustering were extracted and classification was provided with Kanchana and Menaka (2020), however, provided the detection, characterization, and classification of ischemic stroke lesions with optimal feature selection in CT images. In the study, the classification of extracted features was carried out using machine learning methods such as SVM, RF, ANN, and logistic regression.

In recent years, various deep learning methods have been commonly used for automatic detection and segmentation of stroke lesions, and many studies have been proposed. Karthik et al. (2020) proposed a fully convolutional network for ischemic stroke lesion segmentation. In the study, experimental analyses were performed on the ischemic Stroke Lesion Segmentation Challenge (ISLES, 2015) dataset. In another study (Qi et al., 2019), they developed a decoder-encoder-based X-Net method with a change in the U-Net deep learning architecture for segmentation of brain stroke lesions. They used in their study Anatomical Tracings of Lesions After Stroke (ATLAS) dataset. In another study (Liu et al., 2019) conducted using the ATLAS dataset, they proposed a decoder-encoder-based multi-scale deep fusion network architecture for segmentation of stroke lesions. In another study (Xue et al., 2020), they developed a convolutional neural network (CNN)-based method for segmentation of stroke lesions on brain MRI images. Tomita et al. (2020), however, achieved automatic stroke lesion segmentation with a 3D CNN architecture, again using the ATLAS dataset. Clèrigues et al. (2020) performed the segmentation of acute and subacute stroke lesions with U-Net, a 3D decoder-encoder deep learning network. In the study, ISLES 2015, an open-source publicly available dataset, was used. In another study conducted using the ISLES 2015 dataset, Amin et al. (2020) proposed a CNN model for the detection of stroke lesions from MR images. In another study Zhang et al. (2021) proposed on the ATLAS dataset, segmentation of stroke lesions from T1-w MR images was performed with the multi-inputs U-Net method. Zhou et al. (2021) proposed a new U-Net deep learning architecture for chronic stroke lesion segmentation in their study. They used the ATLAS dataset in their studies. In the ATLAS dataset, chronic stroke lesions were automatically segmented in another proposed study (Shin et al., 2022) with the efficient U-Net deep learning method.

The success of deep learning-based automatic segmentation methods is evident in the precise identification of abnormalities in the human brain, especially after stroke attacks (onset), accurately determining their boundaries and follow-up lesions. Therefore, in this chapter, a fully automated computer-aided method based on Mask R-CNN architecture is proposed for segmentation of chronic stroke lesions on brain MR images. In the experimental studies, images obtained from T1-w MR sequences in the ATLAS dataset are used. In our study, segmentation of chronic stroke lesions is achieved by highlighting the advantages of the Mask R-CNN method in medical image segmentation. The next sections of the chapter are organized as follows: In the second section, the methodology and dataset proposed within the scope of the study are detailed. In the third section, the findings and results obtained as a result of the experimental analyses are presented and discussed. In the final section, the conclusions reached in the study are presented.

8.2 MATERIALS AND METHODS

In this chapter, a method based on Mask R-CNN deep learning architecture using the ResNet50 backbone structure is proposed to segment chronic stroke lesions automatically. In experimental studies, ATLAS 2.0 publicly available dataset was used and the performance of the proposed system was verified with measurement metrics. In this study, the methodology of the Mask R-CNN approach proposed for automatic segmentation of stroke lesions is shown in Figure 8.2. In the methodology of the system, firstly, the MR images obtained from the ATLAS 2.0 dataset were divided into two subgroups for the training and testing phases, and training and test sets were created from random slices. Afterward, the proposed Mask R-CNN network, set with the ResNet50 backbone structure, was trained with the MR images in the training set, and the optimal weights of the network were determined. Finally, automatic segmentation and precise boundaries of stroke lesions in the images in the test set are provided.

In this section of the chapter, information about the structure of the proposed Mask R-CNN architecture, the ResNet50 backbone structure, and the dataset used in this study are presented.

8.2.1 IMAGING DATASET AND DATA ACQUISITION

In this chapter, Anatomical Tracings of Lesions After Stroke v2.0 (ATLAS v2.0), a publicly available (open-source) dataset (Liew et al., 2022) consisting of T1-w stroke MR scans to develop and evaluate the proposed method for automatic segmentation of stroke lesions (Liew et al., 2022) were used. Stroke lesions in MR slices in the ATLAS v2.0 dataset are manually segmented, and there are a total of 955 MR scans in the dataset, both training (public) and test (hidden) data. In addition, the ATLAS v2.0 dataset is a more advanced and larger version of the previously presented ATLAS v1.2 dataset (Liew et al., 2018), which is frequently used in many studies proposed for stroke detection. ATLAS v1.2 dataset, consisting of 304 T1-w MR scans, has become a prominent dataset in studies such as anomaly detection and comparison of developed architectures, as well as segmentation of stroke lesions. However, previous studies have reported that the ATLAS

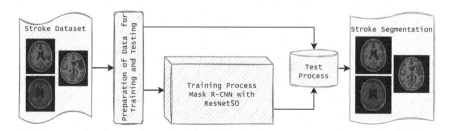

FIGURE 8.2 Methodology of the proposed Mask R-CNN method in this study for automatic segmentation of stroke lesions.

v1.2 dataset has low accuracy, cannot be accessed publicly, and cannot be verified because its measurements are inconsistent. Therefore, the ATLAS v2.0 dataset has been released, considering the benefits of larger datasets in studies. ATLAS v2.0 is a more advanced stroke imaging dataset than ATLAS v1.2. ATLAS v2.0 is a dataset consisting of MR images obtained in post-stroke T1-w sequences of patients collected from 33 different groups from 20 institutions around the world. The ATLAS v2.0 dataset consists of 955 MR scans in NifTI format, and there are 655 MR scans in the training set and 300 completely hidden MR scans in the test set.

In the experimental studies within the scope of this chapter, T1-w MR images in the training set of the ATLAS v2.0 dataset and 600 MR images with public masks and expert labels (masks) were used. For this reason, on the slices obtained from the training set, 3,160 slices were randomly divided into the training set (75%) and the 1,052 slices test set (25%). In this study, some MR images with stroke lesions used for experimental studies in the ATLAS v2.0 dataset are shown in Figure 8.3. In the first column of Figure 8.3, the original MR slices are presented, in the second column, the ground truth mask delineated by the expert, and in the third column, the boundaries of the ground truth mask are marked on the MR slices.

8.2.2 Mask Region-Based Convolutional Neural Network (Mask R-CNN)

Deep learning architectures used in medical image segmentation are mostly based on CNN architecture (Weimer et al., 2016). These architectures are created by various combinations of the general structures of CNNs, such as the convolution operation, which provides output from different angles by passing various filters on the image (Ravì et al., 2016), the padding operation where the missing places are filled in the changes on the data, and the ReLu operation to reset the negative results caused by the filters on the result data (Albawi et al., 2017; Nielsen, 2015). In the later stages of CNN architectures, the pooling process is applied to flatten the data (Sun et al., 2017). Then, the classification of the data is performed with the fully connected layer, which is an artificial neural network structure, on the more meaningful and the obtained flat data (Wu, 2016). As a result of these processes, data are classified successfully with softmax to a certain extent (Liu et al., 2016). The development of the network is ensured by repeating the operations one after the other until the classification performance reaches the expected level or the specified number of iterations (Albawi et al., 2017). The layered block diagram of a typical CNN deep learning architecture is denoted in Figure 8.4.

Region-based convolutional neural network (R-CNN) is proposed by developing a region-based system on the developed CNN architectures (Girshick et al., 2014). An important progress was performed in the structure of CNN by highlighting the Region of Interest (RoI) possible areas in R-CNN. Although this development increased the performance, it caused a density in the amount and process of the transaction. Fast R-CNN was proposed to eliminate problems

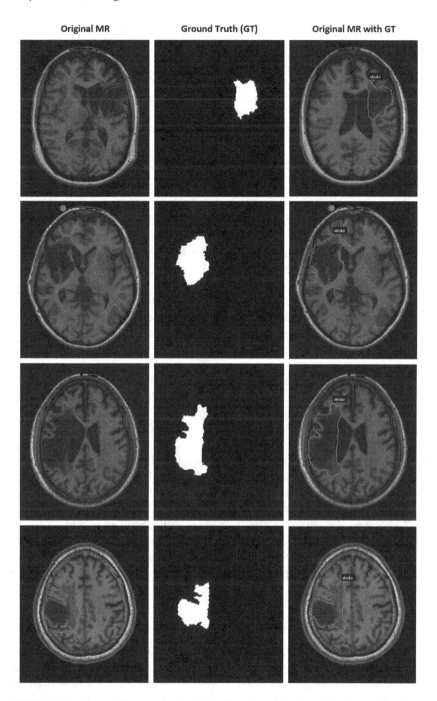

FIGURE 8.3 Some MR images with stroke lesions used for experimental studies in the ATLAS v2.0 dataset. Original MR slices in the first column, stroke lesion masks (ground truth) delineated by the expert in the second column, and ground truth mask boundaries marked manually on the MR slice in the third column.

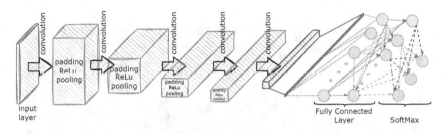

FIGURE 8.4 Layered block diagram of a typical CNN deep learning architecture.

like this (Girshick, 2015). With the Fast R-CNN architecture, Region Proposal Network (RPN) architecture, which is a secondary network structure, was added to determine the areas with the possibility of RoI, and the processing time was reduced and the speed increased. With the Faster R-CNN architecture developed afterwards, the operating speed of the system was increased with a special pooling system for RoIPool and RoI areas (Ren et al., 2015). As a result of all these developments, the mask feature was added to the classification results with the mask region-based convolutional neural network (Mask R-CNN) architecture, which provides an important performance in the segmentation process (He et al., 2017).

Mask R-CNN is a deep learning architecture that has come to the fore in segmentation studies in recent years. The Mask R-CNN architecture consists of a two-stage detection structure. In the first stage, the important regions are determined on the data passing through the backbone containing the general structures of the CNN. This stage has the same features as faster R-CNN and feature mapping is done using RPN. In addition, performance is increased in the selection of important regions on the feature map created with RoIAlign, and the first stage is completed by producing a fixed size feature map. In the second stage, the boundaries and class of the searched object are extracted with fully connected layer (FCL) using fixed size feature map (Long et al., 2015; Shelhamer et al., 2016). In addition, a mask is extracted covering the boundaries of the object with the fully convolutional network (FCN) (Long et al., 2015). In this study, the architecture of the Mask R-CNN method proposed for segmentation of stroke lesions is shown in Figure 8.5.

8.2.3 BACKBONE STRUCTURE

ResNet backbone structure is a prominent convolution structure in convolutional neural networks. It has a structure that consists of a combination of convolution, padding and ReLu operations used in convolution and provides data augmentation between blocks by skip. The most important feature of this structure is that it enables the data to be increased and smoothed by the consecutive use of blocks. ResNet backbone structure is named by the number of blocks such as

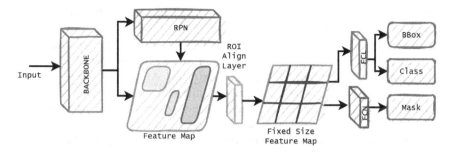

FIGURE 8.5 Architecture of the proposed Mask R-CNN method for segmentation of stroke lesions.

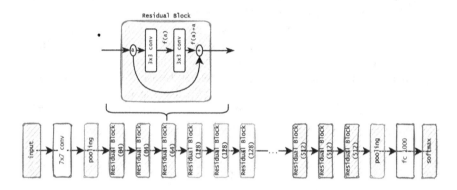

FIGURE 8.6 Block diagram of ResNet50 backbone used in Mask R-CNN architecture.

ResNet50, ResNet101, and ResNeXt used in a row (Targ et al., 2016). In Mask R-CNN architecture, Feature Pyramid Network (FPN) structures can be used as well as ResNet networks as backbone structure. A top-down architecture is created in FPN with lateral connections to create a pyramid structure from a single-scale input (He et al., 2017). In this study, ResNet50 structure shown in Figure 8.6 was used as the backbone structure for segmentation of stroke lesions with Mask R-CNN architecture.

8.3 RESULTS AND DISCUSSION

In this chapter, segmentation of stroke lesions from T1-w MR scans with Mask R-CNN architecture was achieved using the ATLAS v2.0 dataset. In the experimental studies for this study, Mask R-CNN architecture was trained on the training set for 50 epochs using the ResNet50 backbone structure. The weights in each epoch were saved, and the results were validated by measuring the segmentation performance with metrics in the test set. In experimental studies, it was applied on a workstation with RTX2080Ti GPU with Linux operating system. In addition, Python programming language and Keras environment were used for programming.

In the slices taken from the ATLAS v2.0 dataset in NifTI format, the slices with stroke area exceeding the determined threshold value and the expert masks (ground truth) of these slices were visually extracted. After these data were separated as training and test sets, the coordinate information of the areas with lesions on the masks was automatically taken and converted into *json*-based format for use in Mask R-CNN architecture. In this way, the training and test sets of the dataset were organized in accordance with the format of the experimental study.

In experimental studies, dice, recall, precision, average symmetrical surface distance (ASD) and Hausdorff distance 95 (HD95) metrics were used to measure and evaluate the performance of the Mask R-CNN method in segmenting stroke lesions. In the equations of the metrics, A_{gt} shows the ground truth, and A_{seg} shows the segmentation area of the Mask R-CNN method. In addition, TP represents the areas of stroke that are defined as stroke and FP represents the areas of stroke that are not strokes. Moreover, FN represents the areas where stroke is not detected although there is a stroke, and TN represents the areas that are detected as stroke but not stroke. Dice is used to determine ground truth overlap performance with segmented lesion areas with the proposed method (Mask R-CNN in this study) and is shown in Eq. (8.1) (Zou et al., 2004). Precision and recall, however, are metrics showing the rate of accurate determination of the area defined as stroke and are given in Eqs. (8.2) and (8.3), respectively.

$$\text{Dice} = \frac{2\left|A_{gt} \cap A_{seg}\right|}{\left|A_{gt}\right| \cup \left|A_{seg}\right|} \tag{8.1}$$

$$\text{Precision} = \frac{TP}{TP + FP} \tag{8.2}$$

$$\text{Recall} = \frac{TP}{TP + FN} \tag{8.3}$$

The ASD indicates the overlap accuracy, and the distance between each point outside the two areas to be measured is calculated by using the Euclidean formula $d(x, A)$ in Eq. (8.4) and comparing their sums with respect to the overall success rate (Kavur et al., 2020) and is shown in Eq. (8.5).

$$d(x,A) = \min_{y \in A}\left(d(x,y)\right) \tag{8.4}$$

$$\text{ASD} = \frac{1}{\left|A_{gt}\right| + \left|A_{seg}\right|} \times \left(\sum_{x \in A_{seg}} d\left(x, A_{gt}\right) + \sum_{y \in A_{gt}} d\left(y, A_{seg}\right)\right) \tag{8.5}$$

The HD95 metric is used for the overlap distance between ground truth and the segmentation method (Mask R-CNN in this study). The distances $hd(A_{seg}, A_{gt})$

and hd(A_{gt}, A_{seg}) in Eqs. (6) and (8.7) are calculated by the method of overlapping, determining the points between the intersections of the two fields. It is evaluated as the HD95 result, which is the largest among the measured distances between the fields, and it is called this because it is calculated by ignoring the 5% error while doing this, and it is considered that noises are prevented from affecting the measurements (Karimi and Salcudean, 2019). As the error measurement scores zero in HD95, the performance increases and it is seen in the HD95 metric Eq. (8.8).

$$hd(A_{seg}, A_{gt}) = \max_{x \in A_{ref}} \min_{y \in A_{gt}} x - y_2 \tag{8.6}$$

$$hd(A_{gt}, A_{seg}) = \max_{y \in A_{gt}} \min_{x \in A_{ref}} x - y_2 \tag{8.7}$$

$$HD(X,Y) = \max\left(hd(A_{seg}, A_{gt}), hd(A_{gt}, A_{seg})\right) \tag{8.8}$$

In experimental studies, there are some loss values that show the performance of the network during 50 epoch training of the Mask R-CNN method. These loss values, which show the errors in segmentation, start from a certain value and decrease over time. In Figure 8.7, the change of mask loss, region loss, class loss, and total loss values during 50 epoch training of the Mask R-CNN method for automatic segmentation of stroke lesions is shown. Total loss represents the sum of all errors that occurred during the training of the Mask R-CNN architecture. In addition, the error of the masked area as a result of FCN is measured by mask loss, the error in identifying important region areas is measured by region loss,

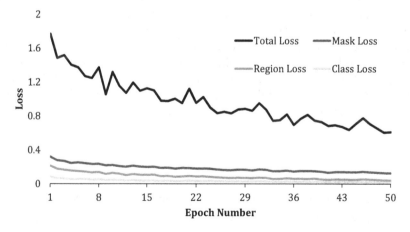

FIGURE 8.7   For automatic segmentation of stroke lesions, mask loss, region loss, class loss, and total loss values created during the training phase of the Mask R-CNN network for 50 epochs.

and the error in classification is measured by class loss. As seen in Figure 8.7, the loss rapidly approached zero during the training process. This shows that Mask R-CNN has achieved a significant success in training.

The performance of the Mask R-CNN proposed method on the test set was evaluated with the most appropriate weights obtained when the training process of the method was completed. In the experimental studies carried out for the detection of stroke lesions, it was determined that Mask R-CNN got the best dice score at the 50th epoch, considering the step with the highest dice coefficient calculated for each epoch. In this study, the performance measurements of the best epoch obtained with Mask R-CNN in experimental studies on the ATLAS v2.0 dataset are presented in Table 8.1. According to the table, the best results for dice, recall, and precision in measurements on the test set were obtained as 78.50%, 77.47%, and 81.98%, respectively. In addition, 16.75 mm and 4.16 mm scores were obtained for HD95 and ASD metrics, respectively. The obtained scores show that the difference between Mask R-CNN segmentation and ground truth is low.

For the experimental studies in segmentation of stroke lesions, the changes in the dice, precision, recall, ASD, and HD95 metrics in the evaluations made in the test set for the best epoch are shown with the box plots in Figure 8.8. When these graphs are examined, it is seen that the performance for dice similarity coefficient, recall, and precision approaches 100%. In addition, it is seen that ASD is below 3 mm and HD95 is below 15 mm. These results show that stroke segmentation was successfully performed in tests using proposed Mask R-CNN deep learning architecture with ResNet50 backbone structure on ATLAS v2.0 dataset.

In Figure 8.9, stroke lesions that were successfully segmented with the proposed Mask R-CNN method in several MR slices in the test set for experimental studies are seen. Here, in each column of Figure 8.9, respectively, the original MR slices, the stroke lesions delineated by the expert in the original MR slices colored in green (original MR with ground truth), the segmentation of the stroke lesions in the MR slices with the proposed Mask R-CNN method (colored in red), and overlap of ground truth and Mask R-CNN segmentation (colored in brown) are shown. When the segmentation results are examined, it is clearly seen that the segmentation of stroke lesions was successfully achieved using Mask R-CNN method. In addition, when the images segmented with ground truth and Mask R-CNN are compared, the boundaries of the segmented images are smoother, but the ground truth mask boundaries determined by the physicians are more detailed. However, some MR images in which stroke lesions were segmented with less success (low

TABLE 8.1

Scores reached in metrics with proposed Mask R-CNN method for the best epoch

Dice [%]	Recall [%]	Precision [%]	HD95 [mm]	ASD [mm]
78.50	77.47	81.98	16.751	4.16478

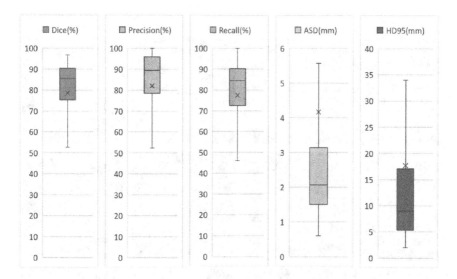

FIGURE 8.8 Box plots for dice, precision, recall, ASD, and HD95 metrics in test set evaluations for best epoch.

dice score) using the proposed method in experimental studies conducted for the test set are presented in Figure 8.10. Here, it is seen that one of the stroke lesions in the MR image in the first row of Figure 8.10 cannot be segmented using the Mask R-CNN method, while another lesion cannot be segmented very success-fully. In contrast, the MR image in the second row of Figure 8.10 shows that the stroke lesion was successfully segmented, but another non-lesion area was seg-mented. Finally, in the MR slice in the third row, it is seen that some small lesions cannot be segmented.

8.4 CONCLUSION

In this chapter, a fully automated Mask R-CNN deep learning method-aided was proposed for segmentation of chronic stroke lesions on brain MR images provided in T1-w MR sequences in the ATLAS v2.0 dataset. In the study, segmentation of chronic stroke lesions was achieved with high accuracy by highlighting the advantages of the Mask R-CNN method in medical image segmentation. In the experimental studies on the test set, the best scores for dice, recall, and precision were obtained as 78.50%, 77.47%, and 81.98%, respectively. At the same time, 16.75 and 4.16 mm scores were obtained for HD95 and ASD metrics, respectively. The achieved scores show that the proposed Mask R-CNN method was successful in segmenting stroke lesions. In addition, it is seen that the proposed method can be used as a secondary tool that can assist physicians in the diagnosis of stroke dis-ease. In this way, physicians can be facilitated in the detection of stroke and deci-sion processes on MR slices. Moreover, it was seen that the ATLAS v2.0 dataset

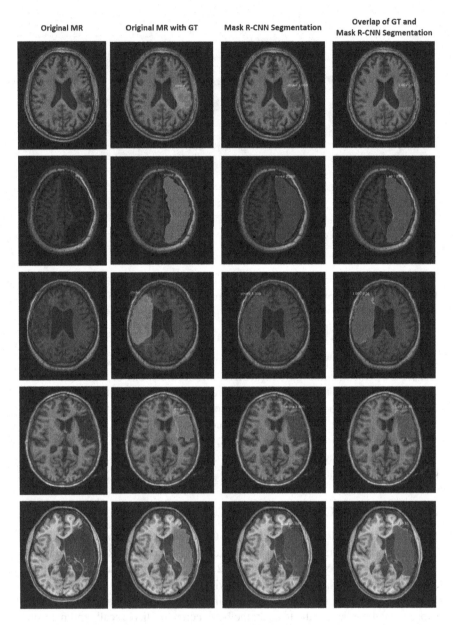

FIGURE 8.9   Stroke lesions successfully segmented using Mask R-CNN-based method on several MR slices in the test set.

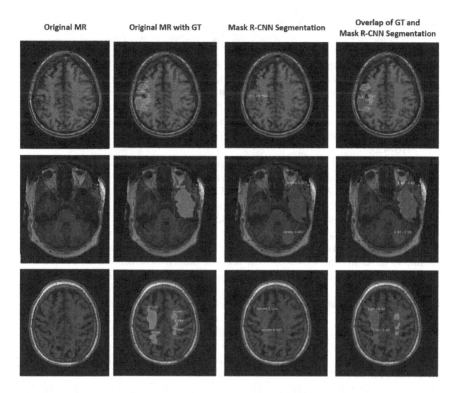

FIGURE 8.10 Some MR images in which stroke lesions are segmented with lower success (lower dice score) using the Mask R-CNN method for the test set.

is more advanced, detailed, and larger in size than the previous version, ATLAS v1.2, and is one of the commonly used datasets for the detection of stoke lesions.

In the future scope of the study, we plan to create our own stroke dataset and make it publicly available. In addition, the accuracy of other state-of-the-art deep learning methods such as U-Net used for medical images in segmentation of brain stroke lesions from datasets can also be investigated, and the obtained results may be compared with each other.

ACKNOWLEDGMENTS

The authors of this chapter would like to thank the team that created and shared the ATLAS v2.0 dataset used in the experimental studies for their support and efforts.

REFERENCES

Albawi, S., Mohammed, T. A., & Al-Zawi, S. (2017). Understanding of a convolutional neural network. In: *2017 International Conference on Engineering and Technology* (ICET), IEEE, Antalya, Turkey.

Allen, L. M., Hasso, A. N., Handwerker, J., & Farid, H. (2012). Sequence-specific MR imaging findings that are useful in dating ischemic stroke. *Radiographics*, *32*(5), 1285–1297.

Amin, J., Sharif, M., Anjum, M. A., Raza, M., & Bukhari, S. A. C. (2020). Convolutional neural network with batch normalization for glioma and stroke lesion detection using MRI. *Cognitive Systems Research*, *59*, 304–311.

Bharathi, P. G., Agrawal, A., Sundaram, P., & Sardesai, S. (2019). Combination of hand-crafted and unsupervised learned features for ischemic stroke lesion detection from magnetic resonance images. *Biocybernetics and Biomedical Engineering*, *39*(2), 410–425.

Clèrigues, A., Valverde, S., Bernal, J., Freixenet, J., Oliver, A., & Lladó, X. (2020). Acute and sub-acute stroke lesion segmentation from multimodal MRI. *Computer Methods and Programs in Biomedicine*, *194*, 105521.

Coutts, S. B. (2017). Diagnosis and management of transient ischemic attack. *Continuum: Lifelong Learning in Neurology*, *23*(1), 82.

De Haan, B., Clas, P., Juenger, H., Wilke, M., & Karnath, H.-O. (2015). Fast semi-automated lesion demarcation in stroke. *NeuroImage: Clinical*, *9*, 69–74.

Feigin, V. L., et al. (2014). Global and regional burden of stroke during 1990–2010: Findings from the global burden of disease study 2010. *The Lancet*, *383*(9913), 245–255.

Girshick, R. (2015). Fast r-cnn. In: *Proceedings of the IEEE International Conference on Computer Vision*. pp. 1440–1448, IEEE, Santiago, Chile.

Girshick, R., Donahue, J., Darrell, T., & Malik, J. (2014). Rich feature hierarchies for accurate object detection and semantic segmentation. In: *Proceedings of the IEEE Conference on Computer Vision and Pattern Recognition*, IEEE, Columbus, OH, USA. pp. 580–587.

Griffis, J. C., Allendorfer, J. B., & Szaflarski, J. P. (2016). Voxel-based Gaussian naïve Bayes classification of ischemic stroke lesions in individual T1-weighted MRI scans. *Journal of Neuroscience Methods*, *257*, 97–108.

He, K., Gkioxari, G., Dollár, P., & Girshick, R. (2017). Mask r-cnn. In: *Proceedings of the IEEE International Conference on Computer Vision*. pp. 2961–2969, IEEE, Venice, Italy.

Kanchana, R., & Menaka, R. (2020). Ischemic stroke lesion detection, characterization and classification in CT images with optimal features selection. *Biomedical Engineering Letters*, *10*(3), 333–344.

Karimi, D., & Salcudean, S. E. (2019). Reducing the hausdorff distance in medical image segmentation with convolutional neural networks. *IEEE Transactions on Medical Imaging*, *39*(2), 499–513.

Karthik, R., Menaka, R., Johnson, A., & Anand, S. (2020). Neuroimaging and deep learning for brain stroke detection-A review of recent advancements and future prospects. *Computer Methods and Programs in Biomedicine*, *197*, 105728.

Kavur, A. E., et al. (2020). Comparison of semi-automatic and deep learning-based automatic methods for liver segmentation in living liver transplant donors. *Diagnostic and Interventional Radiology*, *26*(1), 11.

Kiran, S. (2012). What is the nature of poststroke language recovery and reorganization? *International Scholarly Research Notices*, *2012*, 1–13.

Liew, S.-L., et al. (2018). A large, open source dataset of stroke anatomical brain images and manual lesion segmentations. *Scientific Data*, *5*(1), 1–11.

Liew, S. L., Lo, B. P., Donnelly, M. R., Zavaliangos-Petropulu, A., Jeong, J. N., Barisano, G., … & Yu, C. (2022). A large, curated, open-source stroke neuroimaging dataset to improve lesion segmentation algorithms. *Scientific Data*, *9*(1), 1–12.

Liu, W., Wen, Y., Yu, Z., & Yang, M. (2016). Large-margin softmax loss for convolutional neural networks. In: *ICML. arXiv preprint arXiv:1612.02295.*

Liu, X., et al. (2019). MSDF-Net: Multi-scale deep fusion network for stroke lesion segmentation. *IEEE Access, 7,* 178486–178495.

Long, J., Shelhamer, E., & Darrell, T. (2015). Fully convolutional networks for semantic segmentation. In: *Proceedings of the IEEE Conference on Computer Vision and Pattern Recognition.* pp. 3431–3440, IEEE, Boston, MA, USA.

Nabizadeh, N., John, N., & Wright, C. (2014). Histogram-based gravitational optimization algorithm on single MR modality for automatic brain lesion detection and segmentation. *Expert Systems with Applications, 41*(17), 7820–7836.

Nielsen, M. A. (2015). *Neural Networks and Deep Learning,* Vol. 25. Determination Press: San Francisco, CA, USA.

Pustina, D., Coslett, H. B., Turkeltaub, P. E., Tustison, N., Schwartz, M. F., & Avants, B. (2016). Automated segmentation of chronic stroke lesions using LINDA: Lesion identification with neighborhood data analysis. *Human Brain Mapping, 37*(4), 1405–1421.

Qi, K., Yang, H., Li, C., Liu, Z., Wang, M., Liu, Q., & Wang, S. (2019). X-net: Brain stroke lesion segmentation based on depthwise separable convolution and long-range dependencies. In: *International Conference on Medical Image Computing and Computer-Assisted Intervention.* Springer, Cham, pp. 247–255.

Rajini, N. H., & Bhavani, R. (2013). Computer aided detection of ischemic stroke using segmentation and texture features. *Measurement, 46*(6), 1865–1874.

Ravì, D., Wong, C., Deligianni, F., Berthelot, M., Andreu-Perez, J., Lo, B., & Yang, G.-Z. (2016). Deep learning for health informatics. *IEEE Journal of Biomedical and Health Informatics, 21*(1), 4–21.

Ren, S., He, K., Girshick, R., & Sun, J. (2015). Faster r-cnn: Towards real-time object detection with region proposal networks. *Advances in Neural Information Processing Systems, 28,* 1–9.

Shelhamer, E., Long, J., & Darrell, T. (2016). Fully convolutional networks for semantic segmentation. *IEEE Transactions on Pattern Analysis and Machine Intelligence, 39*(4), 640–651.

Shin, H., Agyeman, R., Rafiq, M., Chang, M. C., & Choi, G. S. (2022). Automated segmentation of chronic stroke lesion using efficient U-Net architecture. *Biocybernetics and Biomedical Engineering, 42*(1), 285–294.

Subudhi, A., Acharya, U. R., Dash, M., Jena, S., & Sabut, S. (2018). Automated approach for detection of ischemic stroke using Delaunay triangulation in brain MRI images. *Computers in Biology and Medicine, 103,* 116–129.

Sun, M., Song, Z., Jiang, X., Pan, J., & Pang, Y. (2017). Learning pooling for convolutional neural network. *Neurocomputing, 224,* 96–104.

Targ, S., Almeida, D., & Lyman, K. (2016). *Resnet in Resnet: Generalizing Residual Architectures. arXiv preprint arXiv:1603.08029.*

Tomita, N., Jiang, S., Maeder, M. E., & Hassanpour, S. (2020). Automatic post-stroke lesion segmentation on MR images using 3D residual convolutional neural network. *NeuroImage: Clinical, 27,* 102276.

Unnithan, A. K. A., & Mehta, P. (2020). *Hemorrhagic Stroke,* StatPearls Publishing, Treasure Island, FL.

Vos, T., et al. (2020). Global burden of 369 diseases and injuries in 204 countries and territories, 1990–2019: A systematic analysis for the global burden of disease study 2019. *The Lancet, 396*(10258), 1204–1222.

Wajngarten, M., & Silva, G. S. (2019). Hypertension and stroke: Update on treatment. *European Cardiology Review, 14*(2), 111.

Wang, P., Zhang, C., Yang, X., Yang, L., Yang, Y., HE, H., & HE, C. (2014). Whole body vibration training improves limb motor dysfunction in stroke patients: Lack of evidence. *Chinese Journal of Tissue Engineering Research*, *18*(38), 6205–6209.

Weimer, D., Scholz-Reiter, B., & Shpitalni, M. (2016). Design of deep convolutional neural network architectures for automated feature extraction in industrial inspection. *CIRP Annals*, *65*(1), 417–420.

Wilke, M., de Haan, B., Juenger, H., & Karnath, H.-O. (2011). Manual, semi-automated, and automated delineation of chronic brain lesions: A comparison of methods. *NeuroImage*, *56*(4), 2038–2046.

WSO (2022). The World Stroke Organization – Learn about stroke. Accessed 26 April, 2022, available: https://www.world-stroke.org/world-stroke-day-campaign/why-stroke-matters/learn-about-stroke

Wu, J.-N. (2016). Compression of fully-connected layer in neural network by kronecker product. In: *2016 Eighth International Conference on Advanced Computational Intelligence (ICACI)*. IEEE, Chiang Mai, pp. 173–179.

Wu, P., et al. (2015). Changes of resting cerebral activities in subacute ischemic stroke patients. *Neural Regeneration Research*, *10*(5), 760.

Xue, Y., Farhat, F. G., Boukrina, O., Barrett, A., Binder, J. R., Roshan, U. W., & Graves, W. W. (2020). A multi-path 2.5 dimensional convolutional neural network system for segmenting stroke lesions in brain MRI images. *NeuroImage: Clinical*, *25*, 102118.

Zhang, Y., Wu, J., Liu, Y., Chen, Y., Wu, E. X., & Tang, X. (2021). MI-UNet: Multi-inputs UNet incorporating brain parcellation for stroke lesion segmentation from T1-weighted magnetic resonance images. *IEEE Journal of Biomedical and Health Informatics*, *25*(2), 526–535.

Zhou, Y., Huang, W., Dong, P., Xia, Y., & Wang, S. (2021). D-UNet: A dimension-fusion U shape network for chronic stroke lesion segmentation. *IEEE/ACM Transactions on Computational Biology and Bioinformatics*, *18*(3), 940–950.

Zou, K. H., et al. (2004). Statistical validation of image segmentation quality based on a spatial overlap index1: Scientific reports. *Academic Radiology*, *11*(2), 178–189.

9 Efficient Classification of Schizophrenia EEG Signals Using Deep Learning Methods

Subha D. Puthankattil and Marrapu Vynatheya
National Institute of Technology Calicut

Ahsan Ali
Indian Institute of Technology Madras

CONTENTS

9.1 INTRODUCTION

Schizophrenia (SZ) is a psychological brain disorder [1]. Schizophrenia is characterized by a symptom constellation that includes cognitive impairment, disordered speech, nonexistent hearing sounds, hallucinations, changes in sleep patterns, etc. [2,3]. The common symptoms of schizophrenia are impaired concentration, mental

DOI: 10.1201/9781003315452-9

chaos, lack of motivation, unfocused facial expressions, delusions, and hallucinations. According to a WHO report [4], 24 million people (1 in 300) are affected by schizophrenia, while in adults, the rate is 1 in 222. Schizophrenic patients can have two symptoms, namely positive symptoms and negative symptoms. Delusions, hallucinations, and disorganized thinking indicate positive symptoms, whereas lack of motivation, no energy, feeling uncomfortable with people, and facial expressions indicate negative symptoms of schizophrenia disease [5]. Cognitive impairment is also a type of negative symptom, where SZ patient lacks in decision-making, learning new things, and remembering new things in regular life. Paranoid, hebephrenic, catatonic, undifferentiated, and residual are the types of schizophrenia [6]. Psychiatrists diagnose schizophrenia by conducting interviews during the course of multiple sittings and hence require a certain amount of expertise. This issue has now been overcome with the introduction of machine learning and deep learning methods.

Electroencephalogram (EEG) signals represent the scalp recorded electrical impulses from the human brain. EEG is a noninvasive physiological method to record the electrical activity of the brain under various pathological states. The EEG signals are divided into five different frequency bands, namely Delta (freq: <3 Hz), Theta (freq: 3 – 7 Hz), Alpha (freq: 7 – 13 Hz), Beta (freq: 13–30 Hz), and Gamma (freq: >30 Hz). EEG signals are non-stationary, highly random, nonlinear in nature and contain essential information about the status of the brain [7]. EEG is a widely acclaimed method to diagnose neurological diseases such as schizophrenia, depression, Alzheimer's, epilepsy, seizures, sleep problems, death of the brain, coma, tumor, etc. [8].

Machine learning (ML) implements more straightforward principles, such as statistical models, while deep learning (DL) uses artificial neural networks (ANNs) to mimic the way people think and learn [9]. ML uses an algorithm to analyze data, learn from the data, and make an intelligent choice based on what it has learned from data, whereas DL structures lay algorithms to develop an artificial neural network that can learn and make intelligent decisions [10]. DL learns hidden patterns from hidden layers, and it requires more data to make the right decision. That is why the DL approach is acceptable over ML to diagnose EEG signals. The acquired signals always have artifacts in the form of heartbeats, EMG signals, sweating, power line noises, etc. The artifacts had to be removed to minimize the misinterpretation of signals. Total variation denoising (TVD) technique [11] has been implemented for the removal of artifacts from SZ EEG signals.

Schizophrenic cognitive impairment and other psychological symptoms are difficult to diagnose [12,13]. Automatically classifying brain disorders such as Parkinson's disease, schizophrenia, Alzheimer's disease, and epilepsy using an automated procedure will be extremely useful [14–17]. Early schizophrenia diagnosis and timely medical intervention will improve the physical and social well-being of a patient [18,19]. Computer-aided diagnosis (CAD) enables automatic identification to activate quick and efficient medical interventions [12,20,21], thus helping to mitigate neurodisorder progression. As with extracting features and training, the network for detection of SZ by LSTM [22,23], CNN [24], VGG-16, and AlexNet [25] saves much time.

This chapter focuses on the early detection of schizophrenia using deep learning models which would help us to distinguish patients from healthy controls. Early detection is possible with deep learning models as it has the capability to detect the hidden traits and patterns in the signal. These plausible studies would help to improve the quality of life of a SZ patient by initiating early and timely medical interventions. This work is carried out by employing LSTM, a recurrent neural network (RNN) architecture, by inputting the network with feature vectors of Katz Fractal Dimension, approximate entropy, and variance to detect SZ. VGG-16 and AlexNet, both being CNN models, are also being used for the classification of SZ. A comparison of the performance of these deep learning models in classifying SZ from healthy controls is discussed in this chapter.

9.2 DATA RECORDING

This scientific study included 14 paranoid schizophrenia patients (seven young men: 27.9 ± 3.3 years, seven young women: 28.3 ± 4.1 years) and 14 healthy controls (seven young men: 26.8 ± 2.9 years, seven young women: 8.7 ± 3.4 years) who were hospitalized at the Institute of Psychiatry and Neurology in Warsaw, Poland [26]. All subjects had 15-minute EEG datasets recorded with their eyes closed and in a relaxed resting state with 19 different electrodes (Fp1, Fp2, F7, F3, Fz, F4, F8, T3, C3, Cz, C4, T4, T5, P3, Pz, P4, T6, O1, O2) at a sampling frequency of 250 Hz employing standard 10–20 electrode placement methods. The EEG signals were obtained from the database of https://doi.org/10.18150/repod.0107441. TVD technique was used to suppress the artifacts, and a 50 Hz notch filter was used for the removal of power line interference.

9.3 METHODOLOGY

The EEG signals of SZ patients and healthy controls were preprocessed using TVD algorithm, and the efficiency of the noise removal technique was assessed using signal-to-noise ratio (SNR). Binary classification of the signals using LSTM was accomplished extracting nonlinear features, namely Katz Fractal Dimension, approximate entropy, and the statistical feature of variance. These were fed as input features to the LSTM algorithm. VGG-16 and AlexNet models used for classification were fed with spectrogram (images) of the EEG signals, which gives a visual representation of the strength of the signals. The nonlinear time domain and statistical time domain feature vectors used for training the LSTM network are discussed in the following section.

9.3.1 TIME DOMAIN FEATURES

i. **Katz Fractal Dimension:** This is a nonlinear time domain technique proposed by M. Katz, which measures the complexities in non-stationary signals [27]. It gives an indication of the randomness or the unpredictability of the time series.

Step 1: Calculate Euclidian distance

Let $P = \{P_1, P_2,....P_n\}$ be the points on a curve, and (x_i, y_i) denotes the coordinates of the sequence P_i, then Euclidian distance between the points can be written as

$$\text{dis}(P_i, P_j) = \sqrt{(x_i - x_j)^2 + (y_i - y_j)^2} \qquad (9.1)$$

Step 2: Define greatest distance

Let L be the total length of the curve (which is the sum of the distance between successive points) and d be the diameter of the curve (or planar extension), calculated as the distance between the first point in the sequence and the point in the sequence that offers the greatest distance. d can be written as

$$d = \max\{dist(P_i, P_j)\} \qquad (9.2)$$

Step 3: Calculation of Dimension D

The Fractal dimension of the curve represented by "D" is given as

$$D = \frac{\log(L)}{\log(d)} \qquad (9.3)$$

Step 4: If the number of steps in the curve is n, and a being the average distance between successive points, then

$$a = L/n \qquad (9.4)$$

Step 5: Calculation of KFD

So Eq. (9.3) becomes

$$D = \frac{\log n}{\log\left(\dfrac{d}{L}\right) + \log n} \qquad (9.5)$$

Hence Eq. (9.5) helps in the estimation of Katz Fractal Dimension for a waveform.

ii. **Approximate Entropy (ApEn):** Approximation entropy is a nonlinear method for determining the degree of regularity and predictability of variations in time-series data [28].

Step 1: Consider the time series data with the data sequence, *(V1), V(2), ..., V(N)* which are equally spaced in time.

Step 2: Let *X(i)* be a subsequence of *V* such that

$$X(i) = [V(i), V(i+1), ...V(i+m-1)], i = 1, 2,...N-m+1 \qquad (9.6)$$

where m denotes the length of the runs to be compared

Let $\{X(j)\}$ represents a subsequence of X. Each attribute in $X(j)$ is compared with $X(i)$, and parameters are defined as follows.

Step 3: Define $C_i^m(r)$: $\displaystyle C_i^m(r) = \frac{\sum_{j=1}^{N-m+1} k_j}{N-m+1}$ \hfill (9.7)

where $\qquad r = k \times SD$ \hfill (9.8)

where r indicates the noise filter level and SD, the standard deviation of X, respectively.

and

$$K = \begin{cases} 1; \; if \; \left|x(i)-x(j)\right| for \; 1 \le j \le N-m \\ 0; \; otherwise \end{cases}$$ \hfill (9.9)

Step 4: Define $\varphi^m(r)$ as:

$$\varphi^m(r) = (N-m+1)^{-1} \sum_{i=1}^{N-m+1} ln\left(C_i^m(r)\right)$$ \hfill (9.10)

Step 5: ApEn (m, r, N) is calculated using $\varphi^m(r)$ and $\varphi^{m+1}(r)$ as follows:

$$ApEn(m, r, N) = \varphi^m(r) - \varphi^{m+1}(r)$$ \hfill (9.11)

where, $\varphi^{m+1}(r)$ can be obtained by increasing the dimension to $m+1$ and repeating the above steps (1) through (3).

An m of 1 and r of 0.5 have been employed for the calculation of ApEn in this work.

iii. **Variance:** It is a measure which gives the spread of data points from its mean value, and it is calculated as given below:

$$Var(X) = \frac{1}{n} \sum_{i=1}^{n} (x_i - \mu)^2$$ \hfill (9.12)

where, μ, n, and x_i are the mean, sample frequency, and i^{th} sample, respectively.

9.3.2 CREATING SPECTROGRAM IMAGES USING SHORT-TIME FOURIER TRANSFORM (STFT)

A spectrogram is a 2D visual representation of a spectrum of signal frequencies as a function of time. It gives an interpretation of how the strength of the signal is distributed among various frequencies. The intensity of different points in the images represents the amplitude of a particular frequency at a particular time.

The EEG signals were recorded for a 15 minutes duration from each electrode at a sampling frequency of 250 Hz, resulting in a total of $250 \times 60 \times 15$ (2,25,000) data points from one electrode. Using the Hanning window, these data points are plotted as a spectrogram image (224×224), generating 14×19 spectrogram images from healthy individuals and 14×19 spectrogram images from SZ patients. The spectrogram of a healthy control and a SZ patient is shown in Figure 9.1a and b, respectively.

9.3.3 Architecture of LSTM

A more sophisticated variation of the RNN is the LSTM. The LSTM, unlike the RNN, can remember information for an extended period and has overcome the vanishing gradient problem. As illustrated in Figure 9.2, an LSTM has three gates: forget gate, input gate, output gate, and one cell state. The job of the forget gate is to update the information in the cell using the sigmoid layer, the input gate is used to update the information in the cell using the sigmoid layer, and the output gate is used to get the output. The work of the cell state is to update the information in the cell using the sigmoid layer.

where σ and $\tanh$ denote the sigmoid function and hyperbolic tangent function, $x^{(t)}$ and $h^{(t-1)}$ are the ith input and output, and "$\times$" and "$+$" are the pointwise multiplication and addition operators, respectively [29].

Forget sigmoid layer:

$$f^{(t)} = \sigma\left(w_f\left[y^{(t-1)}, x^{(t)}\right] + b_f\right) \tag{9.13}$$

where
$$f^{(t)} \in [0,1]$$

$$f^{(t)} = \begin{cases} 1, & \text{keep all the past information} \\ 0, & \text{remove all the past information} \end{cases} \tag{9.14}$$

Input sigmoid layer:

$$i^{(t)} = \sigma(w_i.[y^{(t-1)}, x^{(t)}] + b_i) \tag{9.15}$$

$$z^{(t)} = \tanh(w_c\left[y^{(t-1)}, x_t\right] + b_c)z^{(t)}\epsilon[-1,1] \tag{9.16}$$

Cell state $c^{(t)}$ has been updated from $c^{(t-1)}$

Updated cell state:

$$c^{(t)} = f^{(t)} * c^{(t-1)} + i^{(t)} * z^{(t)} \tag{9.17}$$

Final output

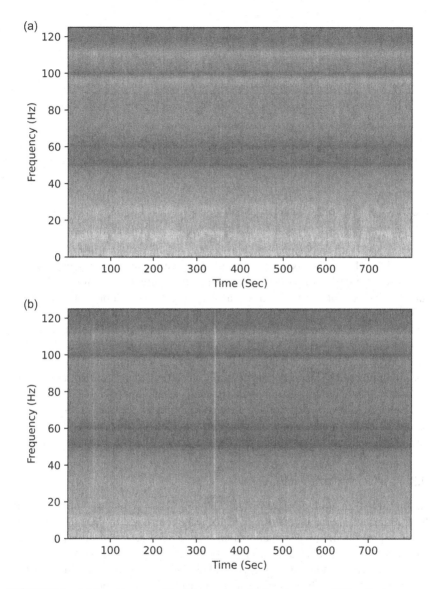

FIGURE 9.1   (a) Spectrogram of healthy control. (b) Spectrogram of SZ patient.

Output sigmoid layer:

$$o^{(t)} = \sigma\left(w_o \left[h^{(t-1)}, x^{(t)} \right] + b_0 \right) \tag{9.18}$$

Current hidden layer:

$$y^{(t)} = o^{(t)} * \tanh\left(c^{(t)} \right) \tag{9.19}$$

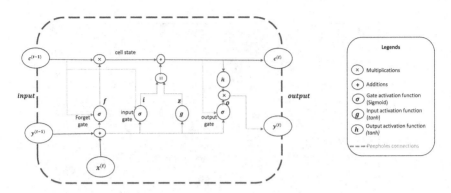

FIGURE 9.2   One cell structure of LSTM.

where w and b are the weights and biases in a particular hidden layer.

The LSTM model consisted of four hidden layers, each with 32 neurons. The structure proposed in this work is represented in Figure 9.3. A total of 6,000 feature vectors were utilized for training and 790 for testing, out of a total sample of 6,790 feature vectors. These feature vectors of FD, ApEn, and variance are calculated from each electrode of the EEG signals recorded from 14 SZ patients and 14 healthy controls. For each LSTM layer, a 30% dropout was employed. A total of 250 epochs were used for training the model with a learning rate of 0.0001. The loss function used was binary cross-entropy, and the model was fit with the Adam optimizer. These parameters aided in efficiently reaching the global minimum.

Four LSTM layers were trained for hyperparameter adjustment, and the performance of the model was assessed. The complete dataset was split into two parts: 89% was used for training, and the remaining 11% was used for testing.

9.3.4 Architecture of VGG-16

Karen Simonyan et al. developed the VGG-16 (Visual Geometry Group with 16 layers adjustable parameters) form of CNN architecture in 2014 [25]. The VGG-16 architecture contains 16 convolutional layers and a 3×3 size receptive field. It has a max pooling layer of size 2×2. There are three wholly linked layers. It employs softmax classifier as the last layer. All hidden layers are activated with Rectified Linear unit (ReLU). The proposed architecture of VGG-16 is shown in Figure 9.4.

VGG-16 model is provided with spectrogram images of all electrodes (19×14×2) for categorization of SZ from healthy controls. Figure 9.5 illustrates a simplified form of the Visual Geometry Group (VGG-16) architecture used in this work, comprising of 16 layers and three fully connected dense layers. The input for the first convolution layer is a fixed size of 224×224 RGB image, and the image goes through a stack of convolution layers. The input to the network is image of dimension (224, 224, 3). A filter size of 3×3 and max pool layer of stride (2, 2) is used for all the layers. The first two convolution layers have a dimension of 224×224×64, and with the application of pooling layer, reduces the dimension

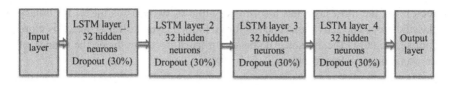

FIGURE 9.3 Proposed structure of LSTM.

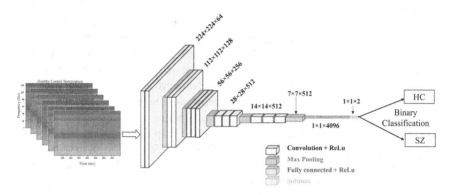

FIGURE 9.4 Proposed architecture of VGG-16 network.

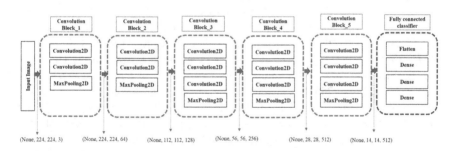

FIGURE 9.5 Summary of VGG-16 architecture network.

of the image to $112 \times 112 \times 64$. Two more convolutional layers are applied with 128 filters leading to $112 \times 112 \times 128$ and results in a dimension of $56 \times 56 \times 128$ on the application of max pooling.

Three convolution layers are added with 256 filters with each having a size of $56 \times 56 \times 256$ followed by the reduction of size to $28 \times 28 \times 256$ on down sampling. Three more stacks of convolution layer with 512 filters of size $28 \times 28 \times 512$ are maxpooled to $14 \times 14 \times 512$. Again 512 filters are employed with three more convolution layers of each $14 \times 14 \times 512$ which on down sampling reduces to $7 \times 7 \times 512$ which is further flattened to make a (1, 25088) feature vector. Following which, there are three fully connected layers: the first takes input from the last feature vector and outputs a (1, 4096) vector, the second layer also outputs a (1, 4096) vector, but the third layer has a softmax output of two classes meant for binary classification. The activation function for all hidden layers is ReLU. ReLU is more computationally efficient since it speeds up learning and reduces the chance of the vanishing gradient problem.

9.3.5 ARCHITECTURE OF ALEXNET

AlexNet network was developed in 2012 by Alex Krizhevsky et al. [30]. In AlexNet architecture, eight layers are there, of which five are convolutional and three are fully connected layers. The network depth in this model is more, compared with the previous models. The first layer of the architecture is used to input filtered images with a dimension of $27 \times 27 \times 3$. The first convolution layer comprises 96 filters of size $11 \times 11 \times 3$ with strides of four pixels. The dimension of the produced feature map is $55 \times 55 \times 96$. The number of filters becomes the channel in the output feature map. The next layer consists of maximum pooling with a dimension of 3×3 and stride of two pixels. This results in a feature map of dimension $27 \times 27 \times 96$. Now the second convolution process is applied with 256 filters with the filter size being lowered to 5×5 and a stride of 1, and padding being 2. The activation function used is ReLU. The output dimension is now $27 \times 27 \times 256$. The generated feature map is $13 \times 13 \times 256$ when max pooling layer of 3×3 with stride of 2 is applied. The third convolution operation takes place with 384 filters of size 3×3 employing stride and padding of 1 each, respectively. The size of the feature vector generated is $13 \times 13 \times 384$. The fourth convolution process also employs 384 kernels of size 3×3 with the stride and padding of 1 each, respectively. The output dimension is $13 \times 13 \times 384$ which is the same as before. The final convolution layer has 256 kernels of size 3×3 with the stride and padding both being set to 1, respectively. The third max pooling layer employed has a size of 3×3 and a stride of 2, resulting in a feature map of the size $6 \times 6 \times 256$. It is flattened to make a (1, 9216) feature vector. AlexNet can generate a 4,096-dimensional feature vector for each input picture containing the hidden units' activations before the output layer is applied. It consists of two fully connected layers with 4,096 neurons and ReLU activation function. The last connected output layer with two neurons and a softmax activation function having an output of 2, is employed for binary classification. The AlexNet model, consists of convolutional layers and fully connected layers. Convolution layers comprise the first five layers, while the last three are fully connected layers. This structure appears challenging to comprehend; hence, a summary model is depicted in Figure 9.6.

In the proposed work, five convolutional layers with ReLU activation function are coupled with cross-channel norms and maximum pooling layers.

9.4 RESULTS AND DISCUSSION

In this study, the performance of the different deep learning models in efficiently classifying schizophrenia from healthy controls is evaluated. The EEG signals from 19 electrode locations recorded under resting state eyes closed condition from 14 SZ patients, and 14 healthy controls were employed for the study. The

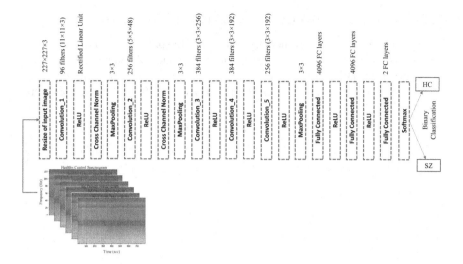

FIGURE 9.6   Proposed AlexNet architecture.

efficiency of LSTM, a mode of RNN architecture in identifying schizophrenia, is compared with two CNN models of VGG-16 and AlexNet. The capability of these deep learning models in learning the representation of features from the data is assessed using the performance measures. The performance measures used are accuracy, precision, recall, and F1-score.

(a) Accuracy is the ratio of correct predictions to the total number of predictions

$$Accuracy = (TP + TN)/(TP + TN + FP + FN)$$

(b) Precision gives an indication of the accuracy of the model in correctly making positive identifications

$$Precision = TP/(TP + FP)$$

(c) Recall is the ratio of positive identifications to the total number of positive samples

$$Recall = TP/(TP + FN)$$

(d) F1-score is an indication of the accuracy of the model on a dataset

$$F1 - score = (2 \times precision \times recall)/(precision + recall)$$

where TP = True Positive, TN = True Negative, FP = False Positive, and FN = False Negative.

9.4.1 RESULTS OF BINARY CLASSIFICATION USING LSTM MODEL

EEG data of SZ patients and healthy controls were split into windows of 4 seconds duration, each consisting of 1,000 epochs. The time domain feature vectors of Katz Fractal Dimension, approximate entropy, and variance were extracted from these epochs. Of the 6,790 features extracted, 6,000 feature vectors were

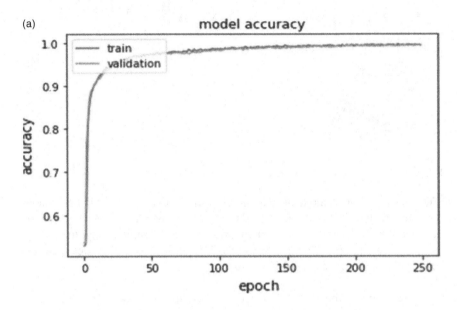

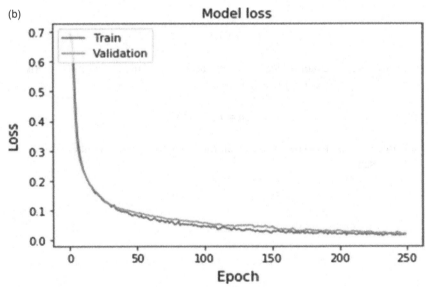

FIGURE 9.7 (a) Model accuracy vs. no. of epochs. (b) Model loss vs. no. of epochs.

TABLE 9.1

Performance measures of LSTM model

Performance Measures	LSTM (%)
Accuracy	99.0
Precision	99.2
Recall	98.9
F1-Score	99

used for training the model, and the remaining employed for testing the network. LSTM network model was built with four layers and 32 hidden neurons. The learning rate was fixed as 0.0001. The plots of model accuracy vs number of epochs and the model loss vs number of epochs are shown in Figure 9.7a and b, respectively. The performance measures calculated for the LSTM model are represented in Table 9.1. A classification accuracy of 99% is obtained for identifying schizophrenia from healthy controls.

9.4.2 RESULTS OF BINARY CLASSIFICATION USING VGG-16 AND ALEXNET MODELS

The performance of the CNN models, namely VGG-16 and AlexNet, in classifying schizophrenia patients from healthy controls is discussed in this section. Eighty percent of the total dataset consisting of the spectrogram images was used for training, and the remaining 20% was used for testing. The loss function used is binary cross-entropy, and Adam optimizer gave the optimum gradient descent. The number of epochs selected for the training dataset, both for VGG-16 and AlexNet, is 50, and the batch size is fixed at 64. The learning rate adopted for VGG-16 is 0.001, and that for AlexNet is 0.0001. The performance of VGG-16 and AlexNet models in terms of accuracy and loss calculated with respect to epochs, are shown in the plots of Figures 9.8 and 9.9, respectively.

The plots of Figures 9.8a and 9.9a represent the changes in accuracy of the training and testing model as a function of the number of epochs for VGG-16 and AlexNet model, respectively, while the plots of Figures 9.8b and 9.9b represent the model loss as a function of the number of epochs for VGG-16 and AlexNet, respectively. The loss for VGG-16 is 0.067, and that for AlexNet is 0.011, which gives an assessment of the error incurred in the model on the application of the training dataset, which ascertains the efficacy of the performance of the classification models. Table 9.2 represents the performance measures calculated for the models of VGG-16 and AlexNet. The outstanding performance of AlexNet over VGG-16 in terms of performance measures gives an indication of the efficiency of the model in correctly classifying schizophrenia from healthy controls.

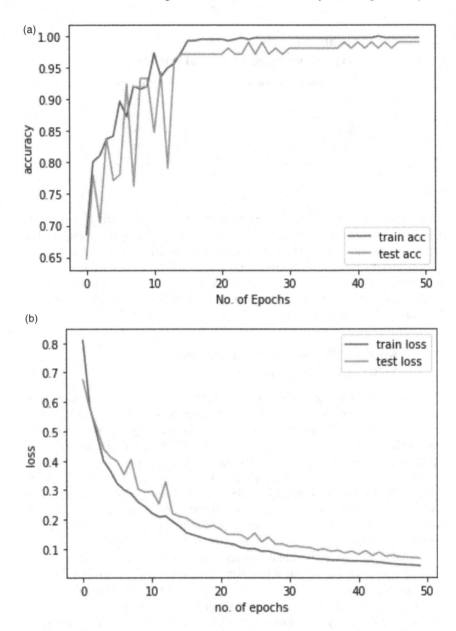

FIGURE 9.8   (a) Accuracy vs. no. of epochs. (b) Loss vs. no. of epochs.

9.4.3 FIVE-FOLD CROSS-VALIDATION

Cross-validation is a technique employed in machine learning algorithms to evaluate the performance of the models on a completely new set of unseen data. A k-fold cross-validation generally assumes a value of k to be 5 or 10, which refers

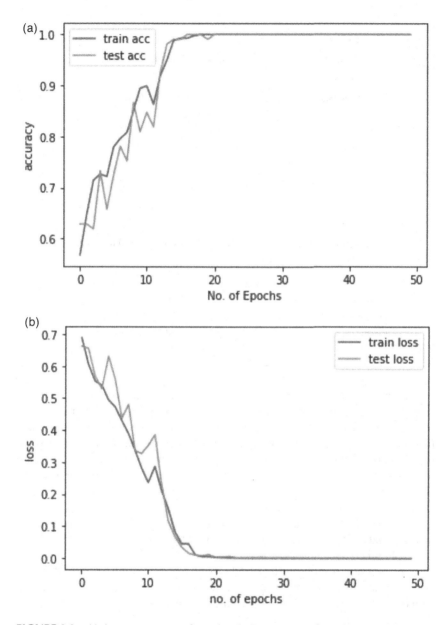

FIGURE 9.9   (a) Accuracy vs. no. of epochs. (b) Loss vs. no. of epochs.

to the number of groups to which the data sample must be split. This study utilizes a five fold cross-validation which greatly reduces the bias of the model. Cross-validation is attempted to ensure that the performance of the model is accurate. The performance measures of LSTM, VGG-16, and AlexNet models based on five fold cross-validation are shown in Table 9.3.

TABLE 9.2

Performance measures of VGG-16 and AlexNet models

Performance Parameters	VGG-16 (%)	AlexNet (%)
Accuracy	99.05	100
Precision	100	100
Recall	98.3	100
F1-Score	99.1	100

TABLE 9.3

Performance measures of LSTM, VGG-16, and AlexNet models based on five fold cross-validation

Performance Parameters	LSTM (%)	VGG-16 (%)	AlexNet (%)
Accuracy	99.1	99.81	99.61
Precision	99.4	100	100
Recall	99.0	98.3	100
F1-Score	99.2	99.1	100

The hyperparameters for both VGG-16 and AlexNet under five fold cross-validation models are tuned to the same value as that of the original model. It is observed from the results that there is only a nominal variation in the classification accuracies of the three different algorithms employed in this work for the classification of EEG signals from SZ and healthy controls. A significant decrease in the value of model loss is a good indication of better classification ability. The results of five fold cross-validation posit a higher classification accuracy for VGG-16 in comparison to AlexNet model.

An overview of the classification accuracies achieved using various machine learning and deep learning algorithms reported by various authors in identifying schizophrenia is shown in Table 9.4.

It is observed from the current study that CNN algorithms surpassed LSTM in identifying SZ from the database, with a classification accuracy of 99.81% employing VGG-16 and 99.61% using AlexNet, respectively.

9.5 CONCLUSION

The performance capability of different deep learning models of LSTM, VGG-16, and AlexNet in classifying schizophrenia from healthy controls is evaluated through this study. The EEG signals of schizophrenia patients and healthy controls were accessed from an open database. The signals were preprocessed, and the time domain feature vectors of Katz Fractal Dimension, approximate entropy,

TABLE 9.4

Summary of studies carried out for the binary classification of SZ EEG signals from that of healthy controls

Author's Name	EEG Database	ML/DL Algorithms	Extracted Features	Classification Accuracy (%)
Johannesen et al. [12]	HC: 12 & SZ: 40	SVM	Alpha, beta, theta-1, theta-2, gamma frequency bands	87.00
Shim et al. [14]	HC: 34 & SZ:34	SVM	Source- and sensor-level features	88.25
Thilakvathi et al. [31]	HC:23 & SZ: 55	SVM	Higuchi's fractal, Kolmogorov, complexity, approximate entropy, Shannon entropy, and dimension	88.50
Santos-Mayo et al. [21]	HC: 31 & SZ: 16	SVM	EEGLAB feature extraction, J5 feature extraction	92.23
Aslan et al. [17]	HC: 39 & SZ: 45	KNN	Relative wavelet energy	90.00
Naira et al. [16]	HC: 39 & SZ: 45	CNN	-	90.0
Oh et al. [9]	HC: 14 & SZ: 14	CNN	-	89.59
Singh et al. [32]	HC: 39 & SZ: 45	CNN-LSTM	-	98.56
Afshin et al. [23]	HC: 14 & SZ: 14	1D CNN-LSTM	-	99.25
Aristizabal et al. [33]	HC: 40 & SZ: 65	CNN-LSTM	-	72.54
Pinaya et al. [20]	HC: 83 & SZ: 143	DBN (deep belief network)	Morphometry	73.6
Latha et al. [34]	HC: 74 & SZ: 72	DBN (deep belief network)	Morphometry	90.0
Han et al. [19]	HC: 31 & SZ: 39	Autoencoder	FC: functional connectivity.	90.0
Qureshi et al. [35]	HC: 72 & SZ: 72	CNN	ICA maps	98.0
Alimardani et al. [3]	SZ: 23 and Bipolar Disorder: 23	KNN	Steady-state visual evoked potential (SSVEP), SNR	91.30
Suily et al. [15]	HC: 32 & SZ: 49	Empirical mode decomposition (EMD)	Statistical features and Kruskal–Wallis (KW) test	89.59
Jahmunah et al. [18]	HC: 14 & SZ: 14	SVM-RBF	Nonlinear features & t-test	92.90

(Continued)

TABLE 9.4 (*Continued*)

Summary of studies carried out for the binary classification of SZ EEG signals from that of healthy controls

Author's Name	EEG Database	ML/DL Algorithms	Extracted Features	Classification Accuracy (%)
Devia et al. [36]	HC: 9 & SZ: 11	Linear discriminant analysis (LDA)	Event-related potential (ERP) features	71.00
Prabhakar et al. [37]	HC: 14 & SZ: 14	Adaboost	Isomap + optimization methods	98.77
Piryatinska et al. [13]	HC: 39 & SZ: 45	Random Forest (RF)	ε-complexity of a continuous vector function	85.3
Phang et al. [24]	HC: 39 & SZ: 45	CNN	-	93.06
Nikhil et al. [22]	HC: 14 & SZ: 14	LSTM	Katz Fractal Dimension (KFD), approximate entropy (ApEn), variance	99.0
Present work	HC: 14 & SZ: 14	VGG-16	-	99.81
Present work	HC: 14 & SZ: 14	AlexNet	-	99.61

and variance extracted were fed to the LSTM classifier. The spectrogram images of the EEG signals of schizophrenia patients and healthy controls were fed as input samples for VGG-16 and AlexNet models. The classification abilities of these deep learning models are evaluated based on the performance measures of accuracy, precision, recall, and F1-score. A five fold cross-validation is employed in order to reduce the bias of the model. The results of five fold cross-validation reveal a better classification accuracy of 99.81% for VGG-16 in comparison to 99.61% for AlexNet in distinguishing schizophrenia from healthy subjects. Hence, an efficient mode of computer-based automated deep learning algorithm could help in identifying schizophrenia, thus reducing the cost burden on the patient.

REFERENCES

1. S. Saha, D. Chant, J. Welham, and J. McGrath, A systematic review of the prevalence of Schizophrenia, *PLOS Med.*, vol. 2, no. 5, p. e141, 2005, doi: 10.1371/JOURNAL. PMED.0020141.
2. R. A. McCutcheon, T. Reis Marques, and O. D. Howes, Schizophrenia – An overview, *JAMA Psychiatry*, vol. 77, no. 2, pp. 201–210, 2020, doi: 10.1001/JAMAPSYCHIAT RY.2019.3360.
3. F. Alimardani, J. H. Cho, R. Boostani, and H. J. Hwang, Classification of bipolar disorder and Schizophrenia using steady-state visual evoked potential based features, *IEEE Access*, vol. 6, pp. 40379–40388, 2018, doi: 10.1109/ACCESS.2018.2854555.
4. WHO report on schizophrenia (2022). https://www.who.int/news-room/fact-sheets/detail/Schizophrenia (Accessed on 1 July 2022)

5. H. L. Provencher and K. T. Mueser, Positive and negative symptom behaviors and caregiver burden in the relatives of persons with Schizophrenia, *Schizophr. Res.*, vol. 26, no. 1, pp. 71–80, 1997, doi: 10.1016/S0920-9964(97)00043-1.

6. C. M. Harding, Course types in Schizophrenia: An analysis of European and American studies, *Schizophr. Bull.*, vol. 14, no. 4, pp. 633–643, 1988, doi: 10.1093/SCHBUL/14.4.633.

7. D. P. Subha, P. K. Joseph, R. Acharya U, and C. M. Lim, EEG signal analysis: A survey, *J. Med. Syst.*, vol. 34, no. 2, pp. 195–212, 2010, doi: 10.1007/s10916-008-9231-z.

8. F. A. Alturki, K. Alsharabi, A. M. Abdurraqeeb, and M. Aljalal, EEG signal analysis for diagnosing neurological disorders using discrete wavelet transform and intelligent techniques, *Sensors*, vol. 20, no. 9, p. 2505, 2020, doi: 10.3390/S20092505.

9. S. L. Oh, J. Vicnesh, E. J. Ciaccio, R. Yuvaraj, and U. R. Acharya, Deep convolutional neural network model for automated diagnosis of Schizophrenia using EEG signals, *Appl. Sci.*, vol. 9, no. 14, p. 2870, 2019, doi: 10.3390/app9142870.

10. A. Shalbaf, S. Bagherzadeh, and A. Maghsoudi, Transfer learning with deep convolutional neural network for automated detection of Schizophrenia from EEG signals, *Phys. Eng. Sci. Med.*, vol. 43, no. 4, pp. 1229–1239, 2020, doi: 10.1007/s13246-020-00925-9.

11. I. W. Selesnick, H. L. Graber, D. S. Pfeil, and R. L. Barbour, Simultaneous low-pass filtering and total variation denoising, *IEEE Trans. Signal Process.*, vol. 62, no. 5, pp. 1109–1124, 2015, doi: 10.1109/TSP.2014.2298836.

12. J. K. Johannesen, J. Bi, R. Jiang, J. G. Kenney, and C.-M. A. Chen, Machine learning identification of EEG features predicting working memory performance in Schizophrenia and healthy adults, *Neuropsychiatr. Electrophysiol.*, vol. 2, no. 1, pp. 1–21, 2016, doi: 10.1186/S40810-016-0017-0.

13. A. Piryatinska, B. Darkhovsky, and A. Kaplan, Binary classification of multi-channel-EEG records based on the ε-complexity of continuous vector functions, *Comput. Methods Programs Biomed.*, vol. 152, pp. 131–139, 2017, doi: 10.1016/J.CMPB.2017.09.001.

14. M. Shim, H. J. Hwang, D. W. Kim, S. H. Lee, and C. H. Im, Machine-learning-based diagnosis of Schizophrenia using combined sensor-level and source-level EEG features, *Schizophr. Res.*, vol. 176, no. 2–3, pp. 314–319, 2016, doi: 10.1016/j.schres.2016.05.007.

15. S. Siuly, S. K. Khare, V. Bajaj, H. Wang, and Y. Zhang, A computerized method for automatic detection of Schizophrenia using EEG signals, *IEEE Trans. Neural Syst. Rehabil. Eng.*, vol. 28, no. 11, pp. 2390–2400, 2020, doi: 10.1109/TNSRE.2020.3022715.

16. C. A. T. Naira and C. J. L. Del Alamo, Classification of people who suffer Schizophrenia and healthy people by EEG signals using deep learning, *Int. J. Adv. Comput. Sci. Appl.*, vol. 10, no. 10, pp. 511–516, 2019, doi: 10.14569/IJACSA.2019.0101067.

17. Z. Aslan and M. Akin, A deep learning approach in automated detection of Schizophrenia using scalogram images of EEG signals, *Phys. Eng. Sci. Med.*, vol. 45, no. 1, pp. 83–96, 2022, doi: 10.1007/s13246-021-01083-2.

18. V. Jahmunah, S. Lih Oh, V. Rajinikanth, E. Ciaccio, K. Hao Cheong, N. Arunkumar, U. Rajendra Acharya, Automated detection of Schizophrenia using nonlinear signal processing methods, *Artif. Intell. Med.*, vol. 100, p. 101698, 2019, doi: 10.1016/J.ARTMED.2019.07.006.

19. S. Han, W. Huang, Y. Zhang, J. Zhao, and H. Chen, Recognition of early-onset Schizophrenia using deep-learning method, *Appl. Informatics*, vol. 4, no. 1, pp. 1–6, 2017, doi: 10.1186/s40535-017-0044-3.

20. W. H. Pinaya, A. Gadelha, O. M. Doyle, C. Noto, A. Zugman, Q. Cordeiro, A.P. Jackowski, R. A. Bressan, Using deep belief network modelling to characterize differences in brain morphometry in Schizophrenia, *Sci. Rep.*, vol. 6, p. 38897, 2016, doi: 10.1038/srep38897.

21. L. Santos-Mayo, L. M. San-Jose-Revuelta, and J. I. Arribas, A computer-aided diagnosis system with EEG based on the p3b wave during an auditory odd-ball task in Schizophrenia, *IEEE Trans. Biomed. Eng.*, vol. 64, no. 2, pp. 395–407, 2017, doi: 10.1109/TBME.2016.2558824.

22. A. Nikhil Chandran, K. Sreekumar, and D. P. Subha, EEG-based automated detection of Schizophrenia using long short-term memory (LSTM) network. In: *Advances in Machine Learning and computational Intelligence*, 2021, Springer, Singapore, pp. 229–236. doi: 10.1007/978-981-15-5243-4_19.

23. A. Shoeibi, D. Sadeghi, J. M. Gorriz, Automatic diagnosis of Schizophrenia in EEG signals using CNN-LSTM models, *Front. Neuroinform.*, vol. 15, p. 777977, 2021, doi: 10.3389/fninf.2021.777977.

24. C. R. Phang, F. Noman, H. Hussain, C. M. Ting, and H. Ombao, A multi-domain connectome convolutional neural network for identifying Schizophrenia from EEG connectivity patterns, *IEEE J. Biomed. Heal. Informatics*, vol. 24, no. 5, pp. 1333–1343, 2020, doi: 10.1109/JBHI.2019.2941222.

25. K. Simonyan and A. Zisserman. Very deep convolutional networks for large-scale image recognition. In: *3rd International Conference on Learning Representations, ICLR 2015- Conference Track Proceedings*. International Conference on Learning Representations (ICLR), 2015, doi: 10.48550/arXiv.1409.1556.

26. E. Olejarczyk and W. Jernajczyk, Graph-based analysis of brain connectivity in Schizophrenia, *PLoS One*, vol. 12, no. 11, p. e0188629, 2017, doi: 10.1371/JOURNAL.PONE.0188629.

27. M. J. Katz, Fractals and the analysis of waveforms, *Comput. Biol. Med.*, vol. 18, no. 3, pp. 145–156, 1988, doi: 10.1016/0010-4825(88)90041-8.

28. S. M. Pincus, I. M. Gladstone, and R. A. Ehrenkranz, A regularity statistic for medical data analysis, *J. Clin. Monit.*, vol. 7, no. 4, pp. 335–345, 1991.

29. G. Van Houdt, C. Mosquera, and G. Nápoles, A review on the long short-term memory model, *Artif. Intell. Rev.*, vol. 53, no. 8, pp. 5929–5955, 2020, doi: 10.1007/s10462-020-09838-1.

30. A. Krizhevsky, I. Sutskever, and G. E. Hinton. Imagenet classification with deep convolutional neural networks. In: *Proceedings of the 25th International Conference on Neural Information Processing Systems* (NIPS 2012), vol.1, pp:1097–1105, 2012, doi: doi.org/10.1145/3065386.

31. B. Thilakvathi, S. S. Devi, K. Bhanu, and M. Malaippan, EEG signal complexity analysis for Schizophrenia during rest and mental activity, *Biomed. Res.*, vol. 28, no. 1, pp. 1–9, 2017.

32. K. Singh, S. Singh, and J. Malhotra, Spectral features based convolutional neural network for accurate and prompt identification of schizophrenic patients, *Proc. Inst. Mech. Eng. Part H J. Eng. Med.*, vol. 235, no. 2, pp. 167–184, 2021, doi: 10.1177/0954411920966937.

33. D. Ahmedt-Aristizabal., T. Fernando, S. Denman, J. E. Robinson, S. Sridharan, P. J. Johnston, C. Fookes, Identification of children at risk of Schizophrenia via deep learning and EEG responses, *IEEE J. Biomed. Heal. Informatics*, vol. 25, no. 1, pp. 69–76, 2021, doi: 10.1109/JBHI.2020.2984238.

34. M. Latha and G. Kavitha, Detection of Schizophrenia in brain MR images based on segmented ventricle region and deep belief networks, *Neural Comput. Appl.*, vol. 31, no. 9, pp. 5195–5206, 2019, doi: 10.1007/s00521-018-3360-1.

35. M. N. I. Qureshi, J. Oh, and B. Lee, 3D-CNN based discrimination of Schizophrenia using resting-state fMRI, *Artif. Intell. Med.*, vol. 98, pp. 10–17, 2019, doi: 10.1016/j. artmed.2019.06.003.

36. J. I. Devia, C., Mayol-Troncoso, R., Parrini, J., Orellana, G., Ruiz, A., Maldonado, P. E., & Egana, EEG classification during scene free-viewing for Schizophrenia detection, *IEEE Trans. Neural Syst. Rehabil. Eng.*, vol. 27, no. 6, pp. 1193–1199, 2019, doi: 10.1109/TNSRE.2019.2913799.

37. S. K. Prabhakar, H. Rajaguru, and S. W. Lee, A framework for Schizophrenia EEG signal classification with nature inspired optimization algorithms, *IEEE Access*, vol. 8, pp. 39875–39897, 2020, doi: 10.1109/ACCESS.2020.2975848.

10 Implementation of a Deep Neural Network-Based Framework for Actigraphy Analysis and Prediction of Schizophrenia

Vijayalakshmi G V Mahesh
BMS Institute of Technology and Management

Alex Noel Joseph Raj
Shantou University

Chandraprabha R
BMS Institute of Technology and Management

CONTENTS

10.1 INTRODUCTION

Schizophrenia is a neurological disorder affecting 20 million people globally [1] and is found to be one of the major causes of mental disability/illness. The continuous study on Schizophrenia has found the variations in the levels

DOI: 10.1201/9781003315452-10

of neurotransmitters: Dopamine and Glutamate play a key role in triggering the disease. It is also observed that people with Schizophrenia have abnormalities in the brain. A study [2] reported that the abnormalities can be noticed in the frontal and temporal lobes of the brain that differentiate from that of healthy people. Schizophrenia affects the cognition skills, emotion and behavior of the person when active.

The symptoms of the disorder are not the same; instead, they are variable. Some prevail while others get reduced. These symptoms include hallucinations, delusions, disordered speech, disorganized thinking, abnormal behavior, lack of response or motivation, unnecessary movements and lack of expressions/emotions. There is no cure for Schizophrenia, however if diagnosed at early stage, it can be treated with the improved technology and therapies. A timely and effective treatment can further prevent the deterioration of the mental health. Diagnostic and Statistical Manual of Mental Disorders (DSM-5) provides details about the mental disorders and diagnosis methods, which can be used to identify and classify the disorders and can be directed toward appropriate treatments. Various methods exist to diagnose Schizophrenia. (i) Psychiatric test is the traditional method of diagnosing where the psychological evaluations will be done based on an interview to understand the behavioral changes and the duration of the illness. Further tests are also done to analyze cognitive skills of the person. The intensity of the illness based on the symptoms can be measured based on positive and negative syndrome scale. This method cannot be completely relied upon as the patients may not provide accurate information fearing social stigma. Therefore, it is important to devise and develop methods that can quantitatively assess the intensity of the disease. (ii) Electroencephalogram (EEG), a non-invasive method, can be used to record the electrical activities of the brain. These recordings are then analyzed to find the patterns that correlate with Schizophrenia. (iii) Brain scans use imaging modalities such as magnetic resonance imaging (MRI), computed tomography (CT) to observe the abnormalities in brain structure. The abnormalities differentiate Schizophrenic individuals from the healthy controls. (iv) Blood sample analysis is also preferred to identify the presence of the toxins as some of the toxins such as heroin or cocaine, alcohol can trigger psychotic symptoms. (v) Actigraphy (AG) recordings provide the motor activity of a person, when monitored continuously they are more suitable for diagnosis of Schizophrenia. Compared with other methods, actigraphy is proved to be [3] a widely accepted tool to monitor activities, assess patterns related to psychotic disorders to identify the presence of Schizophrenia.

These methods when combined with machine learning (ML)/deep learning (DL) can provide a reliable clinical decisive system (CDS) to predict the presence of the disease. ML/DL, a subset of artificial intelligence with its large set of algorithms, is contributing significantly to health care. The machine learning algorithms learns from the clinical data, identifies the complex patterns of the data and creates the model that can aid clinicians to take accurate decision. ML/DL blends well with healthcare in analyzing data collected from various modalities such as spatial data from brain scans or temporal data from EEG/AG recordings to support clinical decisive systems. This paper proposes to use deep neural network with AG recordings to identify Schizophrenia. The objectives of this chapter include (i) analyzing and investigating the use of actigraphy data to identify the presence of Schizophrenia and (ii) evaluating the performance of statistical features derived from actigraphy using ablation study in discriminating the Schizophrenic from healthy controls.

The rest of the chapter is organized as follows: Section 10.2 presents a brief review of the related works on Schizophrenia detection based on machine learning/deep learning. Section 10.3 covers the materials and methodology used in this study. Experimental results and discussions based on the performance metrics are provided in Section 10.4. Finally, Section 10.5 concludes the chapter.

10.2 RELATED WORK

To carry out the proposed work, related research works were referred principally to explore the application of machine learning and deep learning algorithms to diagnose Schizophrenia and next to investigate the relevance of activity recordings from actigraphy to identify Schizophrenia.

An orderly review of the research works using ML algorithms was done in reference [4]. The study analyzed the performance of all the algorithms with performance metrics: Accuracy, sensitivity and accuracy from each work found that support vector machine (SVM) is the frequently used method. The review identified that (i) SVM when combined with other methods provided an accuracy till 100%. (ii) Ensemble classifier model devised by combining a set of classifiers from different ML algorithms is significant in detecting the illness early. (iii) ML can aid clinical decision towards accurate diagnosis.

A study on detecting Schizophrenia using ML algorithms was conducted by Shim et al. [5] where both sensor level and source level features were extracted from EEG signals. The sensor and source level features were extracted from frontal area and temporal area, respectively. The work demonstrated the improvement in the performance of identifying Schizophrenia with an accuracy of 88.24% using the combination of the features.

As observed, analysis of EEG recordings provides a diagnostic method for Schizophrenia. The following work [6] revealed that the analysis can also give clinical interpretation of the data. The study explored the use of measures: generalized partial directed coherence and direct directed transfer function as the features to train random forest algorithm for disease prediction. The results identified (i) the signals related to occipital region play a key role in diagnosing the disease, and (ii) theta and beta waves provided more relevant features to be trained by the ML algorithm for model creation.

A recent work was conducted on EEG data by Buettner et al. [7] to identify paranoid Schizophrenic individuals from healthy controls. This approach provided insights toward working on paranoid Schizophrenia. The experiment was conducted on the EEG data acquired from neurological and psychiatric repository that has 499 recordings obtained from 28 participants. Spectrum analysis of the data combined with Random Forest classifier provided a better accuracy of 96.77%.

Further ML algorithms have also been coupled with brain imaging methods to identify abnormal patterns which reveal the prime differences between Schizophrenia and non-Schizophrenia. These methods are identified to be more reliable in clinical decision. Yassin et al. [8] studied brain scans obtained from Freesurfer. The scans included the imaging data of Schizophrenia, autism spectrum disorder and few images of disease under development. From the images, features such as cortical thickness, subcortical volume and surface area were extracted to train six ML algorithms. The output of the classifiers is then associated with the intensity of the illness. The analysis of the results found the performance of SVM and logistic regression (LR) to be better. Also the features such as cortical thickness and subcortical volume contributed significantly toward the discrimination of the disease categories compared with surface area.

Further, de Mouraet et al. [9] investigated the application of Maximum Uncertainty Linear Discriminant Analysis (MULDA) on structural brain patterns derived from MRI images to identify and categorize first episode psychosis (FEP), Schizophrenia and healthy controls. The prediction of the classifier was analyzed with Cohen's d and p-value. The analysis of the results found that (i) performance score of FEP was more similar to Schizophrenia with p-value$=0.461$ and Cohen's $d=-0.15$ compared with healthy controls with p-value$=0.003$ and Cohen's $d=0.62$, and (ii) the patterns of volumetric changes are distinct that can effectively discriminate between Schizophrenia and healthy controls.

Structural magnetic resonance images were studied by Chen et al. [10] to distinguish Schizophrenic patients from healthy people. The work involved extracting gray matter and white matter features, then application of coarse to fine feature selection method and finally elimination of irrelevant and redundant features using recursive feature elimination. The selected features were then applied to SVM for training and model creation. The proposed framework reported to have diagnosed the Schizophrenic disorder with a classification accuracy of 85% and pronounces to be extended to identify other disorders also.

It is observed that the illness can also affect the linguistic ability of a person leading to changes in patterns of speech and abnormalities in language. ML can be incorporated with language indicators to detect the presence of Schizophrenia. This involves collecting the data from social media feeds, analyze, extract the linguistic features that describe and differentiate the disorder from healthy ones. Zomick et al. [11] used data from Reddit discussion forum and developed a ML model to predict self-identified users with Schizophrenic on the social media. Birnbaum et al. [12] reported to have used Twitter feeds in association with clinical data to derive a ML model for accurately identifying the illness. The analysis from the results concludes that the model was effective in distinguishing the disclosed users only with linguistic features with an accuracy of 88%.

A brief review on the developments of deep learning methods and its collaboration toward Schizophrenia research in its diagnosis and prediction is provided in reference [13]. It also mentions about the appropriate use of the models in proper prediction and reduction in errors. For clinical data analysis, it is very much essential to choose the right features/descriptors and ML/DL algorithm as the mispredictions may create needless anxiety. As mentioned, a study on related research works was done to examine the application of machine learning and deep learning algorithms to identify Schizophrenia. The study provided the evidence of its capability in making reliable diagnostic decisions. Thus, the proposed chapter aims to employ deep neural network (DNN) on the activity recordings obtained from actigraphy to learn from the data and to identify the presence of Schizophrenia. Further, the chapter contributes toward (i) selecting appropriate architecture of DNN and optimizing it to approximate the function from the data and (ii) quantifying the performance of the DNN model in identifying Schizophrenia using actigraphy data.

10.2.1 ACTIGRAPHY

A review on Schizophrenia symptoms has reported unusual motor behavior [14]. Variations in the motor activities bring out issues with their regular activities where people with Schizophrenia become less active that hinders their day-to-day activities. Also they are deprived from good sleep. This is an issue of concern, thus if regular activities are monitored and recorded can aid in detecting the presence of the disorder to initiate early treatment. Actigraphy, a non-invasive motor activity recording-wearable device, is proved to be a potential device to assess and monitor an individual's patterns of motions. A systematic review on using electronic health devices to analyze motor activities related to Schizophrenia can be found in reference [15]. The review found several works on using actigraphy to assess the abnormalities in the activities and wasable to correlate the patterns to relapses and negative symptoms.

Schizophrenia was detected and quantitatively assessed by Boekeret et al. [16] using the measured activities for a fixed amount of time. The work was also able to distinguish between active and resting durations by application of hidden Markov model using the statistical features derived from the actigraphy recordings. Further, the features adopted in this work proved to outperform other methods by providing a better performance. Disturbed sleep is found in people with Schizophrenia; a critical review on sleep disorders with Schizophrenia is done by Mulligan et al. [17] to identify the symptoms and motivate for better treatment. Fasmeret et al. [18] conducted an actigraphy based study to correlate the sleep and day-to-day activities of Schizophrenic people. The analysis reported that greater sleep disturbance resulted in increased the level of auditory hallucinations, delusions and paranoia. Klingamanet al. [19] used similarity graph algorithm to analyze actigraphy data for depression and Schizophrenia. The work investigated changes in the complexity of the recordings to find that (i) the activity patterns are significantly different for depression as compared with Schizophrenia and healthy controls, and (ii) the control systems regulating the motor activities of Schizophrenia and depression are different.

Actigraphy is a wearable devise usually housed in wrist watches to monitor and analyze an individual's patterns of motion or activities. It is based on accelerometer technology where the acceleration is converted into a measurable signal that can be quantified. The electrical signal produced is proportional to the experienced acceleration. Piezoelectric transducer is most widely used in actigraphy to convert the physical motion into its equivalent electric signal. The electric signal has to undergo several stages of processing to provide reliable measurements. Figure 10.1 displays the filtering and sampling process of actigraphy.

The data from accelerator has to be sampled along with filtering to produce activity counts [20]. The data is initially band limited using anti aliasing filter for proper sampling and reconstruction. A careful selection of sampling frequency is required as it affects the activity counts and to reduce the errors [21]. The other factors to be considered are: resolution of analog-to-digital converter, dynamic range, resolution and sensitivity.

10.3 MATERIALS AND METHOD

The process flow of the DNN-based framework for actigraphy analysis and prediction of Schizophrenia is displayed in Figure 10.2. The data flow and the description of the framework are as presented hereinafter.

Actigraph-activity Data and Preprocessing: The actigraph dataset for the proposed work was obtained from reference [22] where the activity recordings were collected from actiwatch using piezoelectric transducer. The actiwatch recorded the combination of the intensity, amount and duration of the activities in x, y and z axes. The recordings were sampled at a rate of 32 Hz to obtain samples $x(n)$. Each sample is an integer proportional to activity proportional to 1 minute epoch.

The data was recorded from 22 Schizophrenic and 32 healthy controls for an average of 12.7 days. The data was labeled using clinical experts using psychiatric test conducted using DSM-IV. The details of the distribution of the data recorded are provided in Table 10.1. Figure 10.3 displays the sample activity data of a healthy control and Schizophrenic recorded for 15 hours in a day.

Computation of Statistical Measures: The actigraphy data measured from every individual that includes Schizophrenic and healthy control for an average of 12.7 days is divided into slots such that each slot

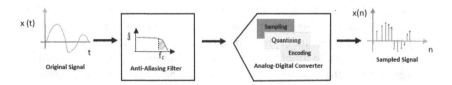

FIGURE 10.1 Process flow of actigraphy.

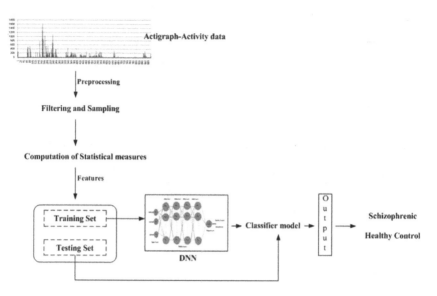

FIGURE 10.2 Process flow of the proposed framework.

TABLE 10.1
Details of Actigraphy dataset

Class Labels	Schizophrenic (22)	Healthy Controls (32)
Female	3	20
Male	19	12
Average age	27–69 years	21–66 years

comprises of the activity data of a day, from every slot three statistical measures: mean (f.mean), standard deviation (f.sd) and proportion of zeros (f.propZeros) were computed that form data descriptors [22]. These descriptors/features have the better ability of discriminating the categories.

Data Partition: The set of features derived from the actigraphy data of both Schizophrenic and healthy controls is subsequently divided into training and testing sets. The training set is a feature matrix, where every row corresponds to the data sample and columns are the features. For supervised learning, every row is labeled with "0" and "1", where 0 indicates healthy controls and 1 maps to Schizophrenia. The features in the training set along with class labels are provided to the classifier algorithm for training. During training, the learnable parameters are tuned to create the model. The model is later tested for its usefulness using the members of the testing set with statistical features.

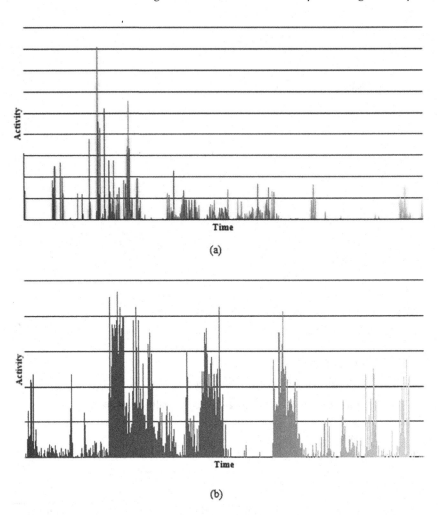

FIGURE 10.3 Sample actigraphy activity level measurement of 15hours for a day. (a) Schizophrenic and (b) healthy control. Here every value indicates the intensity of the activity for every minute in a 15-hour duration.

Classification and Evaluation: The proposed framework uses DNN for learning from examples and classifier model creation. The architecture of DNN (number of hidden layers and neurons in each layer) is carefully selected as it indicates the number of learnable parameters to be trained and plays a significant role in deciding the generalization and approximation ability of the network. During training, dataset with class labels is provided to DNN for training. During training process, the network learns the function underlying the data. Subsequently, the model is tested with unseen samples from testing data set. The binary output provided by the model during testing is mapped to the class labels [Healthy controls, Schizophrenia]. Finally, the performance of the model is quantitatively assessed using the metrics: Classification accuracy, Precision, Recall, F1-score, Matthew's Correlation Coefficient (MCC) and Area Under the Curve (AUC) obtained from RoC.

10.4   RESULTS AND DISCUSSION

The work uses DNN with AG recordings to identify Schizophrenia. The statistical features: mean, standard deviation and proportion of zeros extracted from actigraphy activity data were initially analyzed to find their distribution and relation between the features. Hence, pair plot was used to create a matrix of histograms and scatter plots for analysis. The pair plot for the data considered is depicted in Figure 10.4.

In the matrix displayed in Figure 10.4, the diagonal represents the distribution of the individual features, whereas other units depict the correlation between the features through scatter plots. The units at the location (2,1) and (1,2) indicate higher correlation between mean and standard deviation, while the cells at (3,1), (3,2), (1,3) and (2,3) indicate low correlation among proportion of zeros

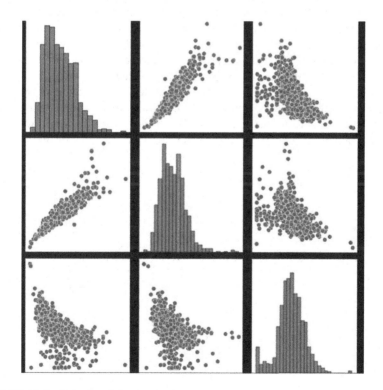

FIGURE 10.4   Pair plot of the features.

with mean and standard deviation, respectively. Thus, the work was carried out with ablation study to identify the combination of best feature descriptors that discriminates the classes significantly: (i) At first highly correlated features: mean and standard deviation considered to form $F_1 = \{$f.mean, f.sd$\}$. This F1 is provided to DNN where it is trained with these features, tested and model is assessed. (ii) Next proportion of zeros feature is added to highly correlated features to form $F_2 = \{$f.mean, f.sd, f.propZeros$\}$ to train, test and assess the model. Next the assessment of the models is compared with identify the effect of including proportion of zeros to F1 in identifying the presence of the disease.

10.4.1   Case (i)

The feature set F_1 is split into two non-overlapping sets for training and testing. The training set F_{1_tr} is labeled with y = {"0"/Healthy controls, "1"/Schizophrenia}. The feature set is scaled to have zero mean and variance of one ($F_{1\_tr\_s}$). The neural network architecture is defined with the required number of layers and neurons. The network has an input layer with neurons mapped to the number of features (f.mean, f.sd, f.propZeros), output layer with neurons equal to the number of outputs (binary) and four hidden layers with the number of neurons in each hidden layer = [20, 10, 6, 4]. The architecture of DNN is illustrated in Figure 10.5. The neurons of each layer are connected to the neurons of the next layer and previous layer with their associated weights and biases. Except the input layer, other layers are provided with non-linear activation functions. The network uses rectified linear unit (ReLU) activation function in the hidden layers which provides the output = maximum of (0, x) for the input x. Now the scaled labeled set [$F_{1\_tr\_s}$, y] is provided to DNN for training.

The network is trained with back propagation with maximum number of iterations set to 5,000. At every iteration, the data is transformed with the corresponding weights, biases and activation function at each layer. During training the learning rate η was set to 0.001, Further with back propagation, the gradients are

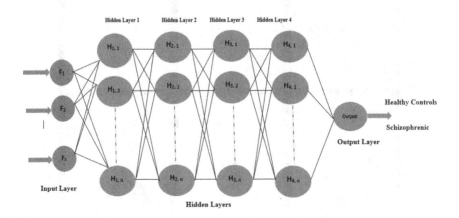

FIGURE 10.5   Architecture of DNN.

calculated to adjust the weights thereby minimizing the cross-entropy loss function to achieve optimization.

The cross-entropy loss between the actual label y_i and the predicted label y_i^p is calculated as

$$CE_{loss} = \frac{1}{M} \sum_i n_i \, w_i \, l_i \tag{10.1}$$

where M is the normalization factor,
  n_i is ith mask value
  w_i is ith weight value and

$$l_i = -\left(y_i \, lnln \; y_i^p + \left(1 - y_i\right) ln\left(1 - y_i^p\right) \right) \tag{10.2}$$

The DNN model is optimized using L-BFGS optimizer which has faster convergence.

After training, the classifier model is created. The model is provided with scaled testing set $F_{1\_te\_s}$ for testing. For every sample of testing test, the model produces a set of probabilities. Each probability value indicates the closeness of the input sample to each category. So the output label of the sample is the category with highest probability. Later, the output label is mapped to the presence of the Schizophrenia disorder.

The model is now quantitatively assessed for its performance, for which metrics [23] Classification Accuracy, Precision, Recall, F1-score, MCC and AUC are computed. The metrics are computed using the elements of the confusion matrix (CM) framed [24] after testing. The elements of the CM are True Positive (TP), True Negative (TN), False Positive (FP) and False Negative (FN) that indicate:

- True Positive: A sample belonging to class of healthy controls predicted as healthy control.
- True Negative: A sample that belongs to the class of Schizophrenia is also predicted as Schizophrenia.
- False Positive: Schizophrenic sample is predicted as healthy control.
- False Negative: Healthy control sample is predicted as Schizophrenic.

The matrix with all the details is indicated in Figure 10.6. From the CM, the performance metrics are computed for performance evaluation.

$$\text{Classification Accuracy } (CA) = (TP+TN)/(TP+TN+FP+FN) \tag{10.3}$$

$$\text{Precision} = TP/(TP+FP) \tag{10.4}$$

$$\text{Recall} = TP/(TP+FN) \tag{10.5}$$

$$\text{F1-score} = (2 \times \text{Precision} \times \text{Recall})/(\text{Precision} + \text{Recall}) \tag{10.6}$$

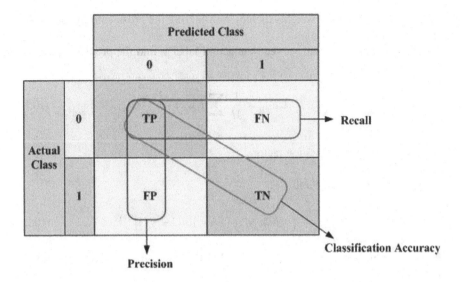

FIGURE 10.6 Confusion matrix.

$$MCC = (TP \times TN - FP \times FN)/A \qquad (10.7)$$

$$A = \sqrt{((TP+FP) \times (TP+FN) \times (TN+FP) \times (TN+FN))} \qquad (10.8)$$

AUC is found from the receiver operating characteristics.

The performance metrics obtained from $F_{1\_te\_s}$ is tabulated in Table 10.2.

10.4.2 CASE (II)

Now, the feature proportion of zeros is integrated with mean and standard deviation to form F_2. A similar type of process mentioned under case (i) is carried out here for training, testing and assessment. The results obtained are presented in Table10.2. An analysis of the results indicates the better performance of the DNN model under F2. The model provided a CA of 84.05% with Precision and Recall of 84.09% and 84.05%, respectively. The values of Precision and Recall signify least error rates. The agreement between the actual label and predicted label is provided by MCC score which is found to 0.6584 specifying the better performance of the model. The combination of all the features was found to be appropriate to detect the Schizophrenia from actigraphy activity recordings.

10.5 CONCLUSION

A DNN-based framework for identifying the presence of the Schizophrenia disorder is presented in this chapter. The work considered the use of the time series

TABLE 10.2
Performance metrics obtained for $F_{1\_te\_s}$ and $F_{2\_te\_s}$

Performance Metrics	$F_{1\_te\_s}$	$F_{2\_te\_s}$
CA(%)	82.60	84.05
Precision(%)	82.60	84.09
Recall(%)	82.60	84.05
F1-score	0.8260	0.8376
MCC	0.6324	0.6584

data, i.e., the actigraphy activity recordings from the individuals. The activity levels are statistically analyzed to compute the statistical features that formed the features of the data. The features include mean, standard deviation and proportion of zeros. Here the features mean and standard deviation were found to be correlated, so an ablation study was conducted based on presence and absence of proportion of zeros feature. The features were provided to DNN algorithm, and the parameters were tuned and optimized during the training process to generate the classifier model. The model was tested and then assessed for its performance. Analysis of the results using the quantitative measures: Classification Accuracy, Precision, Recall, F1-score, AUC and MCC demonstrated the better performance of the DNN model. Further it is also observed that the statistical features derived from actigraphy measurements proved to have good discrimination ability to recognize Schizophrenia and healthy controls.

The proposed framework provided a better predictive performance incorporating the statistical features derived from actigraphy data and DNN. The work asserted use of activity recordings as a modality that can aid in identifying the presence of Schizophrenia. In future, the performance of identifying this neurological disorder could be enhanced by fusing the data acquired from different modalities (spatiotemporal signals) and ensemble classifier methods.

REFERENCES

1. He, H., Liu, Q., Li, N., Guo, L., Gao, F., Bai, L., Gao, F & Lyu, J. (2020). Trends in the incidence and DALYs of schizophrenia at the global, regional and national levels: Results from the global burden of disease study 2017. *Epidemiology and Psychiatric Sciences*, 29, e91.
2. Lieberman, J. A., Girgis, R. R., Brucato, G., Moore, H., Provenzano, F., Kegeles, L., Javitt, D., Kantrowitz, J., Wall, M. M., & Small, S. A. (2018). Hippocampal dysfunction in the pathophysiology of schizophrenia: A selective review and hypothesis for early detection and intervention. *Molecular Psychiatry*, 23(8), 1764–1772.
3. Tahmasian, M., Khazaie, H., Golshani, S., & Avis, K. T. (2013). Clinical application of actigraphy in psychotic disorders: A systematic review. *Current Psychiatry Reports*, 15(6), 1–15.

4. de Filippis, R., Carbone, E. A., Gaetano, R., Bruni, A., Pugliese, V., Segura-Garcia, C., & De Fazio, P. (2019). Machine learning techniques in a structural and functional MRI diagnostic approach in schizophrenia: A systematic review. *Neuropsychiatric Disease and Treatment*, 15, 1605.

5. Shim, M., Hwang, H. J., Kim, D. W., Lee, S. H., & Im, C. H. (2016). Machine-learning-based diagnosis of schizophrenia using combined sensor-level and source-level EEG features. *Schizophrenia Research*, 176(2–3), 314–319.

6. Vázquez, M. A., Maghsoudi, A., & Mariño, I. P. (2021). An interpretable machine learning method for the detection of schizophrenia using EEG signals. *Frontiers in Systems Neuroscience*, 15, 652662.

7. Buettner, R., Beil, D., Scholtz, S., & Djemai, A. (2020). Development of a machine learning based algorithm to accurately detect schizophrenia based on one-minute EEG recordings. In *53rd Hawaii International Conference on System Sciences, HICSS 2020*, Maui, HI, January 7–10, 2020, pp. 1–10. ScholarSpace, 2020.

8. Yassin, W., Nakatani, H., Zhu, Y., Kojima, M., Owada, K., Kuwabara, H., & Koike, S. (2020). Machine-learning classification using neuroimaging data in schizophrenia, autism, ultra-high risk and first-episode psychosis. *Translational Psychiatry*, 10(1), 1–11.

9. de Moura, A. M., Pinaya, W. H. L., Gadelha, A., Zugman, A., Noto, C., Cordeiro, Q., & Sato, J. R. (2018). Investigating brain structural patterns in first episode psychosis and schizophrenia using MRI and a machine learning approach. *Psychiatry Research: Neuroimaging*, 275, 14–20.

10. Chen, Z., Yan, T., Wang, E., Jiang, H., Tang, Y., Yu, X., & Liu, C. (2020). Detecting abnormal brain regions in schizophrenia using structural MRI via machine learning. *Computational Intelligence and Neuroscience*, 2020, Article ID 6405930. https://doi.org/10.1155/2020/6405930.

11. Zomick, J., Levitan, S. I., & Serper, M. (2019). Linguistic analysis of schizophrenia in Reddit posts. In: *Proceedings of the Sixth Workshop on Computational Linguistics and Clinical Psychology* (pp. 74–83), Association for Computational Linguistics, Minneapolis, Minnesota.

12. Birnbaum, M. L., Ernala, S. K., Rizvi, A. F., De Choudhury, M., & Kane, J. M. (2017). A collaborative approach to identifying social media markers of schizophrenia by employing machine learning and clinical appraisals. *Journal of Medical Internet Research*, 19(8), e7956.

13. Cortes-Briones, J. A., Tapia-Rivas, N. I., D'Souza, D. C., & Estevez, P. A. (2021). Going deep into schizophrenia with artificial intelligence. *Schizophrenia Research*, 245, 122–140

14. Walther, S., & Strik, W. (2012). Motor symptoms and schizophrenia. *Neuropsychobiology*, 66(2), 77–92.

15. Molina-Madueño, R. M., Porras-Segovia, A., Ruiz, M., & Baca-Garcia, E. (2021). eHealth tools for assessing psychomotor activity in schizophrenia: A systematic review. *Brazilian Journal of Psychiatry*, 43, 102–107.

16. Boeker, M., Riegler, M. A., Hammer, H. L., Halvorsen, P., Fasmer, O. B., & Jakobsen, P. (2021). Diagnosing schizophrenia from activity records using Hidden Markov model parameters. In: *2021 IEEE 34th International Symposium on Computer-Based Medical Systems (CBMS)* (pp. 432–437), IEEE, Aveiro. USA.

17. Mulligan, L. D., Haddock, G., Emsley, R., Neil, S. T., & Kyle, S. D. (2016). High resolution examination of the role of sleep disturbance in predicting functioning and psychotic symptoms in schizophrenia: A novel experience sampling study. *Journal of Abnormal Psychology*, 125(6), 788.

18. Fasmer, E. E., Fasmer, O. B., Berle, J. Ø., Oedegaard, K. J., Hauge, E. R. (2018) Graph theory applied to the analysis of motor activity in patients with schizophrenia and depression. *PLoS ONE*, 13(4), e0194791. https://doi.org/10.1371/journal. pone.0194791

19. Klingaman, E. A., Palmer-Bacon, J., Bennett, M. E., & Rowland, L. M. (2015). Sleep disorders among people with schizophrenia: Emerging research. *Current Psychiatry Reports*, 17(10), 1–8.

20. Miller, J. (2013). Accelerometer technologies, specifications, and limitations. In *Proceedings of Internationational Conference on Ambulatory Monitoring and Physical Activity Measurement*. IOP Publishing Ltd., Bristol.

21. Brønd, J. C., & Arvidsson, D. (2016). Sampling frequency affects the processing of Actigraph raw acceleration data to activity counts. *Journal of Applied Physiology*, 120(3), 362–369.

22. Jakobsen, P., Garcia-Ceja, E., Stabell, L. A., Oedegaard, K. J., Berle, J. O., Thambawita, V., & Riegler, M. A. (2020). Psykose: A motor activitaxes.y database of patients with schizophrenia. In: *2020 IEEE 33rd International Symposium on Computer-Based Medical Systems (CBMS)* (pp. 303–308), IEEE, Rochester, MN.

23. Selvaraj, D., Venkatesan, A., Mahesh, V. G., & Joseph Raj, A. N. (2021). An integrated feature frame work for automated segmentation of COVID-19 infection from lung CT images. *International Journal of Imaging Systems and Technology*, 31(1), 28–46.

24. Han, J., Pei, J., & Kamber, M. (2011). *Data Mining: Concepts and Techniques*. Elsevier, Netherlands.

11 Evaluating Psychomotor Skills in Autism Spectrum Disorder Through Deep Learning

Ravi Kant Avvari
National Institute of Technology Rourkela

CONTENTS

11.1 INTRODUCTION

Autism spectrum disorder relates to a spectrum of developmental disorders that impairs the normal function of social, communication, and cognition skills in a developing child. It is well described as a "developmental disorder" due to the appearance of the symptoms in course of the development during the first 18 months after birth [3,4]. ASD is highly prevalent in children during the early development, with a prevalence of 1 in 100 children [1]. Boys are more prone to the disorder with 1 in 27 compared with the girls affecting 1 in 116 [2]. With growing age, the deficits in the intellectual disability become prominent and diagnosable; reports indicating an intelligence quotient (IQ) <70 in about 31% of children having the disorder. According to the Diagnostic and Statistical Manual of Mental Disorders (DSM-5), nature of symptoms, recordable and diagnosable are laid as under the following considerations – lack of/reduced interest in communication; deficit in response whether social interaction, emotional and verbal or nonverbal responses; deficits in gestures, facial and nonverbal communicative behaviors; stereotype responses; repetitive motor movements and other responses that are indicative of clear deficits in social communication and intellectual impairments. Overall, there is a drastic reduction in the psychomotor skills which are vital for the child development during the early phase. While measurement of the psychomotor skills itself is a challenges, coming up with a method of measurement and determining the extent of reduction in the skill is another level of challenge.

Despite advances in the technology, the cause of ASD is still not clear. A number of studies have been performed till date searching for mechanisms leading to the development and progression of the disorder. Various imaging techniques used for investigating the shape, structure, and function of the brain in autistic compared with a typically developing child are well documented. Better course and prognosis of neurodevelopmental disorders seem to be confusing with no clear indication of the key biomarkers leading to diagnosis. With increasing capabilities of deep learning, there is growing evidence of scoping for key biomarkers that may essentially help in diagnosis and more specifically the facilitation of the measurement of psychomotor skill for early diagnosis before an onset of the visible symptoms. Evaluation solely on the basis of deep learning alone does not suffice for effective diagnosis of the autism, an improvisation is wanting. Recent evidence suggests that the diagnosis has to be more corroborated with the morphological (structure), functional, and behavioral (psychomotor skill) specifics. The motivation of the chapter relies on understanding the context of how the method of measurements helps in the facilitation of the diagnosis and where do we miss identifying those key biomarkers that would potentially discriminate the autism from typically developing individuals. The chapter details key observations on the use of the deep learning techniques toward an effective diagnosis with reference the recent works.

This chapter is organized in the following: firstly, an overview of the work is presented indicating the keywords in the area and the associated techniques/terms/disorders that are addressed in the literature, following this, a global view of the clinical works in the area is introduced providing details of the various means of measuring/estimating the level of reduction in the psychomotor skills compared with typically developing child. Since the key idea is to connect the method of measurement of the psychomotor skills to the diagnostic measures, due importance has been given understand the technology and the limitations thereof. Following this, prominent works in the area are reviewed and discussed with reference to the application of deep learning techniques in terms of accuracy of detection. Different models adopted are introduced with reference to the challenges and the state of art strategies as speculated by the authors to make an effective diagnosis during the early phase of the onset of autism. This is followed by conclusion.

11.2 SEARCH METHODOLOGY

The study focused on the works published in the recent years from 2015 to March 2022 using following electronic databases – PubMed, Science Direct, MEDLINE, EMBASE, and Google Scholar for research articles published in journal; articles in the proceedings and other sources including preprint were not considered. Search string included the terms – Autism, ASD, deep learning, machine learning, neural network, attention, brain areas, and functional connectivity. A combination of these terms was used for search in the title and abstract of articles.

The study was limited to the include only those studies reporting significant change in the outcome measures or reported to observe significance difference in the ASD compared with typically developed (TD) child. Duplicate studies, irrespective of the author or source of origin of the work, were excluded, where possible.

11.3 CLINICAL STUDIES OF ASD

The basis of diagnosis relies on the way the child responds to the stimuli involving social, behavioral patterns (including non-specific and disturbed), attention disorders, disabilities in interpretation, and defects in motor/sensory responses. The first approach to clinical observation involves monitoring the child over a period of time on how the child responds, learns, and acquires new skills/abilities and

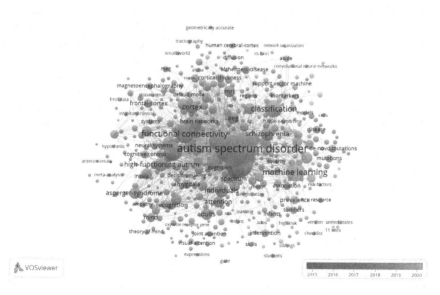

FIGURE 11.1 Keywords analysis using VOSviewer of the articles (1,350 numbers) published during the period from 1 January 2000 to 1 January 2022.

the nature of communication with people. Engaging the child in sportive activities provides further information. A sequence of test may be administered using various diagnostic tools for screening – Indian Scale for Assessment of Autism (ISAA), Denver Development Screening Test (DDST), Vineland Social Maturity Scale (VSMS), Social Communication Questionnaire (SCQ), Autism Diagnostic Observation Schedule (ADOC), Attention-Deficit Hyperactivity Disorder (ADHD), Intellectual Disability (ID), and Diagnostic Statistical Manual (DSM-IV, DSM-V). Observation requires monitoring the child over a long period of time while observing the responses to the stimuli, making the diagnosis difficult.

With increasing technological developments, various tools have been adopted to automate the process of monitoring and data collection, thereby improving the speed of diagnosis; preferably more accurately. Machine learning (ML) has been applied to autism research in various studies to make an intelligence guess about the outcome of an event in course of time. For large datasets which are typically generated by the monitoring systems over a long period of time across various subjects, it is difficult to consolidate the huge amount of data into meaningful information. DL typically uses more layers of neural networks to process and learn from such huge amount of the information. The information typically includes a time-varying signal, images taken from various imaging modalities such as MRI, ultrasound, and X-ray. The DL methods have gained a more popularity due to its ability to identify the key features from the dataset and produce a meaningful data which can form the basis of diagnosing the disease. The learning is basically done by training the neural networks with a fraction of the dataset, typically unbiased, so the weights of the networks are adjusted in accordance to nature of hidden information. Typically feedforward training is employed to study the information by reducing the cost function to its minima using gradient descent method. Later, new models were introduced differing in choice of activation function and the mode of updating weights/training methods. Convolutional neural network (CNN), a class of artificial neural networks, has gained popularity in the neuroimaging due to its ability to learn spatial hierarchies [6]. It employs convolution to extract features from a large dataset. CNN performs well in image classification such as identifying common features in the MRI across the subjects. This in combination with other machine learning algorithms has proved to be very useful in identifying the biomarkers for diagnosing various neurodegenerative diseases. In view of ASD, we seek to utilize various imaging and non-imaging modalities to scope for changes in the brain (both structural and functional), behavioral changes, and observations as recording via questionnaire. Various modalities of measuring and diagnosing the ASD are discussed in the following subsections.

11.3.1 Robot-Assisted Diagnosis

Behavioral studies may be facilitated precisely, in contrast to traditional, with assistance from robots through interaction; preferably passive mode. During various stimuli, the robots can be programmed to register the information in the form of speech signal/voice, logging the facial expression using camera, gesture, and gaze responses of the child. Such data forms a strong basis of evaluating the extent of the disorder in the child as the information is meaning and can lead to clear indications of the nature of neurological deficits.

11.3.2 EYE TRACKING

Eye tracking is a non-invasive modality for measuring eye movement response to visual stimuli. The subject with ASD shows a different pattern for processing the visual information, such as by fixing to certain area of the image in contrast to a typical developing child. Eye tracking gives quantified information on the nature of the gaze patterns of subject which is the key to the understanding of the behavioral and psychological insights of the disorder. Tracking can potentially provide clues to the reasons for atypical behavior of the child especially the sociability communication, body language, attention, and emotional response.

11.3.3 FACIAL SCANNING

In facial scanning, the images of the faces are registered and analyzed using computer methods for features that are distinguishable. The tool provides an effective way of monitoring the faces as a primary source of information for preliminary screening of the ASD. Using stimuli, the behavioral pattern is also studied to assess the deficits in social interaction and interests.

11.3.4 GAIT ANALYSIS FOR STEREOTYPICAL MOVEMENTS

Measurement of the gait is centered on capturing the spatio-temporal changes of the body movement as accurate as possible. There are various methods for measuring the locomotion – goniometer, force platform, 3D motion analysis system, and inertial sensors. Goniometer is a device that measures the extent to rotation of a joint, also known as the joint angle. Joint angle information provides the postural and locomotion change of the upper and lower extremity. The force platform is a platform laid on the floor to capture the ground reaction forces (GRFs) which are impressed by virtue of the individual standing or doing some activity on the force platform. The GRF captures the force that is equal to the person's weight. An array of these force platforms is used to assist in measurement of the forces during static (when the person is not moving or stationary) and during motion. Since the forces exerted are due to the activity of the person, it allows one to capture the dynamics involved. Such as during running, the GRF increases due to acceleration forces which can increases up to two or three times the weight of the person. Likewise, the measurement can be taken to characterize activities such as walking, running, and jumping. However, the use of high-speed camera (in 3D motion capture system) can enable tracking of the body parts (reflective of the skeletal movements) in 3D space to facilitate the measurement of kinematics data. A combination of force plate with 3D motion registration helps to capture both the orientation details of the body parts and forces details during the movement. As an alternative to gait measurement, many wearable systems (employing inertial sensors) have been proposed recently to facilitate the easy use of the technology in gait analysis. This would not only provide recoding of the gait in lab setting, however, also in the outdoors for record the gait pattern over longer duration of time. Inertial sensor is potentially useful in identifying the stereotypical motor activities such as the hand flapping, head banging, body rocking, mouthing, and repetitive dropping. Whereas data collection through observational means is qualitative, the SMM measurement using inertial sensor provides quantified information on the nature of movement over a long period of time. This has an advantage of collecting the data without consent of the parent/ expert. Characterizing challenging behaviors through motion sensing could provide more insights into the psychomotor deficits the child is currently suffering from. Phases of repetitive motor patterns can be easily observed, and the recurrence can be noticed for purpose of diagnosis.

11.3.5 FACIAL FUSED GAIT ANALYSIS

Whereas the gait alone provides information about the motor movement which is useful in assessing for any deficits in the motor activity, the details of the social and cognition aspects are not derivable. A simultaneous recoding of the facial changes with the motor patterns will supplement the information to make an analysis on the nature of coordination between the social, cognition, and motor patterns. Studies involving visual stimuli can shed more light into the nature of defects. Skills involving flexibility to manipulate objects using the hand and play games can infer intactness of the musculoskeletal system and its coordination with the nervous system. Receptors involve in the assessment of the posture of the body and the sensory feedbacks involved in the control of the joints can be clearly visualized for deficits and presented for clinical assessment.

11.3.6 ELECTROENCEPHALOGRAPHY

Electroencephalography is a method for measuring the surface potential appearing on the scalp. It is indicative of some kind of neural activity taking place in the brain, where resulting from no activity or task driven. These are, in fact, the potentials average over several millions of neurons just adjacent to the region of interest from where the potentials are recorded. Despite being averaged information, it allows capturing the neural activity in real time. Signals acquired are reflective of the neural activity, conduction and networks interactions which are used in assessing the activity of the brain from macroscopic point of view. EEG recordings are typically identifiable in the frequency range 0–100 Hz, which correlates to intellectual disability or deficits in cortical region of the brain.

11.3.7 Functional Near-Infrared Spectroscopy (f-NIRS)

The f-NIRS is a non-invasive technique for imaging the details of the oxygenation supply to the tissue using near-infrared radiation. By measuring the amount of light absorbed by the chromophores, such as oxyhemoglobin and deoxyhemoglobin (wavelength region of 650–925 nm), the information pertaining to the hemodynamic changes in the tissue of interest; where deoxyhemoglobin show high tendency of absorption below 790 nm and oxyhemoglobin above 790 nm. The method has been employed to investigate the hemodynamic changes in the cortical region to assess the local neural activity.

11.3.8 MR Imaging (Structural and Functional)

The invention of MRI has given the clinicians with an immense opportunity to explore the structure of the deep tissues hidden inside the body [5]. Given that this imaging modality avoids use of any potentially dangerous ionizing radiation, it has been used for observing the tissue for a long duration. The principle behind the imaging is the use of a very strong magnetic field (1.5T, 3T, 7T) to align the free hydrogen nuclei along the direction of this strong magnetic field. Since the proton (a positively charged particle) spinning about its axis creates a magnetic field around it, the proton present in the material behaves as the tiny magnet (strength of this magnetic field is known as the magnetic moment). Many such protons present confer the material of its net magnetic moment. When a tiny magnet (considering the example of proton) is placed in a magnetic field, it experiences a torque that tends to exhibit additional movement of precession at some frequency known as the Larmor frequency that is characteristic of the nucleus. Since the frequency falls in the range of radiofrequency (*rf*), an external *rf* pulse can be applied to cause the nuclei to tilt away from its axis. This *rf* signal is used as a probe to investigate the region of interest (ROI) of the specimen. Considering that the removal of the *rf* pulse gives signature of the relaxation of the proton back to its original position as without *rf* excitation, it gives details of the property of the tissue in terms of the relaxation (T1: spin-lattice; T2: spin-spin). To facilitate reconstruction of the 3D structure of the specimen, the response signal is encoded by creating a gradient of the magnetic field along the dimension, let us consider X-axis. Since the field is encoded with space, the precession and the Larmor frequency also change in accordance to the magnetic field strength provided along this dimension. Thus, by taking an axial slice where the frequency is same, the axial scanning can be performed, and the information can be processed to construct the image.

With different settings, MR images can be obtained specifically for the type of application [5]. In spin echo mode, depending on the type of tissue under imaging such as fatty or tissue with more water content, the choice of sequence may be adopted as T1 or T2 weighted. In T1 weighted, the tissue is allowed for spin-lattice relaxation (magnetization in the same direction as the static magnetic field) by using a short repetition time (TR) and echo time (TE). In T2 weighted, the tissue is allowed for spin-spin relaxation (transverse to the static magnetic field) by using long TR and TE times. Specific structural information can be deduced with getting into the details of the imaging modality and exploiting the changes in diffusion of the proton in the tissue. In diffusion-weighted imaging (DWI), the interest is to keep track of the movement of the water to assess the local changes or diffusion of water. Since the movement of water (basically the nuclei part) is not random and takes place following various biochemical and mechanical diffusion (including thermal agitation), the local motion of the molecules provides details of relevant of some action in the local region (preferably the cellular events). A similar variant of the DWI is the diffusion tensor imaging (DTI) which captures the local diffusion of the water by ensuring the directionality of diffusion. DTI is a powerful technique to visualizing the white matter of the brain where the water molecules tend to diffuse along the direction of the neural connectivity (axonal directions) rather than being random. The diffusion mobility of water is highly directional and driven by the structural orientation of the neuronal fiber tracts in the brain. The underlying method employs mathematical analysis to assess the diffusion anisotropy of the tissue local to the region. The directionality of the diffusion has allowed for imaging the tract-specific regions of the white matter for assessing any changes in the brain from typically developed brain. A newer method known as the diffusion spectrum imaging (DSI) was also introduced to improve the imaging of the nerve tracks, including the ones with multiple fiber bundle crossings. This method of nerve fiber tracking has enabled visualizing the whole bundle such as the corticospinal tract whereby significant clinical studies can be performed. Such advanced MR imaging has led to the development of Human Connectome Project (HCP) funded by NIH, to map the networks of the brain essential for processing the information received by the nerve fibers of sensory and motor function.

Whereas the structural information is reflective of the static structure of the brain, details of the information processing during the resting state (*rs*) or task-driven (*td*) cannot be perceived. Functional MRI allows measurement of the local changes in the brain owing to local metabolic processes arising from basal state and during activity. These time-varying changes in brain metabolism are observed through local changes in blood flow in the region of interest, hence the name blood oxygen level dependent (BOLD) signal. The neuronal events owing to the nature of task being processed by the brain takes some time to become visible in the MRI. During the activity, there is a more demand for the local blood supply to the neurons processing the information. This demand for more amount of blood supply is supplemented by the feedback-induced vasodilation which allows arterioles to expand and draw in more blood. The response time to peak typically is of the order of seconds before the signal falls to the baseline BOLD. The *rs* and *td* MRI provides valuation information on the local activity of the brain to a good spatial resolution (millimeter) at moderate temporal resolution (seconds). The *f*MRI distinguishes the local blood flow by measuring the changes in magnetization between oxygen-rich and oxygen-deficit blood.

With potential modalities of imaging various details, information derived from DWI and *f*MRI has been studied to assess both the structural and functional information about the brain, thus providing simultaneous/concurrent view of the structure and functional relationship during health and pathology. Such information could help study the functional regions of the brain thorough imaging of the white matter pathways toward diagnosing various disorders of the brain. Combined EEG and ƒMRI are also explored to scope for brain functional at higher temporal resolution [7,8,9,10,11,12,14,15,16,17,18,19,23,20,24,26,25,21,22].

TABLE 11.1

Summary of the clinical studies involving screening of ASD using DL/ML

Author	Intervention	Dataset	Method	Outcome Measures	Observations
Lu and Perkowski (2021) [7]	FI	East Asian dataset, Kaggle	VGG16	Landmark features – facial images	95% F1-score, highlighting feature differences in ASD from normal
Liu et al. (2016) [8]	M test, rs-fMRI, FI	ABIDE	k-means, SVM	Facial discrimination	88.51% accuracy in classification
Ke et al. (2020) [9]	rs-fMRI	ABIDE, YUM	RAM, STN, CAN, CNN, RNN	Image classification	Structural changes in the ASD observed which are key to social and cognitive skills
Heinsfeld et al. (2017) [10]	rs-fMRI	ABIDE	SVM, RF, DNN	Functional connectivity of brain areas	Facilitative identification of the areas of the brain differentiating the ASD
Guo et al. (2022) [11]	MRI, DWI	Acquired	ASM, SSM, DSM, attention -3D ResNet-18	Brain regions	DSM showed best in AUC and further improvement observed with attention-based 3D ResNet-18
Ahmed et al. (2022) [12]	Eye tracking	Figshare dataset	FFNN, ANN, CNN, SVM	Eye movement	CCN-SVM (GoogleNet + SVM and ResNet-18 + SVM) allowed for better diagnosis – 95.5% and 94.5%

(Continued)

TABLE 11.1 (*Continued*)

Summary of the clinical studies involving screening of ASD using DL/ML

Author	Intervention	Dataset	Method	Outcome Measures	Observations
Subah et al. (2021) [14]	rs-fMRI	ABIDE	BASC atlas, AAL, Power atlases, DNN	Functional connectivity	BASC atlas showed best performance
Xu et al. (2021) [15]	fNIR	Acquired	MLNN, LSTM, CNN	IFG, TL area	MLNN allowed better sensitivity and specificity
Yin et al. (2021) [16]	fMRI	ABIDE	Pretrained AE, DNN	Brain regions	Pretrained AE allowed for better diagnosis (AUC of 82.4%)
Rad et al. (2021) [17]	IMU	Acquired	LSTM, CNN	SMM	Combined feature learning proves to be useful in detecting SMM
Kong et al. (2019) [18]	rs-fMRI	ABIDE	DNN	Functional connectivity	AUC of 97.38%
Sherkatghanad et al. (2020) [19]	rs-fMRI	ABIDE	CNN (10 fold CV)	Functional connectivity	Accuracy of 70.22% in detection
Zhang et al. (2022) [23]	fMRI	ABIDE	DL with F-score feature selection	Functional connectivity	Accuracy of 70.9%
Tawhid et al. (2021) [20]	EEG	KAUH	RF, kNN, SVM, CNN	Spectral information	DL is more accurate (99.15%) than ML (95.25%)
Ari et al. (2022) [24]	EEG	KAUH	DP, ELM-AE, CNN	EEG rhythms	Accuracy of 98.88%
Abdolzadegan et al. (2020) [26]	EEG	Acquired	DBSCAN, SVM, kNN	Non-linear features in EEG	Improved feature extraction with accuracy of 90.57% (SVM) and 72.77% (kNN)
Kang et al. (2020) [25]	EEG and eye tracking	Acquired	MRMR, SVM	EEG, heat map	Accuracy maximum of 85.44%, with AUC=0.93

(Continued)

TABLE 11.1 (*Continued*)
Summary of the clinical studies involving screening of ASD using DL/ML

Author	Intervention	Dataset	Method	Outcome Measures	Observations
Eni et al. (2020) [21]	Speech signal	Acquired	DNN, CNN	Prosodic, acoustic, and conversational features	Correlates were best with CNN
Saranya and Anandan (2021) [22]	Facial, gait	Kaggle, KDEF, CASIA, Acquired	DEAF	Gait, facial features	Improved prediction by combining FELM and CNN

Note: f, functional; M, memory; rs, resting state; CV, cross validation; DL, deep learning; FI, facial imaging; AUC, area under receiver operating characteristic curve; SVM, support vector machine; RF, random forest; ADC, apparent diffusion coefficient; ABIDE, autism brain imaging data exchange; DWI, diffusion-weighted imaging; ASM, all-sequence model; SSM, single-sequence model; DSM, dominant-sequence model; ANN, artificial neural networks; FFNN, feedforward neural networks; DNN, deep neural network; IFG, inferior frontal Gyrus; TL, temporal lobe; NIR, near-infrared spectroscopy; MLNN, multi-layer neural network; LSTM, long and short-term memory network; IMU, inertial measurement unit; SMM, stereotypical motor movement; KAUH, King Abdulaziz university hospital; KDEF, Karolinska directed emotional faces; FLEM, fuzzy-based ELM (extreme learning machine); CASIA, Chinese academy of sciences, institute of automation; DEAF, deep extreme adaptive fuzzy; DPA, Douglas–Peucker algorithm; MRMR, minimum redundancy maximum relevance; DBSCAN, density-based spatial clustering of applications with noise.

11.4 RESULTS AND DISCUSSIONS

Despite inconsistency in classification to some degree, the deep leaning strategy appears to be promising method for diagnosing the ASD with a plenty of scope for improvement in terms of accuracy, precision, and F1-score. The state of the art in the diagnosis of autism using deep learning methods is discussed with reference to the architectures and the choice of pipelining/process involved for further processing of the data (refer to Table 3.1 for details of the methods used).

Use of facial morphology in distinguishing disorder from normal is one way of quantifying the morphological changes in the ASD patients. A total of 1,122 (East Asian dataset) and 2,936 facial images (Kaggle dataset) were analyzed using deep convolutional neural networks [7]. Synonymous with the VGG16/VGG19 (Visual Geometry Group from Oxford with 16 convolution layers), Lu and Perkowski [7] preferred to choose VGG16-based deep learning for the pre-training using Keras-VGGFace (implemented using Keras Functional Framework v2+) using VGGFace dataset for setting up the pretrained model for the study. VGG is one of the most preferred choices of modeling as a feature extractor in comparison to the rest. The VGG16 architecture has series of convoluting layers, involving two convolution layers of size of 3×3 (64 filters each) followed by max pooling over a 2×2-pixel window with a stride of two pixels. After series of the stacks, the data is passed through a fully connected layer comprising of 4,096 and 4,096, followed by output layer with softmax activation with 1,000 numbers of neurons signifying 1,000 different classifications. To improve the classification accuracy involving two races, the model was further refined by adjusting the learning rates and the model parameters. With fine-tuning the Lu et al. were able to improve the accuracy by 2% with an F1-score of 0.95 and a high classification accuracy of 95%. The differences in the accuracy across the races were due to the differences in anthropometric measurements of the groups. The author suggested for further study involving race-specific models to ensure that the race-specific anthropometric measures are taken care prior to classification.

Face scanning for visually stimuli was studied for differentiating the ASD from typical developing (TD) subjects [8]. The machine learning technique involving partitioning of the facial images using k-means clustering was used, considering different k values for throughput analysis of the data for accuracy. Histogram was extracted and performed classification of the histogram data using SVM followed by score averaging. The study resulted in exploration of the key discriminating features of the facial image that would be potential useful in diagnosis. Use of scan path representing the trajectory traced by the eye during the activity has been adopted to study the behavior of autism patients [13]. Authors have employed three levels of analysis in screening for autism – one involving feature extraction using LBP and GLCM, second using GoogleNet and ResNet-18 deep feature extraction, and third by merging the SVM/Deep learning methods for classification [12]. The study indicates that hybrid modes involving above systematic data analysis allow for increased accuracy of prediction.

In synonymous with previous work on the functional connectivity of brain areas where the accuracy was relatively low, author has analyzed ABIDE dataset for reliable classification and diagnosis [10]. The method involved denoising using autoencoders (involving 19,900–1,000–600–2 numbers of neurons, with hidden neurons between the input and output layer) followed by training and unsupervised learning. Next stage training involves fine-tuning of the weights via supervised-trained multi-layer perceptron. The objective of the weight's adjustment is to ensure minimization of the error and improvement in accuracy. The deep network allowed for accuracy in the range of 63%–68% for leave-one-site-out cross validation process. Further network architectures involving five types were analyzed where the MRI was analyzed using 2D/3D convolution layers followed by processing with fully connected networks [9]. In other models, slices were processed by 2D gap following CNN. To facilitate the data learning, models using the previous states from CNN and STN were fed to each time step of the RNN. In the modeling process, the advantage is the processing of original MRI voxel data directly by the neural network to identify the structures what well differentiates the autism form normal. Models using recurrent attention model (RAM) +FC appear to show a good correlation in identifying the discriminatory structures in the MRI.

In diagnosis using functional near-infrared spectroscopy, the data is a time-series data where CNN models which are more specific to local based do not fare better with time-series information and do not consider feedbacks. Authors have employed CLAttention model to extract the local features of the time-varying signal followed by long- and short-term memory network (LSTM), a type of temporal recursive neural network, to perform temporal sequence analysis for feature extraction [15]. The study was found to be useful in identifying rather more meaningful features using the above scheme.

Using EEG, the authors have used linear and non-linear features (such as power spectra, FFT, WT for linear; fractal dimension, Lyapunov exponent and entropy for non-linear) [26] as the basis for clustering using density-based spatial clustering of applications with noise (DBSCAN) method [27]. The study facilitated identification of two early symptoms and diagnosis showing better accuracy and sensitivity using SVM. While there are numerous studies performed involving methods scoping for prefixed features extraction, deep learning does not prefixes the features; however, it essentially determines key features with increased accuracy of classification in differentiating subject into autism and typically developing [24,25]. Using Short-Time Fourier Transform (STFT) and Local Binary Pattern (LBP) for feature generation, the spectrogram images were formed and provided to the deep learning network for potential diagnosis [28]. Considering the computational complexity required to perform the analysis, light weight deep learning modeling was adopted by using pretrained models were used to facilitate diagnosis using MobileNetV2 [29], ShuffleNet [30], and SqueezeNet [31]. The study allowed for feasible diagnosis of the subjects with potentially application for its use in early diagnosis in a clinical setting.

11.5 CONCLUSION

Numerous studies have been performed to evaluate the psychomotor skills in child having ASD. In this chapter, we have discussed various modalities of exploring the disorder through study of the gaze, behavioral changes, responses to stimuli facilitated by automation, and neuroimaging modalities scoping for structural and functional changes in the brain. With huge amount of data available, processing the data and performing quick diagnosis is a challenge with good accuracy and specificity. DL/ML comes at great advantage in scooping for key features and classification driven by the intelligence. With use of various pre-processing techniques, segmentation, filtering, key feature extraction and classification, there are good chances to perform better diagnosis. Further methods of evaluation and screening would focus more on standardizing the diagnostic criteria and improve the accuracy of diagnosis which could clinicians in determining diagnosis and the course of treatment.

11.5.1 DECLARATIONS

The author received no financial support for the research, and/or publication of this article. Further, the author declared no potential conflicts of interest with respect to the research, authorship, and/or publication of this article.

REFERENCES

1. WHO Autism spectrum disorders. Available from: https://www.who.int/news-room/fact-sheets/detail/autism-spectrum-disorders, accessed 10 Mar 2022.
2. Speaks A. Autism Statistics and Facts. Available from: https://www.autismspeaks.org/autism-statistics, accessed, 10 Mar 2022.
3. Lipkin, P. H., & Macias, M. M. (2020). Council on children with disabilities, section on developmental and behavioral pediatrics. Promoting optimal development: Identifying infants and young children with developmental disorders through developmental surveillance and screening. *Pediatrics*, 145(1), e20193449.
4. Hyman, S. L., Levy, S. E., & Myers, S. M. (2020). Council on children with disabilities, section on developmental and behavioral pediatrics. Identification, evaluation, and management of children with autism spectrum disorder. *Pediatrics*, 145(1), e20193447.
5. Grover, V. P., Tognarelli, J. M., Crossey, M. M., Cox, I. J., Taylor-Robinson, S. D., & McPhail, M. J. (2015). Magnetic resonance imaging: principles and techniques: Lessons for clinicians. *Journal of Clinical and Experimental Hepatology*, 5(3), 246–255.
6. Khodatars, M., Shoeibi, A., Sadeghi, D., Ghaasemi, N., Jafari, M., Moridian, P., & Berk, M. (2021). Deep learning for neuroimaging-based diagnosis and rehabilitation of autism spectrum disorder: A review. *Computers in Biology and Medicine*, 139, 104949.
7. Lu, A., & Perkowski, M. (2021). Deep learning approach for screening autism spectrum disorder in children with facial images and analysis of ethnoracial factors in model development and application. *Brain Sciences*, 11(11), 1446.
8. Liu, W., Li, M., & Yi, L. (2016). Identifying children with autism spectrum disorder based on their face processing abnormality: A machine learning framework. *Autism Research*, 9(8), 888–898.
9. Ke, F., Choi, S., Kang, Y. H., Cheon, K. A., & Lee, S. W. (2020). Exploring the structural and strategic bases of autism spectrum disorders with deep learning. *IEEE Access*, 8, 153341–153352.
10. Heinsfeld, A. S., Franco, A. R., Craddock, R. C., Buchweitz, A., & Meneguzzi, F. (2018). Identification of autism spectrum disorder using deep learning and the ABIDE dataset. *NeuroImage: Clinical*, 17, 16–23.
11. Guo, X., Wang, J., Wang, X., Liu, W., Yu, H., Xu, L., & Chen, Y. (2022). Diagnosing autism spectrum disorder in children using conventional MRI and apparent diffusion coefficient based deep learning algorithms. *European Radiology*, 32(2), 761–770.
12. Ahmed, I. A., Senan, E. M., Rassem, T. H., Ali, M. A., Shatnawi, H. S. A., Alwazer, S. M., & Alshahrani, M. (2022). Eye tracking-based diagnosis and early detection of autism spectrum disorder using machine learning and deep learning techniques. *Electronics*, 11(4), 530.
13. Carette, R., Elbattah, M., Cilia, F., Dequen, G., Guerin, J. L., & Bosche, J. (2019). Learning to predict autism spectrum disorder based on the visual patterns of eye-tracking scanpaths. In: Proceedings of the 12th International Joint Conference on Biomedical Engineering Systems and Technologies (BIOSTEC 12th International Conference on Health Informatics), SCITEPRESS – Science and Technology Publications, Lda, Portugal (pp. 103–112).

14. Subah, F. Z., Deb, K., Dhar, P. K., & Koshiba, T. (2021). A deep learning approach to predict autism spectrum disorder using multisite resting-state fMRI. *Applied Sciences*, 11(8), 3636.

15. Xu, L., Sun, Z., Xie, J., Yu, J., Li, J., & Wang, J. (2021). Identification of autism spectrum disorder based on short-term spontaneous hemodynamic fluctuations using deep learning in a multi-layer neural network. *Clinical Neurophysiology*, 132(2), 457–468.

16. Yin, W., Mostafa, S., & Wu, F. X. (2021). Diagnosis of autism spectrum disorder based on functional brain networks with deep learning. *Journal of Computational Biology*, 28(2), 146–165.

17. Rad, N. M., Kia, S. M., Zarbo, C., van Laarhoven, T., Jurman, G., Venuti, P., & Furlanello, C. (2018). Deep learning for automatic stereotypical motor movement detection using wearable sensors in autism spectrum disorders. *Signal Processing*, 144, 180–191.

18. Kong, Y., Gao, J., Xu, Y., Pan, Y., Wang, J., & Liu, J. (2019). Classification of autism spectrum disorder by combining brain connectivity and deep neural network classifier. *Neurocomputing*, 324, 63–68.

19. Sherkatghanad, Z., Akhondzadeh, M., Salari, S., Zomorodi-Moghadam, M., Abdar, M., Acharya, U. R., & Salari, V. (2020). Automated detection of autism spectrum disorder using a convolutional neural network. *Frontiers in Neuroscience*, 13, 1325.

20. Tawhid, M. N. A., Siuly, S., Wang, H., Whittaker, F., Wang, K., & Zhang, Y. (2021). A spectrogram image based intelligent technique for automatic detection of autism spectrum disorder from EEG. *Plos One*, 16(6), e0253094.

21. Eni, M., Dinstein, I., Ilan, M., Menashe, I., Meiri, G., & Zigel, Y. (2020). Estimating autism severity in young children from speech signals using a deep neural network. *IEEE Access*, 8, 139489–139500.

22. Saranya, A., & Anandan, R. (2021). FIGS-DEAF: An novel implementation of hybrid deep learning algorithm to predict autism spectrum disorders using facial fused gait features. *Distributed and Parallel Databases*, 40, 1–26.

23. Zhang, J., Feng, F., Han, T., Gong, X., & Duan, F. (2022). Detection of autism spectrum disorder using fMRI functional connectivity with feature selection and deep learning. *Cognitive Computation*, 1–12.

24. Ari, B., Sobahi, N., Alçin, Ö. F., Sengur, A., & Acharya, U. R. (2022). Accurate detection of autism using Douglas-Peucker algorithm, sparse coding based feature mapping and convolutional neural network techniques with EEG signals. *Computers in Biology and Medicine*, 143, 105311.

25. Kang, J., Han, X., Song, J., Niu, Z., & Li, X. (2020). The identification of children with autism spectrum disorder by SVM approach on EEG and eye-tracking data. *Computers in Biology and Medicine*, 120, 103722.

26. Abdolzadegan, D., Moattar, M. H., & Ghoshuni, M. (2020). A robust method for early diagnosis of autism spectrum disorder from EEG signals based on feature selection and DBSCAN method. *Biocybernetics and Biomedical Engineering*, 40(1), 482–493.

27. Ester, M., Kriegel, H. P., Sander, J., & Xu, X. (1996). A density-based algorithm for discovering clusters in large spatial databases with noise. In: *kdd*, AAAI, (Vol. 96, No. 34, pp. 226–231).

28. Baygin, M., Dogan, S., Tuncer, T., Barua, P. D., Faust, O., Arunkumar, N., & Acharya, U. R. (2021). Automated ASD detection using hybrid deep lightweight features extracted from EEG signals. *Computers in Biology and Medicine*, 134, 104548.

29. Sandler, M., Howard, A., Zhu, M., Zhmoginov, A., & Chen, L. C. (2018). Mobilenetv2: Inverted residuals and linear bottlenecks. In: *Proceedings of the IEEE Conference on Computer Vision and Pattern Recognition*, IEEE, Salt Lake City, UT, USA (pp. 4510–4520).

30. Zhang, X., Zhou, X., Lin, M., & Sun, J. (2018). Shufflenet: An extremely efficient convolutional neural network for mobile devices. In: *Proceedings of the IEEE Conference on Computer Vision and Pattern Recognition* (pp. 6848–6856).

31. Iandola, F. N., Han, S., Moskewicz, M. W., Ashraf, K., Dally, W. J., & Keutzer, K. (2016). SqueezeNet: AlexNet-level accuracy with 50× fewer parameters and < 0.5 MB model size. *arXiv preprint arXiv:1602.07360*.

12 Dementia Detection with Deep Networks Using Multi-Modal Image Data

Altuğ Yiğit and Zerrin Işık
Dokuz Eylul University

Yalın Baştanlar
Izmir Institute of Technology

CONTENTS

12.1 INTRODUCTION

Dementia is a neurodegenerative disease that causes changes in cognitive abilities of the brain. Even though there are many subtypes of dementia such as Alzheimer's, vascular dementia, Parkinson, Huntington's disease, and Lewy body. Alzheimer disease is considerably encountered in elderly population; hence the risk increases by age [1]. Identification of subtypes of dementia is quite complicated because of their similar symptoms such as declining memory, personality change, disability of abstract thinking [2]. However, since physiological and

DOI: 10.1201/9781003315452-12

185

mental status changes occur naturally in the brain due to aging, early diagnosis of dementia is quite challenging and may even lead to misdiagnosis in the absence of the patient's history [3]. Cognitive impairment occurs several years ago prior to diagnosis of dementia; at the same time abnormal cognitive decline is similar with decline by natural ageing in early stages [4].

The transitional phase between normal cognitive decline depending on ageing and early dementia is called mild cognitive impairment (MCI). Although MCI patients have some functional cognitive disorders, they do not meet the diagnostic criteria for the disease. In the early stages of the disease, some MCI cases can be diagnosed as normal, because those are slightly different from the normal cognitive declines. Meanwhile, it is quite challenging to detect at the onset of dementia in the advanced stages of the MCI [5]. MCI is likely to progress into dementia. MCI patients who have metabolic disorders such as hypertension, increased cholesterol levels, and diabetes have higher risk of progression to dementia [6]. The key point for early diagnosis of dementia is to accurately detect abnormal cases among all cognitively declined cases.

Although there is no treatment to prevent the progression of many types of neurodegenerative diseases, treatments can be applied to relieve some symptoms and slow down disease progression by early diagnosis [7]. To diagnose earlier stages and distinguish subtypes of dementia, many invasive and non-invasive methods are available. Most employed invasive method for clinical diagnosis is cerebrospinal fluid (CSF) measurement, which reveals biochemical marker levels such as amyloid-β and tau [8]. As a non-invasive method, neuroimaging markers are generally preferred [9]. Several neuroimaging markers with varied modalities are employed to make the correct diagnosis and those allow us to obtain varied neurodegenerative information such as structural, functional, and metabolic. While structural brain imaging modalities, magnetic resonance imaging (MRI), and computed tomography (CT) are commonly used to identify cerebral atrophy in neurodegeneration [10], positron emission tomography (PET) and single-photon emission computed tomography (SPECT) are employed to detect molecular pathophysiological changes in-vivo before symptoms appear and anatomical atrophy begins [11].

Nowadays, automatic diagnostic systems are developed to assist specialists in making the right decisions during clinical diagnosis. Some studies evaluated the brain's electrical activity using electroencephalography (EEG) and clinical data, including cognitive tests such as mini-mental state examination, finger tapping, and continuous performance tests [14,15]. Others mainly employed neuroimaging techniques such as MRI [16–18] and PET [19,20]. Due to PET imaging having an insufficient spatial resolution to focus on anatomical atrophy, as a second modality, structural imaging modalities such as MRI must be examined to take advantage of high-resolution data and disclose anatomical details [12]. Thanks to brain imaging modalities, prognostic data can be acquired in a pre-symptomatic period [13]. As in clinical evaluation, the literature has conveyed that taking advantage of more than one neuroimaging technique enhances computer-assisted diagnostic performance. Researchers employed some machine learning and deep learning algorithms to build diagnosis systems. They need domain-specific knowledge to extract features from volumetric brain scans and apply machine learning classification algorithms. Brain scans are segmented into regions using an anatomical atlas to obtain region-based information. Afterward, feature selection algorithms are applied to identify valuable features before feeding those into a machine learning algorithm [21,22]. However, with the advent of deep learning models, automated feature extraction modules that do not require prior domain-specific knowledge have come into use. 2D and 3D convolutional neural networks [23,24] and stacked autoencoders [25,26] are mainly used in such studies to acquire hierarchical feature representation. With the motivation of investigating the effectiveness of multi-modal deep neural networks for the diagnosis of dementia, 2D and 3D feature fusion (grid-based pixel and voxel intensities) and decision-level ensemble models have been proposed in this study. These models extract features from MRI and PET scans as input. Due to the many achievements reported in the literature, developing a multi-modal system using deep networks was preferred. Two types of classification tasks have been performed to separate Alzheimer's from healthy people and MCI from healthy people again.

A summary of contributions of this chapter is as follows:

- It presents a broad review of multi-modal imaging approaches proposed for dementia diagnosis.
- It proposes a new method for representing volumetric data as 2D brain slices.
- It offers a multi-modal feature fusion solution that focuses on assorted features.
- It introduces a dynamic decision-based ensemble learning approach with deep neural networks.

This chapter is organized as follows: Related work reviews available methods in literature for computerized diagnosis of dementia. Methodology presents details of neuroimaging data and multi-modal imaging networks. Results and discussion section presents results of two and multi-modal deep neural network solutions and compares them with literature by discussing advantages and deficiencies. Conclusion section highlights critical points in the chapter and concludes the study.

12.2 RELATED WORK

Brain imaging modalities are widely employed in clinical diagnosis of various diseases including neurological diseases such as MCI, Alzheimer's disease, other dementia diseases, and brain tumors. Increasing computation power facilitates the application of computer-aided systems developed to diagnose dementia. These systems evaluate brain imaging similar to an expert. These systems support the specialist's decisions via automated predictions based on various machine learning approaches. In terms of diversity of brain imaging modalities, literature studies can be divided into single-modality and multi-modality solutions. Single-modality imaging solutions stand for making decisions concerning just structural, functional, or molecular information using a single brain scan method. The studies for the diagnosis of dementia generally utilize biomarkers based on a single imaging modality, such as MRI [16–18,27–33], CT [38,39], DTI [40,41], and PET [19,20,46–50]. Multi-modality imaging solutions consider distinct features. Depending on the type of imaging, various information can be obtained. Structural brain imaging is employed to identify cerebral atrophy due to neurodegeneration. Molecular imaging provides cellular processes and molecular information [32]. In the remaining part of this section, available solutions will be discussed under three subsections: Structural Imaging, Molecular Imaging, and Multi-Modality Imaging Solutions.

12.2.1 STRUCTURAL IMAGING IN DEMENTIA

Structural imaging modalities indicate cerebral atrophy due to neurodegeneration in the brain. Chague et al. [16] employed volumetric T1-weighted MRI to distinguish subtypes of dementia: early-onset and late-onset Alzheimer's disease, frontotemporal dementia, depression. To specify discriminant atrophy areas, weight maps were obtained for each voxel of MRI scans using a support vector machine (SVM). Manual feature extraction requires domain knowledge and carrying out feature engineering work. On top of that, machine learning approaches are applied to biomarkers obtained by extracting certain features. Cortical thickness measurement is a significant biomarker acquired from structural MRI. It is widely employed in the studies to detect conversion from MCI to dementia in Parkinson's disease [17], to identify subtypes of dementia such as frontotemporal dementia [18], and to differentiate Alzheimer's disease and dementia with Lewy bodies [27]. Measurements are performed on certain regions of interest in a brain atlas via cortical parcellation [28]. Lebedeva et al. [31] employed cortical thickness measurements from 74 different brain regions for estimating MCI or dementia in patients with late-life depression. Hippocampal shape and volume are other substantial biomarkers obtained from structural brain scans. Structural atrophy in the hippocampal area region leads to shape and volume changes, and it is mainly related to the onset of dementia. Costafreda et al. [29] identified volumetric hippocampal shape morphology from MRI for detecting conversion from MCI to Alzheimer's disease. In another study [30], hippocampal shape and volume features were assessed to reveal the development of dementia in participants who did not have dementia initially. After automatic segmentation of the hippocampus region, shape and volume features are combined by equalizing the total variance of feature vectors. It has been reported that structural biomarkers obtained from the hippocampus region are notable in predicting the development of the disease [29,30]. In some of the studies that consider the local intensity values of specific brain regions, the relations between the regions are examined. Tong et al. [32] presented a graph-based multiple instance learning method in which each patch of an image corresponds to an instance, and all images are represented as graphs, which illustrate relationships between the patches of an MRI sample. They performed classification operating with an SVM to detect Alzheimer's disease and distinguish stable and progressive MCI. Bron et al. [33] employed voxel-based morphometry of gray matter features from nine regions of interest from structural MRI. To distinguish dementia, immensely correlated features are identified by SVM-based weight maps.

Recent studies have employed deep learning approaches, as a result of their achievements in related fields [61] and reported higher achievements to differentiate dementia types such as dementia with Lewy bodies and Alzheimer's [36,37]. Those can discover biomarkers automatically without prior domain-specific knowledge. Nemoto et al. [36] applied the ResNet model to gray matter images derived from structural MRI to specify dementia with Lewy bodies and distinguish it from Alzheimer's disease. Similarly, another study [37] employed the VGG-16 model that takes a structural MRI slice for three-way classification of Alzheimer's, MCI, and healthy individuals. To identify the most informative slice, they calculated the entropy for each structural brain scan. Another neuroimaging method is CT; it has lower spatial resolution compared with structural MRI, which is widely accessible. Unlike MRI, it uses X-rays and generates images in a short time [38]. Gao and Hui [39] performed a combination of 2D and 3D convolutional neural networks (CNNs) using CT brain images to discriminate between Alzheimer's disease, lesions, and normal aging.

12.2.2 MOLECULAR IMAGING IN DEMENTIA

Molecular imaging approaches such as PET and single-photon emission computed tomography (SPECT) reveal molecular pathophysiological changes *in-vivo*. These approaches help to detect the disease in the initial period before symptoms appear. The studies reported machine learning-based computer-aided diagnosis approaches that take various brain PET scans as input and predict the presence of dementia. Lizuka et al. [35] feed brain SPECT, which expresses blood flows in the brain regions, into a CNN model to distinguish Lewy bodies from Alzheimer's disease. They indicated that the 2D network is superior to 3D network that accepts whole-brain scans. Studies have also reported that PET imaging approaches have better spatial resolutions and quantification than SPECT [42].

Amyloid-β, tau, and fluorodeoxyglucose (FDG) PET imaging methods are widely used to identify dementia diseases. Molecular targets of PET change according to the radiotracers [43]. Amyloid-β PET scans reveal brain amyloid deposition related to Alzheimer's disease. Mathotaarachchi et al. [46] proposed a random forest classifier that predicts the progression of dementia according to amyloid-β PET biomarkers. They derived biomarkers from specific brain regions such as the angular gyrus, posterior cingulate cortex, and precuneus. Similarly, another random forest classifier [47] identifies positive or negative amyloid deposition. The tau PET is used to assess neurofibrillary pathology and expose tau protein deposition [44]. Jo et al. [20] applied a 3D CNN-based classification strategy that assesses tau deposition for distinguishing Alzheimer's disease and MCI from healthy controls. They also presented a layer-wise relevance propagation algorithm by which most affected brain regions have been specified as the thalamus, hippocampus, parahippocampus, and fusiform on tau PET. Zou et al. [48] represented volumetric tau PET scans as 2D grid images that contain nine coronal slices. They performed 2D and 3D CNN models with data augmentation to classify Alzheimer's disease and reported higher accuracy compared with the standard region of interest-based approaches.

F-18 fluorodeoxyglucose radiotracer is used to generate brain FDG-PET scans that evaluate cerebral metabolic rates of glucose. Patients with Alzheimer's disease have metabolic glucose deficiency in some parts of the brain, such as the posterior cingulate cortex and parietotemporal areas [45]. Xia et al. [19] suggested a hybrid algorithm that can discover differentiating patterns between healthy individuals, Alzheimer's, and frontotemporal dementia. Glucose metabolic rate features were obtained from FDG-PET scans, including spatial variation, average level, and asymmetry. Afterward, they selected features using a genetic algorithm and performed classification by SVMs. Singh et al. [49] conducted binary classification employing a deep multi-layer feed-forward neural network to distinguish dementia. The network evaluates voxel intensities from FDG-PET scans instead of manually extracting specific features. To reduce dimensionality, they performed max pooling, mean pooling, and principal component analysis. Yee et al. [50] constructed a 3D CNN that takes FDG-PET scans as input and predicts the probability scores for dementia types. Studies have reported that deep learning approaches discovering new features are more successful compared with other machine learning algorithms [49,50]. However, automatic feature extraction approaches do not need domain knowledge and uncover hierarchical features that best represent the data.

12.2.3　Multi-Modality Imaging Solutions

The literature has reported that the combination of distinct neuroimaging modalities is more successful than single-modality imaging solutions. Multi-modality gives the ability to evaluate various biomarkers together, such as structural and molecular. Not only are high-resolution anatomical details achieved, but molecular pathophysiological biomarkers are also distilled, including tau, amyloid deposition, and metabolic rates of glucose. The studies offered various fusion strategies for combining multiple neuroimaging modalities. Depending on the application method, fusion strategies can be applied to concatenate extracted features (feature fusion) [21,22,25] or to merge numerous imaging modalities as pixel-based (image fusion) [51,52] as depicted in Figure 12.1. Zhang et al. [21] employed the intensity values of whole MRI and the average intensity values of PET scans to separate dementia types using a multiclass SVM. They developed an embedded feature selection strategy combining the regularization term with the multiclass hinge loss. To concatenate features obtained from different

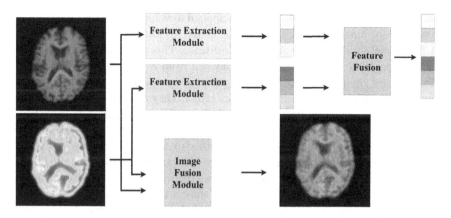

FIGURE 12.1 Application of feature fusion and image fusion on MRI and PET scans.

modalities, a new regularization term is presented, and multiple kernel learning is performed. In another study, Hao et al. [22] introduced a feature selection approach on multiple neuroimaging modalities: voxel-based measure (VBM) MRI and FDG-PET. They calculated similarity in the form of a graph for each modality using a random forest algorithm and selected features with consistent metric constraint. After produced features are combined, classification is performed by a multi-kernel SVM to identify dementia types, including early MCI and late MCI Alzheimer's disease. Kim and Lee [25] designed a multi-modal sparse hierarchical extreme learning machine that evaluates volume and mean intensity values from 93 regions of interest of MRI, FDG-PET, and CSF features for diagnosis of MCI and Alzheimer's disease.

In addition to feature fusion methods, image fusion strategies are also applied to detect subtypes of dementia. Kong et al. [51] proposed an image fusion approach that combines volumetric MRI and PET scans. They generated gray matter images from MRI, and co-registration is applied on PET images to form a fused image. Then, a 3D CNN model was constructed to detect dementia using fused scans. Song et al. [52] created a setup to compare image fusion and feature fusion approaches exploiting volumetric MRI and FDG-PET scans for multiclass dementia detection. They reported that the proposed image fusion method is superior to the feature fusion method.

Deep learning strategies are immensely promising in detecting dementia diseases. CNN, a deep learning model, is extensively used to make a computerized diagnosis on medical images. Medical images are handled directly using CNN models, and no prior feature engineering is required. Deep learning models for detecting dementia diseases can be considered as 2D and 3D approaches in terms of input type. 3D approaches assess volumetric brain scans taking as input and processing voxel values. Vu et al. [54] suggested a CNN and Sparse Automatic Encoder (SAE) networks that take MRI and PET scans to diagnose dementia. For discovering distinct biomarkers, SAE is applied to volumetric scans, and CNN is operated for binary classification. Huang et al. [55] presented a multi-modal 3D CNN model for diagnosing Alzheimer's disease. This model evaluates volumetric hippocampal area intensity values fetched from MRI and FDG-PET. After features are computed by convolution and pooling operations, feature fusion is applied ahead of feeding them into flatten layers. They reported that multi-modal imaging solutions outperform single-modal ones. 2D techniques comprise slices of volumetric images. Fang et al. [24] designed an ensemble framework consisting of deep CNNs and an Adaboost classifier to identify Alzheimer's disease. They picked specific slices from volumetric MRI and PET scans, then fed them into the ensemble model. Although studies broadly employ multi-modal imaging solutions using MRI and PET images, some studies utilize other modalities such as EEG and MRI or FDG-PET and florbetapir (AV-45) PET. A study [26] proposes an artificial neural network (ANN) model with stacked autoencoders that assess resting-state EEG and MRI scans to diagnose Alzheimer's patients with dementia. To estimate the cognitive decline in MCI patients, Choi et al. [53] developed a CNN model that takes FDG-PET and AV-45 PET images as input. They trained the model using data of Alzheimer's and healthy individuals. After that, cognitive decline is estimated via those weights.

This chapter proposes multi-modal deep neural networks for fusion structural and molecular biomarkers. For this reason, 2D or 3D feature fusion and decision-level ensemble networks are proposed that take features from T1-MRI and FDG-PET scans. These networks evaluate structural and molecular information using voxel and grid-based pixel intensities. Multi-modal imaging solution is preferred with deep networks due to many achievements reported in the literature.

12.3 METHODOLOGY

This section provides information about the neuroimaging data used in this study, the processing of the data, and the application of CNN models. Volumetric neuroimaging data are represented as 2D grid data in different ways, as discussed in 12.3.2 Pre-processing of brain scans. Proposed feature fusion and decision-level ensemble networks are presented in 12.3.3 Application of Multi-Modal Imaging Networks.

12.3.1 IMAGE ACQUISITION

This chapter has been prepared with the data obtained from the Alzheimer's Disease Neuroimaging Initiative (ADNI) database.[1] This project started in 2003 as a public–private collaboration under the chairmanship of Michael W. Weiner, MD. It aims to investigate brain scans; MRI, PET, different biological markers, clinical and neuropsychological assessments for measuring MCI and early Alzheimer's disease progression.

Brain MRI scans are generated using Siemens, GE Healthcare, and Philips scanners. T1-weighted volumetric images are created with roughly $1\,mm^3$ target voxel size. The target execution time for the patient scanning phase is 30 minutes, and the phantom scan time is 15 minutes [56]. For FDG-PET scans, frames obtained in 5minutes (six frames between 30-and 60-minutes post-injection) are co-registered to frame 1 using rigid-body translation, rotation, and six degrees of freedom by the NeuroStat "mcoreg" routine. All frames of these are averaged into a single frame, afterward application of co-registration. As a result, these are generated in the form of a $160\times160\times96$ grid with $1.5\,mm^3$ voxels [57]. There are different versions of the project as ADNI 1/2/3 and GO. In this study, to develop multi-modality imaging data and generate distinct biomarkers, we identify participants who have baseline T1-MRI and FDG-PET scans. We built three datasets: T1-MRI, FDG-PET, and a multi-modal set. Participants who have multiple imaging modalities have been filtered out. In total, 751 scans (212 patients with Alzheimer's, 303 MCI, 236 healthy controls) for each modality have been selected.

12.3.2 Pre-Processing of Brain Scans

After obtaining volumetric brain scans, some operations were performed to prepare for evaluation. Reorientation, cropping, bias-field correction, brain extraction or skull stripping, and registration procedures were implemented as pre-processing of T1-MRI scans. To bring all scans to the exact spatial location and obtain an equivalent form of volumetric data, identical steps without bias-field correction were performed on FDG-PET scans as well. FMRIB's Software Library (FSL) [58] was employed as a library, which contains tools for analyzing functional, structural, and DTI brain imaging data, such as analysis of gray matter density, subcortical segmentation, and linear registration.

Initially, Montreal Neurological Institute (MNI) orientation was applied to obtain the same standard and facilitate the manual review. After meeting the same orientation standard, a cropping operation was performed to remove the neck and lower head sections and to perform other operations more efficiently. Then bias-field correction was applied to the cropped data to remedy low signal areas generated by the MRI scanners; this procedure is only suitable for MRI scans. Skull that protects the brain, eyes, fats, and muscles are redundant and not related to the disease. Therefore, the Brain Extraction Tool (BET) was operated to distinguish undeserved information from demanded data. It runs based on histogram density in which the brain scan is represented in binary, defining a threshold value, and the approximate head size is estimated [59]. Inherently, sometimes subjects might move their heads for any reason. It leads to a decrease in quality and change in spatial locations of brain areas. Consequently, segmentation and classification performances might be corrupted because of non-uniform information. To avoid these problems, registration was applied to transform volumetric data into the same MNI space in $91\times109\times91$ voxels with 2 mm isotropic spacing.

Voxel intensities have been normalized into the 0–1 range; it was performed on each channel of T1-MRI and FDG-PET scans. Intermediate results of procedures have been visualized by Mango,[2] which is a medical image viewer and analysis software developed by Lancaster and Martinez. Forasmuch, manual examinations have been performed to evaluate the correctness of the pre-processing methods. Applied procedures are presented in Figure 12.2. Behind volumetric scans were pre-processed, 2D grid-based data were constructed that represent volumetric data reducing dimension. 2D 3×8 grid data were built, by picking eight slices for each perspective: axial, sagittal, coronal from $91 \times 109 \times 91$ voxels, as shown in Figure 12.3. In this process, slices were selected by jumping with two intervals containing the slices close to the middle point of volumetric data. Each slice was cropped from the center with a 45×45 window to acquire informative data. Same method was performed on volumetric scans to reduce dimension to $45 \times 55 \times 45$. In this way, we selected more informative areas which contain atrophied areas.

Thanks to this grid-based data representation, volumetric data is represented differently, containing all perspectives and significant brain regions. Unlike existing data augmentation methods, a new slice-based data augmentation approach, which can be used in multi-dimensional medical images, has been proposed. In this approach, augmented data is generated using different brain slices which are shifted by a fixed amount. In other words, multiple 2D representations are obtained from a single volumetric scan. Spawned data were processed in grayscale and normalized between 0 and 1.

12.3.3 Implementation of Multi-Modal Imaging Networks

CNN models were constructed capable of evaluating multi-modal imaging data, including T1-MRI and FDG-PET. In addition, networks that take single-modal imaging were implemented to highlight the success of multi-modal solutions. For emphasizing effectiveness of the proposed grid-based data, a CNN model was built to assess volumetric brain scans. The convolution and pooling part of Inception V3 was implemented besides 1,024 dense layers before the output layer for extracting features from grid-based data. Furthermore, transfer learning was applied using ImageNet weights instead of starting training with random weights. Adam optimizer, categorical cross-entropy, rectified linear unit function commonly used in deep networks and softmax function calculating class probabilities

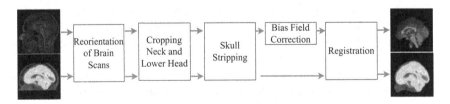

FIGURE 12.2 Applied procedures on T1-MRI and FDG-PET scans.

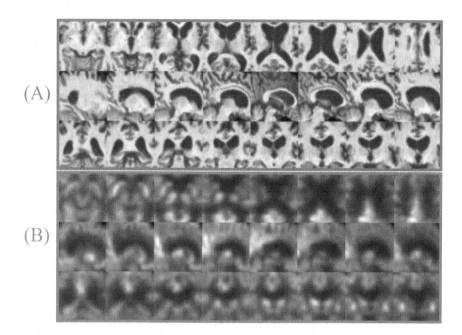

FIGURE 12.3 3×8 slice-based grid data obtained from (a) MRI and (b) PET consists of all cropped perspectives.

were utilized for supervised training. Training was performed for 100 epochs. The implemented loss function is formulated as follows.

$$L(y_a, \hat{y}_a) = -\left(y_a \cdot log(\hat{y}_a) + (1 - y_a).log(1 - \hat{y}_a)\right) \tag{12.1}$$

In Eq. (12.1), ground truth value and *ith* predicted value are denoted as y_i and $\hat{y}_i$. The initial learning rate value was defined as 1e-4. To obstruct overfitting, batch normalization as well as regularization (L2) was applied on networks. Batch normalization reduces the internal covariate shift and normalizes each training minibatch to boost the generalization.

A 3D CNN model that operates on volumetric scans was implemented as a baseline model. It has two convolution layers with 32 units and 256 dense layers. The application of L2 regularization on the loss function is formulated in Eq. (12.2). Data size is represented with K, and the parameter of regularization is indicated with λ. W_j is all weights connected to the of *jth* feature, and the number of features is M.

$$L_r = \frac{1}{K} \sum_{i=1}^{K} L(y_i, \hat{y}_i) + \frac{\lambda}{2.K} \sum_{j=1}^{M} W_j^2 \tag{12.2}$$

Multi-modal networks were developed in two manners: (i) feature fusion-based deep neural networks and (ii) decision-based ensemble deep neural networks as we proposed in our previous study [60]. A feature fusion-based end-to-end deep neural network was designed that combines structural and molecular biomarkers. After discovering biomarkers, a serial fusion is performed to compose multimodal information. Two sets of 2,048 features are serially fused before feeding into the logit layer. However, an ensemble approach was proposed for deep neural networks with a softmax activation function. This approach implies using of dynamic weights rather than static values; the same for all weak learners. Meta learner is created by a combination of decisions of two deep networks. Decisions are analyzed according to the confidence scores.

Softmax function is formulated in Eq. (12.3), where the class amount is pointed out with K. In Eq. (12.4), ensemble strategy is presented. The weight of the base learners (W_β) is changing dynamically. Two base learners are created; the weight of the first learner (s_1) is W_β, and the other (s_2) is $1 - W_\beta$ that changes depending on the first learner.

$$s(z_j) = \frac{e^{z_j}}{\sum_{k=1}^{K} e^{z_k}} \quad for \quad j = 1, ..., K \tag{12.3}$$

$$E_{\text{out}} = \begin{bmatrix} W_\beta.s_1(z_1) + (1 - W_\beta).s_2(z_1) \\ W_\beta.s_1(z_2) + (1 - W_\beta).s_2(z_2) \end{bmatrix} \tag{12.4}$$

When a network makes an overconfident decision, the weight of this network is decreased; therefore, it is punished. Ordinarily, majority voting is performed with equal weights. Overconfident decisions mainly occur in situations where ReLU and softmax activation functions are employed in a neural network. A threshold value of 0.9 is defined to assess overconfidence. If softmax probability value is greater than the given threshold, it is accepted as an overconfident decision. To minimize contribution, W value is set to 0.3 for ensemble decision.

12.4   RESULTS AND DISCUSSION

This section presents experimental results including comparisons with other studies. Experiments were performed on the NVIDIA T4 Tesla core GPU, and the TensorFlow library is used with Python 3.7. Binary classification results are reported that indicate Alzheimer's (AD/HC) and MCI (MCI/HC) diagnosis performances. The experimental results were obtained by a six fold cross-validation as given in Table 12.1. 2D CNN models take grid-based data that consists of slices selected from all perspectives in the size of 135×360. 3D networks interpret the $45 \times 55 \times 45$ volumetric brain regions.

Feature fusion and decision-level ensemble deep neural networks were employed to assess structural and functional information. Multi-modal feature fusion networks are compared with decision-based ensemble networks. In order to take multiple modalities as MRI and PET, neural networks with feature fusion were constructed with two inputs. While features were serially fused in

TABLE 12.1

Comparison of AD and MCI diagnosis performances

Network	Data	AD/HC	MCI/HC
3D CNN	MRI	82.79	66.1
3D CNN	PET	89.62	71.15
3D multi-modal feature fusion	MRI+PET	87.27	68.22
2D CNN	MRI	90.57	67.8
2D CNN	PET	91.04	69.91
2D multi-modal feature fusion	MRI+PET	91.98	71.87
2D multi-modal ensemble	MRI+PET	89.16	69.09

fusion models, independent networks were employed in decision-level ensemble models for decision making. As noticed from Table 12.1, the networks that take grid-based representation containing all perspectives as a 3×8 matrix led to promising results for diagnosing AD and MCI. Although the multi-modal 3D solution for AD identification fails to pass the single-modal 3D PET network, 2D single-modality solutions perform worse than the 2D multi-modal feature fusion network. However, the 2D feature fusion is superior to the 2D ensemble network. Consequently, feature fusion networks using the Inception V3 are much more thriving than the decision-level ensemble models for diagnosis of AD and MCI. The single-modal networks trained with T1-MRI scans perform worse than other networks evaluating FDG-PET scans. The computerized MCI diagnosis is more challenging than Alzheimer's diagnosis based on the predictions of the neural networks. We suggest that metabolic features that provide information about brain metabolism are advantageous for diagnosis of dementia. However, it is more costly to acquire metabolic information compared with structural imaging. In order to develop an accurate diagnostic system for neuroimaging, all atrophy-based features should be employed. Since the accuracy of MRI scans is lower than PET, it also decreases the accuracy of multi-modal systems.

Multi-modal neural networks performed slightly better than the single-modal networks for 2D inputs. More accurate multi-modal systems can be developed if the performances of both modalities are balanced. The pre-trained Inception model with ImageNet weights outperformed the other models including customized CNNs for 3D setups. While multi-modal solutions with 3D data are not as successful as single-modality solutions developed with PET, those achieved more accuracy than the single-modality MRI solutions. Lin et al. [23] proposed a multi-modal strategy for diagnosing Alzheimer's disease using 3D CNN. They reported 89.26% and 92.28% accuracy with real and synthetic MRI and PET scans respectively with the ADNI dataset, similar to this study. As distinct, we proposed a new input representation (i.e., grid-based) that requires less computation power, uses real brain scans, and achieves 91.98%. Huang et al. [55] developed a CNN model for dementia diagnosis. Different from this study, they evaluated hippocampal area intensity. They achieved 90.20% accuracy for diagnosing Alzheimer's disease by using fused features. Volumetric networks require more training time and computation power. It shows that grid-based data might be a great and efficient alternative to 3D solutions at a lower cost. Thanks to those advantages, grid-based inputs can be preferred as an alternative to volumetric data for deep neural networks. An improvement might be achieved with the best representation of volumetric data in 2D space and fine-tuning of networks.

12.5   CONCLUSION

This chapter presents a broad review of studies available for the computerized diagnosis of dementia and a study capable of multi-modal evaluation to efficiently identify dementia types: Alzheimer's and MCI. It discusses the advantages of using multi-modality imaging solutions by presenting studies from the literature. We reported that multi-modal biomarkers, including structural and molecular information, are beneficial for diagnosing dementia. This chapter offered a novel method for representing volumetric data as 2D brain slices, which positively contributed to the final decision of the model. Since this method consists of multiple brain perspectives, it depicts volumetric data excellently in a lower resolution. This study presents a dynamic decision-based ensemble learning approach with deep neural networks. Nevertheless, feature fusion networks performed better than ensemble networks. It is preferable for early diagnosis of dementia. Serial combination of various imaging biomarkers increases diagnostic accuracy. Application of transfer learning to deep networks improves training time and classification performance even though pre-trained weights belong to a different task such as ImageNet. The chapter also proposed a multi-modal feature fusion network which is quite promising model for differentiating AD and MCI. Computerized diagnosis systems create opportunities to identify new biomarkers, discover drugs, assist experts, early detection, and improve the quality of patients' lives. Evaluating multi-modal biomarkers increases early detection probability as well as provides information about the progression of the disease.

   In the future, we planned to apply deep learning strategies to evaluate categorical data such as age, cognitive tests besides structural features representing atrophy, and molecular features in the brain metabolism related to dementia diseases. In order to detect progression of dementia diseases glucose usage and structural changes in the brain scans are effective when used together. It might be advantageous for multi-modal deep neural networks that assess various imaging techniques besides cognitive tests features to diagnose dementia diseases. Thus, multi-modal deep networks will be created to assess varied features, including FDG-PET, T1-MRI scans, and categorical. It is also desirable to compose an extensive dataset for better generalization.

ACKNOWLEDGMENTS

A. Yiğit is supported by the Scientific and Technological Research Council of Turkey (TUBITAK) 2211-C Scholarship. Data collection and sharing for this project was funded by the Alzheimer's Disease Neuroimaging Initiative (ADNI) (National Institutes of Health Grant U01 AG024904) and DOD ADNI (Department of Defense award number W81XWH-12-2-0012). ADNI data are disseminated by the Laboratory for Neuro Imaging at the University of Southern California. As such, the investigators within the ADNI contributed to the design and implementation of ADNI and/or provided data but did not participate in analysis or writing of this report. A complete listing of ADNI investigators can be found at: http://adni.loni.usc. edu/wp-content/uploads/how_to_apply/ADNI_Acknowledgement_List.pdf.

NOTES

1 adni.loni.usc.edu.
2 http://ric.uthscsa.edu/mango.

REFERENCES

1. Hendrie, H. C. (1998). Epidemiology of dementia and Alzheimer's disease. *The American Journal of Geriatric Psychiatry*, *6*(2), S3–S18. https://doi. org/10.1097/00019442-199821001-00002.

2. Brown, R. G., & Marsden, C. D. (1984). How common is dementia in Parkinson's disease? *The Lancet*, *324*(8414), 1262–1265. https://doi.org/10.1016/s0140-6736(84) 92807-1.

3. Gustafson, L. (1996). What is dementia? *Acta Neurologica Scandinavica*, *94*(s168), 22–24. https://doi.org/10.1111/j.1600-0404.1996.tb00367.x.

4. National Collaborating Centre For Mental Health (Great Britain, Social Care Institute For Excellence (Great Britain, & National Institute For Health And Clinical Excellence (Great Britain. (2007). *Dementia: a NICE-SCIE guideline on supporting people with dementia and their carers in health and social care*. British Psychological Society/Gaskell.

5. Petersen, R. C. (2004). Mild cognitive impairment as a diagnostic entity. *Journal of Internal Medicine*, *256*(3), 183–194. https://doi.org/10.1111/j.1365-2796.2004.01388.x.

6. Pal, K., Mukadam, N., Petersen, I., & Cooper, C. (2018). Mild cognitive impairment and progression to dementia in people with diabetes, prediabetes and metabolic syndrome: a systematic review and meta-analysis. *Social Psychiatry and Psychiatric Epidemiology*, *53*(11), 1149–1160. https://doi.org/10.1007/s00127-018-1581-3.

7. Maher, P. (2019). The potential of flavonoids for the treatment of neurodegenerative diseases. *International Journal of Molecular Sciences*, *20*(12), 3056. https://doi. org/10.3390/ijms20123056.

8. Schoonenboom, N. S. M., Reesink, F. E., Verwey, N. A., Kester, M. I., Teunissen, C. E., van de Ven, P. M., Pijnenburg, Y. A. L., Blankenstein, M. A., Rozemuller, A. J., Scheltens, P., & van der Flier, W. M. (2012). Cerebrospinal fluid markers for differential dementia diagnosis in a large memory clinic cohort. *Neurology*, *78*(1), 47–54. https://doi.org/10.1212/WNL.0b013e31823ed0f0.

9. Ahmed, R. M., Paterson, R. W., Warren, J. D., Zetterberg, H., O'Brien, J. T., Fox, N. C., Halliday, G. M., & Schott, J. M. (2014). Biomarkers in dementia: clinical utility and new directions. *Journal of Neurology, Neurosurgery & Psychiatry*, *85*(12), 1426–1434. https://doi.org/10.1136/jnnp-2014-307662.

10. Harper, L., Barkhof, F., Scheltens, P., Schott, J. M., & Fox, N. C. (2014). An algorithmic approach to structural imaging in dementia. *Journal of Neurology, Neurosurgery, and Psychiatry*, *85*(6), 692–698. https://doi.org/10.1136/jnnp-2013-306285.

11. Villemagne, V. L., & Rowe, C. C. (2017). Molecular brain imaging in dementia. In *Dementia* (pp. 139–154). Boca Raton, FL: CRC Press.

12. Kircher, M. F., & Willmann, J. K. (2012). Molecular body imaging: MR imaging, CT, and US. part I. principles. *Radiology*, *263*(3), 633–643. https://doi.org/10.1148/radiol.12102394.

13. Johnson, K. A., Fox, N. C., Sperling, R. A., & Klunk, W. E. (2012). Brain imaging in Alzheimer disease. *Cold Spring Harbor Perspectives in Medicine*, *2*(4), a006213–a006213. https://doi.org/10.1101/cshperspect.a006213.

14. Sharma, N., Kolekar, M. H., & Jha, K. (2020). Iterative filtering decomposition based early dementia diagnosis using EEG with cognitive tests. *IEEE Transactions on Neural Systems and Rehabilitation Engineering*, *28*(9), 1890–1898. https://doi.org/10.1109/tnsre.2020.3007860.

15. So, A., Hooshyar, D., Park, K., & Lim, H. (2017). Early diagnosis of dementia from clinical data by machine learning techniques. *Applied Sciences*, *7*(7), 651. https://doi.org/10.3390/app7070651.

16. Chagué, P., Marro, B., Fadili, S., Houot, M., Morin, A., Samper-González, J., Beunon, P., Arrivé, L., Dormont, D., Dubois, B., Teichmann, M., Epelbaum, S., & Colliot, O. (2021). Radiological classification of dementia from anatomical MRI assisted by machine learning-derived maps. *Journal of Neuroradiology*, *48*(6), 412–418. https://doi.org/10.1016/j.neurad.2020.04.004.

17. Shin, N.-Y., Bang, M., Yoo, S.-W., Kim, J.-S., Yun, E., Yoon, U., Han, K., Ahn, K. J., & Lee, S.-K. (2021). Cortical thickness from MRI to predict conversion from mild cognitive impairment to dementia in Parkinson disease: a machine learning–based model. *Radiology*, *300*(2), 390–399. https://doi.org/10.1148/radiol.2021203383.

18. Kim, J. P., Kim, J., Park, Y. H., Park, S. B., Lee, J. S., Yoo, S., Kim, E.-J., Kim, H. J., Na, D. L., Brown, J. A., Lockhart, S. N., Seo, S. W., & Seong, J.-K. (2019). Machine learning based hierarchical classification of frontotemporal dementia and Alzheimer's disease. *NeuroImage: Clinical*, *23*(2), 101811. https://doi.org/10.1016/j.nicl.2019.101811.

19. Xia, Y., Lu, S., Wen, L., Eberl, S., Fulham, M., & Feng, D. D. (2014). Automated identification of dementia using FDG-PET imaging. *BioMed Research International*, *2014*, 1–8. https://doi.org/10.1155/2014/421743.

20. Jo, T., Nho, K., Risacher, S. L., & Saykin, A. J. (2020). Deep learning detection of informative features in tau PET for Alzheimer's disease classification. *BMC Bioinformatics*, *21*(21), 1–13. https://doi.org/10.1186/s12859-020-03848-0.

21. Zhang, Y., Wang, S., Xia, K., Jiang, Y., & Qian, P. (2021). Alzheimer's disease multiclass diagnosis via multimodal neuroimaging embedding feature selection and fusion. *Information Fusion*, *66*, 170–183. https://doi.org/10.1016/j.inffus.2020.09.002.

22. Hao, X., Bao, Y., Guo, Y., Yu, M., Zhang, D., Risacher, S. L., Saykin, A. J., Yao, X., & Shen, L. (2020). Multi-modal neuroimaging feature selection with consistent metric constraint for diagnosis of Alzheimer's disease. *Medical Image Analysis*, *60*, 101625. https://doi.org/10.1016/j.media.2019.101625.

23. Lin, W., Lin, W., Chen, G., Zhang, H., Gao, Q., Huang, Y., Tong, T., & Du, M. (2021). Bidirectional mapping of brain MRI and PET with 3D reversible GAN for the diagnosis of Alzheimer's disease. *Frontiers in Neuroscience*, *15*, 646013. https:// doi.org/10.3389/fnins.2021.646013.

24. Fang, X., Liu, Z., & Xu, M. (2020). Ensemble of deep convolutional neural networks based multi-modality images for Alzheimer's disease diagnosis. *IET Image Processing*, *14*(2), 318–326. https://doi.org/10.1049/iet-ipr.2019.0617.

25. Kim, J., & Lee, B. (2018). Identification of Alzheimer's disease and mild cognitive impairment using multimodal sparse hierarchical extreme learning machine. *Human Brain Mapping*, *39*(9), 3728–3741. https://doi.org/10.1002/hbm.24207.

26. Ferri, R., Babiloni, C., Karami, V., Triggiani, A. I., Carducci, F., Noce, G., Lizio, R., Pascarelli, M. T., Soricelli, A., Amenta, F., Bozzao, A., Romano, A., Giubilei, F., Del Percio, C., Stocchi, F., Frisoni, G. B., Nobili, F., Patanè, L., & Arena, P. (2021). Stacked autoencoders as new models for an accurate Alzheimer's disease classification support using resting-state EEG and MRI measurements. *Clinical Neurophysiology*, *132*(1), 232–245. https://doi.org/10.1016/j.clinph.2020.09.015.

27. Lebedev, A. V., Westman, E., Beyer, M. K., Kramberger, M. G., Aguilar, C., Pirtosek, Z., & Aarsland, D. (2012). Multivariate classification of patients with Alzheimer's and dementia with Lewy bodies using high-dimensional cortical thickness measurements: an MRI surface-based morphometric study. *Journal of Neurology*, *260*(4), 1104–1115. https://doi.org/10.1007/s00415-012-6768-z.

28. Sørensen, L., Pai, A., Anker, C., Balas, I., Lillholm, M., Igel, C., & Nielsen, M. (2014). Dementia diagnosis using MRI cortical thickness, shape, texture, and volumetry. In *Proc MICCAI Workshop Challenge on Computer-aided Diagnosis of Dementia Based on Structural MRI Data* (pp. 111–118). Berkshire: University of Reading.

29. Costafreda, S. G., Dinov, I. D., Tu, Z., Shi, Y., Liu, C.-Y., Kloszewska, I., Mecocci, P., Soininen, H., Tsolaki, M., Vellas, B., Wahlund, L.-O., Spenger, C., Toga, A. W., Lovestone, S., & Simmons, A. (2011). Automated hippocampal shape analysis predicts the onset of dementia in mild cognitive impairment. *NeuroImage*, *56*(1), 212–219. https://doi.org/10.1016/j.neuroimage.2011.01.050.

30. Achterberg, H. C., van der Lijn, F., den Heijer, T., Vernooij, M. W., Ikram, M. A., Niessen, W. J., & de Bruijne, M. (2013). Hippocampal shape is predictive for the development of dementia in a normal, elderly population. *Human Brain Mapping*, *35*(5), 2359–2371. https://doi.org/10.1002/hbm.22333.

31. Lebedeva, A. K., Westman, E., Borza, T., Beyer, M. K., Engedal, K., Aarsland, D., Selbaek, G., & Haberg, A. K. (2017). MRI-based classification models in prediction of mild cognitive impairment and dementia in late-life depression. *Frontiers in Aging Neuroscience*, *9*, 13. https://doi.org/10.3389/fnagi.2017.00013.

32. Tong, T., Wolz, R., Gao, Q., Guerrero, R., Hajnal, J. V., & Rueckert, D. (2014). Multiple instance learning for classification of dementia in brain MRI. *Medical Image Analysis*, *18*(5), 808–818. https://doi.org/10.1016/j.media.2014.04.006.

33. Bron, E. E., Smits, M., Niessen, W. J., & Klein, S. (2015). Feature selection based on the SVM weight vector for classification of dementia. *IEEE Journal of Biomedical and Health Informatics*, *19*(5), 1617–1626. https://doi.org/10.1109/jbhi.2015.2432832.

34. Weissleder, R., & Mahmood, U. (2001). Molecular Imaging. *Radiology*, *219*(2), 316–333. https://doi.org/10.1148/radiology.219.2.r01ma19316.

35. Iizuka, T., Fukasawa, M., & Kameyama, M. (2019). Deep-learning-based imaging-classification identified cingulate island sign in dementia with Lewy bodies. *Scientific Reports*, *9*(1). https://doi.org/10.1038/s41598-019-45415-5.

36. Nemoto, K., Sakaguchi, H., Kasai, W., Hotta, M., Kamei, R., Noguchi, T., Minamimoto, R., Arai, T., & Asada, T. (2021). Differentiating dementia with Lewy bodies and Alzheimer's disease by deep learning to structural MRI. *Journal of Neuroimaging*, *31*(3), 579–587. https://doi.org/10.1111/jon.12835.

37. Jain, R., Jain, N., Aggarwal, A., & Hemanth, D. J. (2019). Convolutional neural network based Alzheimer's disease classification from magnetic resonance brain images. *Cognitive Systems Research*, *57*, 147–159. https://doi.org/10.1016/j.cogsys.2018.12.015.

38. Hirsch, G. V., Bauer, C. M., & Merabet, L. B. (2015). Using structural and functional brain imaging to uncover how the brain adapts to blindness. *Annals of Neuroscience and Psychology*, *2*, 5. https://www.ncbi.nlm.nih.gov/pmc/articles/PMC6168211/.

39. Gao, X. W., Hui, R., & Tian, Z. (2017). Classification of CT brain images based on deep learning networks. *Computer Methods and Programs in Biomedicine*, *138*, 49–56. https://doi.org/10.1016/j.cmpb.2016.10.007.

40. De, A., & Chowdhury, A. S. (2021). DTI based Alzheimer's disease classification with rank modulated fusion of CNNs and random forest. *Expert Systems with Applications*, *169*, 114338. https://doi.org/10.1016/j.eswa.2020.114338.

41. Torso, M., Bozzali, M., Cercignani, M., Jenkinson, M., & Chance, S. A. (2020). Using diffusion tensor imaging to detect cortical changes in fronto-temporal dementia subtypes. *Scientific Reports*, *10*(1), 1–11. https://doi.org/10.1038/s41598-020-68118-8.

42. Garcia, E. V. (2011). Physical attributes, limitations, and future potential for PET and SPECT. *Journal of Nuclear Cardiology*, *19*(S1), 19–29. https://doi.org/10.1007/s12350-011-9488-3.

43. Landau, S. M., Thomas, B. A., Thurfjell, L., Schmidt, M., Margolin, R., Mintun, M., Pontecorvo, M., Baker, S. L., & Jagust, W. J. (2014). Amyloid PET imaging in Alzheimer's disease: a comparison of three radiotracers. *European Journal of Nuclear Medicine and Molecular Imaging*, *41*(7), 1398–1407. https://doi.org/10.1007/s00259-014-2753-3.

44. Okamura, N., Harada, R., Furumoto, S., Arai, H., Yanai, K., & Kudo, Y. (2014). Tau PET imaging in Alzheimer's disease. *Current Neurology and Neuroscience Reports*, *14*(11). https://doi.org/10.1007/s11910-014-0500-6.

45. Mosconi, L., Berti, V., Glodzik, L., Pupi, A., De Santi, S., & de Leon, M. J. (2010). Pre-clinical detection of Alzheimer's disease using FDG-PET, with or without amyloid imaging. *Journal of Alzheimer's Disease*, *20*(3), 843–854. https://doi.org/10.3233/jad-2010-091504.

46. Mathotaarachchi, S., Pascoal, T. A., Shin, M., Benedet, A. L., Kang, M. S., Beaudry, T., Fonov, V. S., Gauthier, S., & Rosa-Neto, P. (2017). Identifying incipient dementia individuals using machine learning and amyloid imaging. *Neurobiology of Aging*, *59*, 80–90. https://doi.org/10.1016/j.neurobiolaging.2017.06.027.

47. Zukotynski, K., Gaudet, V., Kuo, P. H., Adamo, S., Goubran, M., Scott, C., Bocti, C., Borrie, M., Chertkow, H., Frayne, R., Hsiung, R., Laforce, R. J., Noseworthy, M. D., Prato, F. S., Sahlas, D. J., Smith, E. E., Sossi, V., Thiel, A., Soucy, J.-P., & Tardif, J.-C. (2019). The use of random forests to classify amyloid brain PET. *Clinical Nuclear Medicine*, *44*(10), 784–788. https://doi.org/10.1097/RLU.0000000000002747.

48. Zou, J., Park, D., Johnson, A., Feng, X., Pardo, M., France, J., Tomljanovic, Z., Brickman, A. M., Devanand, D. P., Luchsinger, J. A., Kreisl, W. C., & Provenzano, F. A. (2021). Deep learning improves utility of tau PET in the study of Alzheimer's disease. *Alzheimer's & Dementia: Diagnosis, Assessment & Disease Monitoring*, *13*(1), e12264. https://doi.org/10.1002/dad2.12264.

49. Singh, S., Srivastava, A., Mi, L., Caselli, R. J., Chen, K., Goradia, D., Reiman, E. M., & Wang, Y. (2017). Deep learning based classification of FDG-PET data for Alzheimers disease categories. *Proceedings of SPIE--the International Society for Optical Engineering, 10572*, 105720J. https://doi.org/10.1117/12.2294537.

50. Yee, E., Popuri, K., Beg, M. F., & Alzheimer's Disease Neuroimaging Initiative. (2020). Quantifying brain metabolism from FDG-PET images into a probability of Alzheimer's dementia score. *Human Brain Mapping, 41*(1), 5–16. https://doi.org/10.1002/hbm.24783.

51. Kong, Z., Zhang, M., Zhu, W., Yi, Y., Wang, T., & Zhang, B. (2022). Multi-modal data Alzheimer's disease detection based on 3D convolution. *Biomedical Signal Processing and Control, 75*, 103565. https://doi.org/10.1016/j.bspc.2022.103565.

52. Song, J., Zheng, J., Li, P., Lu, X., Zhu, G., & Shen, P. (2021). An effective multimodal image fusion method using MRI and PET for Alzheimer's disease diagnosis. *Frontiers in Digital Health, 3*, 637386. https://doi.org/10.3389/fdgth.2021.637386.

53. Choi, H., & Jin, K. H. (2018). Predicting cognitive decline with deep learning of brain metabolism and amyloid imaging. *Behavioural Brain Research, 344*, 103–109. https://doi.org/10.1016/j.bbr.2018.02.017.

54. Vu, T. D., Yang, H.-J., Nguyen, V. Q., Oh, A-Ran., & Kim, M.-S. (2017, February 1). Multimodal learning using convolution neural network and sparse autoencoder. In *2017 IEEE International Conference on Big Data and Smart Computing (BigComp)*, IEEE Xplore, Jeju, Korea (South), 309–312. https://doi.org/10.1109/BIGCOMP.2017.7881683.

55. Huang, Y., Xu, J., Zhou, Y., Tong, T., & Zhuang, X. (2019). Diagnosis of Alzheimer's disease via multi-modality 3D convolutional neural network. *Frontiers in Neuroscience, 13*, 509. https://doi.org/10.3389/fnins.2019.00509.

56. Jack, C. R., Bernstein, M. A., Fox, N. C., Thompson, P., Alexander, G., Harvey, D., Borowski, B., Britson, P. J., L. Whitwell, J., Ward, C., Dale, A. M., Felmlee, J. P., Gunter, J. L., Hill, D. L. G., Killiany, R., Schuff, N., Fox-Bosetti, S., Lin, C., Studholme, C., & DeCarli, C. S. (2008). The Alzheimer's disease neuroimaging initiative (ADNI): MRI methods. *Journal of Magnetic Resonance Imaging, 27*(4), 685–691. https://doi.org/10.1002/jmri.21049.

57. Jagust, W. J., Landau, S. M., Koeppe, R. A., Reiman, E. M., Chen, K., Mathis, C. A., Price, J. C., Foster, N. L., & Wang, A. Y. (2015). The Alzheimer's disease neuroimaging initiative 2 PET core: 2015. *Alzheimer's & Dementia, 11*(7), 757–771. https://doi.org/10.1016/j.jalz.2015.05.001.

58. Jenkinson, M., Beckmann, C. F., Behrens, T. E. J., Woolrich, M. W., & Smith, S. M. (2012). FSL. *NeuroImage, 62*(2), 782–790. https://doi.org/10.1016/j.neuroimage.2011.09.015

59. Jenkinson, M. (2005). BET2: MR-based estimation of brain, skull and scalp surfaces. *Eleventh Annual Meeting of the Organization for Human Brain Mapping, 17*(3), 167. https://ci.nii.ac.jp/naid/10030066593/en/.

60. Yiğit, A., Baştanlar, Y., & Işık, Z. (2022). Dementia diagnosis by ensemble deep neural networks using FDG-PET scans. *Signal, Image and Video Processing, 16*, 2203–2210. https://doi.org/10.1007/s11760-022-02185-4.

61. Tekir, S., Baştanlar, Y. (2020). Deep learning: exemplar studies in natural language processing and computer vision. In *Data Mining: Methods, Applications and Systems*. London: InTechOpen Press. https://doi.org/10.5772/intechopen.91813

13 The Importance of the Internet of Things in Neurological Disorder
A Literature Review

Pelin Alcan
Istanbul Okan University

CONTENTS

13.1 INTRODUCTION

Looking at the last 30 years, it is known that the rise of the internet has affected the world very much. Only in the last 15 years, with the increasing processing power and connectivity of electronics, "smart" devices have entered our lives.It is known that the market for IoT devices has reached $3.04 trillion in 2020. This cost seems to increase exponentially (Haghi et al., 2017; Wei, 2014). In the century we live in, healthcare systems stand out with the availability of high-performance computing tools that process abundant biomedical data. The abundance of data and the overdevelopment of computer frameworks bring together chances and threats for investigators and healthcare professionals (Valliani et al., 2020).

Deep learning techniques are a subtitle of presentment learning approaches that create nonlinear functions to translate raw information into more complex dimensions (LeCun et al., 2015). Deep learning approaches are required in different engineering inventions such as self-driving cars, face recognition, and language translations (Valliani et al., 2020). Deep learning tools appear particularly well in neuroscience applications that rely on complex neuroimaging modalities.

IoT represents a network that can gather and transfer information using sensors and communication reports (Meola, 2016). Researchers expect the global

IoT market to grow from $212 billion in 2019 to $1.6 trillion by 2025. In addition, health, insurance, and education are shown as leading areas in IoT spending.

IoT is a system that provides a connection to every object in the physical space. One of its most important features is that it extends the connection not only to computers and mobile tools, but also to everyday devices. IoT creates opportunities in different fields from connected refrigerators, wearables, cars, and cities (Elkhodr et al., 2016). It connects people to the " Internet of things" with wearables, smartwatches, and fitness trackers, or via smart glasses and virtual reality headsets. Example applications of IoT can be shown as in Figure 13.1.

It is seen that the vast majority of 1billionpeople worldwide are affected by epilepsy disease and Alzheimer's disease. Neurological diseases can deeply shake a person's way of life. It is stated that 1million people in the USA are living with Parkinson's disease (Parkinson's Disease Foundation report). In Europe, there are

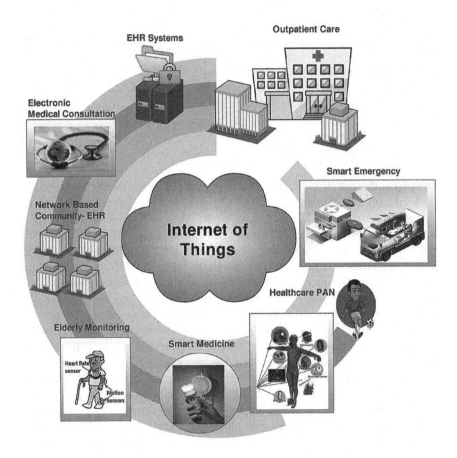

FIGURE 13.1   IoT-based healthcare system application examples (Elkhodr et al., 2016).

1.2 millionpeople with Parkinson's disease. The progression of Parkinson's disorder can be slowed down with stem cell therapy. Although the cause of the disease is still unknown, there are some treatment alternatives, including surgery and medication, to control its indications. Early diagnosis of Alzheimer's, epilepsy, Parkinson's, and most neurological disorders is crucial for patients to lead a better life (Chiuchisan and Geman, 2014).

Research and progresses in information and communication technologies have led to the improvement of many recent technologies and smart tolls that can be utilized in the space of healthcare systems. As computer-based patient monitoring systems advance to assist remote monitoring along with medicinal activities, doctors and medical workers interact with computer networks and utilize special implementations to provide higher standard healthcare services.

As a result of the developments in technology, different healthcare implementations simplify the information exchange between doctors – individuals or corporations, while reducing expenditures. They also expand the scope and reach of medical facilities and improve the quality of services. Today's medical tools are powered by microcontrollers, sensors, mobile communication devices, nanopumps, and much more to enable individuals, doctors, or other medical professionals to make patient tracing and treatment more personalized (Chiuchisan and Geman, 2014). The purpose of this chapter is to summarize the most basic implementations of IoT in neurology and to shed light on the articles written on these subjects. You can see the organization of this section in Figure 13.2.

Thanks to great advances in technology in recent years, scientists are able to simultaneously obtain data fromvarious levels of a lifetime system, while also simulating large-scale brain networks. Of course, one of the fields that contributed the most to this big data is neuroscience (Mahmud et al., 2018).

Today's neuroscience research is managed and guided by data. The information extracted from these information allows the improvement and refinement of data-intensive models, while also providing a better description of underlying biological events. Information analytics and modeling stages are very important and advances in artificial intelligence have made these steps work smoothly (Luo et al., 2016; Hashem et al., 2015). This research progresses from the concepts between the internet of things and neurology and shows the studies on these issues.

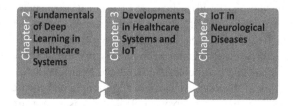

FIGURE 13.2 Overall organization of this chapter.

13.2 FUNDAMENTALS OF DEEP LEARNING IN HEALTHCARE SYSTEMS

Traditional machine learning algorithms are often utilized in the classification and processing of biomedical information. In recent years, the use of a multi-layered learning network has become mandatory due to the rise in the amount of information. Deep learning encompasses all the application parts that distinguish the subclasses with quite good performance, primarily due to the presence of multi-dimensional information and inadequate human judgment operations. These techniques have the feature of examining the interdepartmental interactions of the information in depth and completely. Deep learning is better than traditional machine learning techniques because it learns using high-dimensional observational data.In deep learning, it is inspired by the working structure of the human brain, which shows a multi-layered learning style (Uyulan et al., 2019).

DL techniques are similar in structure to artificial neural network (ANN). A deep neural network (DNN) often consists of three layers such as an input layer, hidden layer, and an output layer. Convolutional neural networks (CNNs) have become especially important in imaging-based medical research. CNNs consist of convolutional layers from which data properties are learned (Saba et al., 2019). Deep learning (DL) has been successfully used to solve disease diagnostic problems. In deep learning, there is no need to extract features separately. DL techniques can also be utilized to analyzes a different problem such as natural language processing systems, drug discovery, and robotic processes (Gautam and Sharma, 2020).

Çevik and Kilimci (2021) evaluated the emotion analysis of people about Parkinson's disease by using deep learning and word placement models in their article. This study is the first to investigate this disease with the help of word placement models and deep learning methods through social media. In their article, Uyulan et al. (2019) gave a general description of deep learning structures utilized in biomedicine and neuroscience and showed the implementations of these structures on EEG-based analytical tasks and the potential complexities encountered.

Over the last decade, deep learning has also been tried in medical applications and has worked better than many varied techniques. In different fields of neuroscience, deep learning algorithms have demonstrated their importance in aiding the anatomical segmentation of brain architectures. It has shown good results in areas such as the identification of brain lesions such as tumors and image-based estimation of different neurological disorders. Although deep learning has different successes, the superiority of this subject in the diagnosis of neurological diseases has not been clearly presented yet. Looking at the literature, it is seen that no special studies have been conducted for the diagnosis of neurological disorders such as Alzheimer's, cerebrovascular diseases, Parkinson's, cerebral palsy, epilepsy, multiple sclerosis, migraine, and autism through DL.

13.3   DEVELOPMENTS IN HEALTHCARE SYSTEMS AND IoT

Progresses in technologies have led to the occurrence of a paradigm called e-Health for healthcare and the integration of network systems into medical procedures. In the century we live in, the connection between engineering and medicine has gotten a little closer, and mechanical parts have been improved to replace missing human parts. In addition, micro tools were utilized as miniature cameras, implants, and real-time systems for the home were also created. Intelligent systems are used in the follow-up of patients in order to automatically process medicinal information and assist medicinal resolutions.

The main goal of combining IoT with the healthcare industry is to improve health and medicinal activity delivery. Thus, more patients can be saved. Remote healthcare tracing activities, smart home systems, smart water and transport systems are some of the other areas to be developed with IoT applications (Atzori et al., 2010).

The healthcare and communications technology industry has growth potential. The IoT suggests many advantages that develop healthcare and processes. IoT addresses the health needs of a society rather than individuals. Ultimately, it helps healthcare services at large by promoting applications that decrease the influences of illness, invalidity, and incidental injury. Also, consolidating health practices with other fields of IoT offers an approach that promotes sustained health systems (Boulos and Al-Shorbaji, 2014). As Shrimali (2020) points out in Figure 13.3, the adoption of IoT has revolutionized the healthcare industry as it has multiple implementations, from remote monitoring systems to medical tolls integration.

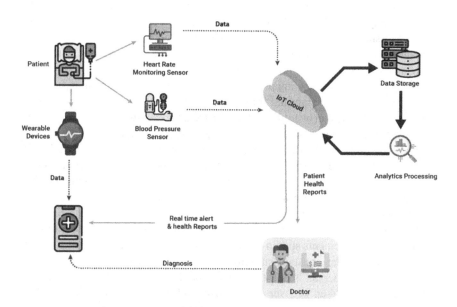

FIGURE 13.3   IoT and healthcare industry (Shrimali, 2020).

In the healthcare field, disease prevention is as important as providing treatment to people (Fries et al., 1998). IoT creates an opportunity to protect sustainable concepts and spaces for a healthier living space.As seen from research, IoT is also about reducing the harmful effects of global warming on the healthcare of the human population (Elkhodr et al., 2016). It is crucial for healthcare services to combine sustainability basis such as energy resources, water efficiency, and global harmony into their organizations.

Considering the implementations of IoT in healthcare, monitoring, and delivery of medicines are among the applications in this field (Laranjo et al., 2012). With the use of IoT, the field of drug is becoming more productive. Today, people can learn and share more efficient information about diseases and treatments (Elkhodr et al., 2016). IoT significantly helps people to learn medical information in real time and early diagnosis of illnesses (Zhao et al., 2011). Thus, individuals can get rid of contact with a disease or seek treatment for their disease as early as possible. With IoT health applications, significant health records of individuals can be kept. This information is defined as Electronic Health Records (EHR) (Kalra and Ingram, 2006). The combination of IoT with the EHR system will develop login to healthcare information and better sharing betweenvaried organizations.

The use of IoT in healthcare will develop remote healthcare tracing processes. Remote healthcare monitoring technologies create some resolutions for tracing individuals at house. All these technologies purpose to provide better care and decrease the expenses on individuals without reducing the quality of health processes provided (Elkhodr et al., 2016). With the help of a remote monitoring system, an individual's biomedical signals during their daily activities can be measured anywhere. This technology helps to bring together signals about people's organisms, such as heart rate, from a distance with the help of the Internet. In addition, this system has great benefits related to the improvement of maintenance and service quality (Elkhodr et al., 2011).

An IoT-based remote tracing process can recognize a change in an individual's body and monitor their staminal functions. It is very sufficient that the data collected by this system can be found on the internet and that this data can be accessed instantly from various systems and organizations (Baig and Gholamhosseini, 2013). When there is a medical emergency, the system is created to warn health professionals, emergency services, and relatives. In addition, the system provides information about the health status of an observed sick person, allowing needed assistance to be provided immediately (Elkhodr et al., 2016).

IoT services can help monitor, diagnose, and treat diseases. These diseases are frequently listed as diabetes, cancer, lung diseases and heart diseases. In such diseases, body movements should be constantly monitored. Therefore, the patient should be kept under constant surveillance. Medical doctors and health workers ensure that the person is constantly monitored. Unfortunately, as anyone can guess, patient follow-up is a very costly task and is often not as effective as it should be (Pang et al., 2015). Healthcare professionals may not be able to monitor a patient continuously among dozens of jobs. Body sensor networks (BSNs) improves patient monitoring by integrating with IoT healthcare systems. This system monitors the body functions of the person using a chip or wearable wireless biosensor devices (Savola et al., 2012).

This chip monitors the vital functions of the person. If there is a change in the patient's body functions, it detects this and reports it to the IoT system. IoT is a system that can perform important activities such as alerting a healthcare worker. When an emergency occurs, an ambulance crew can also be alerted for assistance, depending on how the system is designed. IoT health monitoring systems aim to provide a platform for patients and elderly individuals to monitor and assist them remotely, whether at home or away from home. In this way, it can be said that these systems are an environmental intelligence environment (Elkhodr et al., 2016). Electronic Health Records become digitally accessible with the help of IoT. Thus, with the help of remote monitoring systems, medical errors will be reduced (Scurlock and D'Ambrosio, 2015). If IoT applications in healthcare are examined, personal area networks (PANs) will also be seen (Neuhaeuser and D'Angelo, 2013). With the help of a PAN, people will be able to track their body functions using technologies such as wearable smart sensors and smart wrist devices. As technology advances, wearable technologies in healthcare will also advance (Vermesan and Friess, 2013).

13.4 IoT IN NEUROLOGICAL DISEASES

It is important to support medical decisions that assist medical professionals in disease prevention, treatment, health tracing, diagnosis using health portals, health data networks, telehealth processes, e-health records, personal wearable and portable infectious systems, and a great deal of ICT-based technologies and implementations. The flow of information between an individual with neurological disorders such as Alzheimer's disease, epilepsy, Parkinson's disease and doctors is complicated and quite challenging.

The figure below presents a home monitoring system that monitors Parkinson's patients with the help of a web-based application and wireless sensors. Figure 13.4 shows a web application from Patel et al.'s article that facilitates patient–physician interaction to access sensor data (Patel et al., 2010).

Now, with the concept of IoT, many sensors can be tied to the cloud systems for seamless resource sharing. Cyber Physical Systems provides a frame for information-driven survey while designing optimal medical services for individuals. Today's neuroscience research is based on data. Neuroscience research generates in large quantities of information, and it is very inconvenient to examine this information. With the knowledge that emerges from all these data,the underlying biological events are identified and the experimental design is facilitated (Mahmud et al., 2018).

Considering the computational intensity of data analytics and modeling stages, these steps can be carried out without any problems thanks to the developments in cloud computing. As Luo et al. (2016) and Hashem et al. (2015) say, big data paradigms and cloud computing have transformed context-sensitive work into information-driven search.

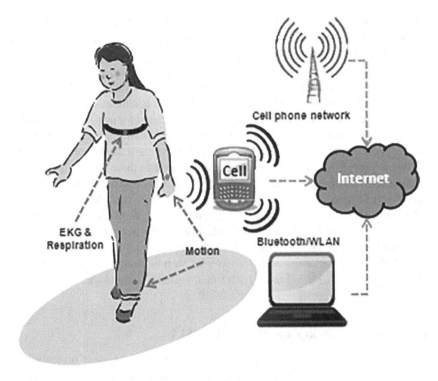

FIGURE 13.4 General home monitoring scenario (Patel et al., 2010).

Neuroscience data is quite different from other data and has high variability. Neuroscience data are often notorious for their variability (e.g., EEG and LFPs). Misidentification and misinterpretation can occur where signals are received unsupervised without an expert (Mahmud et al., 2018). At this point, Mahmud et al. (2012) presented a service-oriented architecture for web-based collaborative biomedical signal analysis. This model, which has three main ingredients: user persons, contributors, and services, assumes the inherent security of the internet and uses a certificate-based security as the authentication scheme.

Mahmud et al. (2018) present an Adaptive Neuro-Fuzzy based TMM (trust management model) that provides reliable information transfer among E2E (end-to-end) instruments and targets cloud-based IoT architecture. This article also examines the effects of cloud-based IoT architecture convenient for neuroscience implementations on QoS (quality of service) issues.

Vergara et al. (2017) investigated some important issues such as the detection of seizures of a neurological disease such as epilepsy and the monitoring of the patient. In epilepsy, there is sudden and uncontrolled discharge of neurons in the cerebrum. As a result, involuntary contractions, some sensory changes, and differences in consciousness are seen in the patient. Epilepsy occurs with seizures. It is thought that there are 65 million people affected by epilepsy in the world.

This disease also has detrimental effects on the patient's quality of life and on their professional or social progress. Vergara et al. (2017) found that many of these approaches do not have proper integration with ergonomics and the healthcare system. They then delved into the basic elements that an epileptic invention and monitoring tool should fulfill. In doing so, they also described the system required for a particular epilepsy invention and tracing platform.

With the help of sensors and IoT technologies, the health status of Alzheimer's patients can also be monitored. These technologies track the condition of targeted individuals at home or outside. Appropriate treatment is very important for Alzheimer's patients. Oskouei et al. (2020) focused on Alzheimer's disease, which is the most widespread neurological disease of the pastyears. Alzheimer's is a widespreadtype of dementia, a progressive neurological illness that causes the devastation of cerebrum parts. Symptoms of this disorder, which causes deterioration in thinking, memory, and behavior, appear with age. In Alzheimer's disease, the person cannot carry out daily tasks independently, and there must always be a person in the family who will take care of this person's behavior and health. For all these reasons, it is very costly for families of Alzheimer's patients to hire a nurse and maintain this patient's care. However, using IoT, the behavior and health situation of these individuals can be easily monitored remotely and intervened in a timely manner. By placing dissimilar parts of smart watches, actuators, and sensors in the homes of the individuals, data about the patients' temperatures, medication intake timings, and movements can be collected.

Figure 13.5 shows the general system of the IoT. The term IoT was first coined by Kevin Ashton in 1998 and has since become an area of interest for many universities and industries.

An individual remote control system using the IoT is seen in Figure 13.6.

Oskouei et al. (2020) explained in their study that necessary information will be gathered fromvarious sensors installed in patients' houses and smart watches to control blood pressure levels and temperatures, which is very sufficient for Alzheimer's patients in the pandemic of Covid-19 disease. Communication protocols such as WebSocket and Message Queue Telemetry Transport (MQTT) have been implemented for sensors and smart watch. The secure backend admin panel is utilized to monitor the whereabouts of healthcare professionals, individuals, and vehicles such as ambulances. All these protocols also protect the privacy of patients.

Epilepsy is a chronic and recurrent illness. Unfortunately, the treatment period is also very long. Unfortunately, a very important part of the patients cannot fully control their attacks even after 3 years of treatment. Conventional treatment can cause mental and psychological disorders, especially depression. Zhang et al. (2021) proposed a clinical trial based on the IoT electronic medical neuroelectrical stimulation in order to improve the condition of patients with epilepsy as soon as possible and to treat their anxiety and depression. McHale and Pereira (2021) examined the future of personalization in epilepsy in their article. That is, they focused on the essence of the individual characteristics of epilepsy patients fromone size to another. The personalized healthcare approach is facilitated by

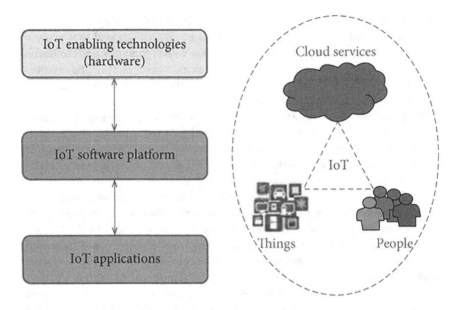

FIGURE 13.5   Architecture of the IoT (Oskouei et al., 2020).

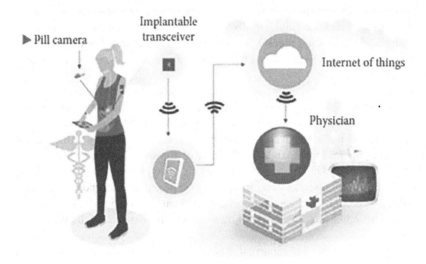

FIGURE 13.6   Telecommunications of individual care process utilizing IoT (Oskouei et al., 2020).

the IoT. Sensor-based IoT devices are of interest in the need for continuous patient monitoring. In epilepsy, patients of various types should be followed exactly according to their identified key symptoms and their treatment should be elaborated. This article demonstrates an IoT-based epilepsy monitoring system that supports a more accurate way of monitoring individual epilepsy patients remotely.

Dementia affected more than 46 million people worldwide in 2018. It was said that there were about 850,000 dementia patients in the UK in the same year. Unfortunately, this number is estimated to reach 1 million by 2025. Enshaeifar et al. (2018) discussed a technical design in the UK called Technology Integrated Healthcare Management (TIHM) for dementia care in their article. TIHM uses the concept of IoT provided by different firms. This project brought together a team of healthcare professionals, businesses with IoT products, and academic groups. Machine learning and data analysis algorithms generate notifications for the well-being of patients. The data is monitored throughout the day by health professionals who make appropriate decisions based on the data collected. Enshaeifar et al. (2018), while discussing the technical design of TIHM, also explained why human practice should be an complementary element of technological design.

One of the most common neurological disorders in young adults is multiple sclerosis (MS). This disorder occurs in the spinal cord, which provides information communication between the central nervous system and organs, which occurs as a result of physical destruction. The prevalence of gait disturbance (pwMS) in people with MS is thought to be between 41% and 75%. Sparaco et al. (2018) investigated different motion sensors embedded in smartphones and wearable mobile devices (MWD) to measure the walking behavior of MS patients, as well as to assess their falls, fatigue, exercise, and sleep quality (Sparaco et al., 2018).

Talboom et al. (2018) summarized last biomedical study utilizing IoT and wearable devices in the field of neurological features and disease. In addition, they also examined where biomedical studies will advance in the future using IoT devices and wearable devices. Wearable devices contain sensors to be able to connect to other devices and collect data. Wearable devices have a screen to access real-time information. In addition, wearable devices can send information to the other instrument or to the cloud to offload heavy information examination. Information entry capability and local storage preferences can frequently be unite into wearable devices. Nowadays, many tools/devices store most of their data in the cloud (Wei, 2014). In recent years, widespread use of commercial IoT devices and wearable devices has been observed. For example, respiration, heart rate, brain waves, diet, exercise status, sleep status, location data, and habits can be gathered from IoT devices and wearable end users. The collected data can be combined with fitness data and diet to define patients from a very large sample for heart and metabolic diseases. With the use of commercial IoT wearables in scientific studies, workgroups can be greatly expanded at minimal cost (Talboom, 2018).

The most important aspects of stroke unit treatment are heart rate (HR) monitoring and maintaining a normal heart rate. Tracing of electrical activity in the cerebrum/brain, recognized as electroencephalography (EEG), is a diagnostic method in stroke. Almarzouki et al. (2021) tested the designed glove wearable device that can examine HR and EEG in their study. Sciarron et al. (2021) demonstrated a prototype of wearable smart glasses that track blinks (EBs) to the end user via the electrooculogram (EOG) signal. The great advantage of such solutions is that the application follows an entirely understandable road to continually trace the characteristic symptoms of neurological disorders. In this application, the frame around the glasses is equipped with sensors to make the device smart. Thus, the aim is to solve the issue of initial invention of neurological symptoms by using IoT wearable technology. Stroke is an important disease that puts the health of middle-aged and elderly people at great risk. As a result of the implementation of IoT technology in home health monitoring and telemedicine, early identification of ischemic stroke is ensured. Thus, preventive medical services are provided for individuals at high risk of stroke. Li et al. (2021), while clarifying the network architecture of the rehabilitation process and the IoT, also present an overall system structure based on intelligent medical care. This article develops and implements cloud computing while summarizing how to implement and advantages of the IoT in the medical care of stroke disease.

IoT devices for remote monitoring, diagnosis, and treatment hold promise for medicine, as in many other subjects, including bipolar disorder and other mental illnesses. It is thought that IoT devices can help detect emotional reactions, moods, and cognitive abilities in the coming years. There are some risks arising from the interconnection between IoT devices and patients, healthcare providers, and device manufacturers. Monteith et al.'s (2021) papers also show some of the key issues with the development of IoT devices.

13.5 CONCLUSIONS AND FUTURE SCOPE

Health is one of the most important parts of countries and indeed society. Healthcare technology covers many systems such as remote patient monitoring systems, electronic health, and home care services. When health technologies are examined one by one in this way, it is seen that IoT offers many opportunities that improve health services and operations. As a result of combining health applications with IoT applications, the understanding of sustainability enters health services. Disease prevention is as important as providing medical treatment. IoT plays an crucial part in the field of neurology and in the study of neurological diseases, as in many other health fields. In the past years, neurological diseases have been at the forefront more than all other diseases. The goal of this chapter is to show the most primary implementations of IoT in neurology and to summarize the different studies on this subject. The future scope of this section will be primarily to explore where deep learning and IoT techniques are more applied in neuroscience.

REFERENCES

Almarzouki, H Z., Alsulami, H., Rizwan, A., Basingab, M.S., Bukhari, H., & Shabaz, M. An internet of medical things-based model for real-time monitoring and averting stroke sensors, *Journal of Healthcare Engineering*, 2021, *2021*, 9, Article ID: 1233166. Doi: https://doi.org/10.1155/2021/1233166.
Atzori, L., Iera, A., & Morabito, G. The internet of things: A survey, *Computer Networks*, 2010, *54*, 15, 2787–2805. doi: 10.1016/j.comnet.2010.05.010.

Baig, M., & Gholamhosseini, H. Smart health monitoring systems: An overview of design and modeling, *Journal of Medical Systems*, 2013, *37*, 2, 1–14, PMID:23321968. doi: 10.1007/s10916-012 9898-z.

Boulos, M. N. K., & Al-Shorbaji, N. M. On the internet of things, smart cities and the WHO healthy cities, *International Journal of Health Geographics*, 2014, *13*, 10, PMID: 24669838.

Chiuchisan, I. & Geman, O. An approach of a decision support and home monitoring system for patients with neurological disorders using internet of things concepts, *WSEAS Transactions on Systems*, 2014, *13*, 460–469, E-ISSN: 2224–2678.

Çevik, F. & Kilimci, Z.H. The evaluation of Parkinson's disease with sentiment analysis using deep learning methods and word embedding models, *Pamukkale University Journal of Engineering Sciences*, 2021, *27*, 2, 151–161.

Elkhodr, M., Shahrestani, S., & Cheung, H. Internet of things applications: Current and future development. In: *Innovative Research and Applications in Next-Generation High Performance Computing*, Qusay F. Hassan (ed.), 2016. Doi: 10.4018/978-1-5225-0287-6.ch016

Elkhodr, M., Shahrestani, S., & Cheung, H. An approach to enhance the security of remote health monitoring systems. In: *4th International Conference on Security of Information and Networks*, Sydney, Australia, 2011. doi: 10.1145/2070425. 2070458.

Enshaeifar, S., Barnaghi, P., Skillman, S., Markides, A., Elsaleh, T., Acton, T., Nilforooshan, R., & Rostil, H. Internet of things for dementia care, *IEEE Internet Computing*, 2018, *22*, 8–17. Doi: 10.1109/MIC.2018.112102418.

Fries, J. F., Koop, C. E., Sokolov, J., Beadle, C. E., & Wright, D. Beyond health promotion: Reducing need and demand for medical care. *Health Affairs*, 1998, *17*, 2, 70–84, PMID: 9558786. Doi: 10.1377/hlthaff.17.2.70.

Gautam, R. & Sharma, M. Prevalence and diagnosis of neurological disorders using different deep learning techniques: A meta-analysis, *Journal of Medical Systems*, 2020, *44*, 2, 49. Doi: https://doi.org/10.1007/s10916-019-1519-7.

Haghi, M., Thurow, K. & Stoll, R. Wearable devices in medical internet of things, scientific research and commercially available devices, *Healthcare Informatics Research*, 2017, *23*, 4–15.

Hashem, I. AT, Yaqoob, I., Anuar, N. B., Mokhtar, S., Gani, A. & Ullah Khan S. The rise of "big data" on cloud computing: Review and open research issues, *Information System*, 2015, *47*, 98–115.

Kalra, D. & Ingram, D. *Electronic Health Records Information Technology Solutions for Healthcare*, Springer, London, 2006, 135–181. Doi: 10.1007/1–84628-141–5_7.

Laranjo, I., Macedo, J., & Santos, A. Internet of things for medication control: Service implementation and testing, *Procedia Technology*, 2012, *5*, 777–786. Doi: 10.1016/j.protcy.2012.09.086.

LeCun, Y., Bengio, Y., & Hinton, G. Deep learning, *Nature*, 2015, *521*, 436–444. Doi: https://doi.org/10.1038/nature14539.

Li, X., Ren, S., & Gu, F. Medical internet of things to realize elderly stroke prevention and nursing management, *Journal of Healthcare Engineering*, 2021, *2021*, 12, Article ID: 9989602. Doi: https://doi.org/10.1155/2021/9989602.

Luo, B., Hussain, A., Mahmud, M., & Tang, J. Advances in brain-inspired cognitive systems, *Cognitive Computing*, 2016, *8*, 5, 795–796.

Mahmud, M., Rahman, M. M., Travalin, D., Raif, P. & Hussain, A. Service oriented architecture based web application model for collaborative biomedical signal analysis, *Biomedical Engineering/Biomedizinische Technik*, 2012, *57*, 780–783. Doi: 10.1515/bmt-2012-4412.

Mahmud, M., Kaiser, M. S., Rahman, M. M., Rahman, M. A., Shabut, A., Al-Mamun, S. & Hussain, A. A brain-inspired trust management model to assure security in a cloud based IoT framework for neuroscience applications, *Cognitive Computing*, 2018, *10*, 864–873. Doi: 10.1007/s12559-018-9543-3.

McHale, S. A. & Pereira, E. Facilitating personalisation in epilepsy with an IoT approach, (IJACSA), *International Journal of Advanced Computer Science and Applications*, 2021, *12*, 9.

Meola, A. 'Internet of Things devices, applications & examples', Business Insider UK, December 19, 2016. http://uk.businessinsider.com/internet-of-things-devices-applications-examples-2016-8?r=US&IR=T.

Monteith, S., Glenn, T., Geddes, J., Severus, E., Whybrow, P. C., & Bauer, M. Internet of things issues related to psychiatry, *International Journal of Bipolar Disorders*, 2021, *9*, 11. Doi: https://doi.org/10.1186/s40345-020-00216-y.

Oskouei, R. J., MousaviLou, Z., Bakhtiari, Z., & Jalbani, K. B. IoT-based healthcare support system for Alzheimer's patients, *Wireless Communications and Mobile Computing*, 2020, *2020*, 15, Article ID: 8822598. Doi: https://doi.org/10.1155/2020/8822598.

Pang, Z., Zheng, L., Tian, J., Kao-Walter, S., Dubrova, E., & Chen, Q. Design of a terminal solution for integration of in-home health care devices and services towards the internet-of-things, *Enterprise Information Systems*, 2015, *9*, 1, 86–116. Doi: 10.1080/17517575.2013.776118.

Patel, S., Chen, B., Buckley, T., Rednic, R., McClure, D., Tarsy, D., Shih, L., Dy, J., Welsh, M. & Bonato, P. Home monitoring of patients with Parkinson's disease via wearable technology and a web-based application, *International Conference of the IEEE EMBS*, IEEE, Argentina, 2010, 4411–4414.

Saba, L., Biswas, M., Kuppili, V., Godia, E. C., Suri, H. S., Edla, D. R., Omerzu, T., Laird, J. R., Khanna, N. N., Mavrogeni, S., Protogerou, A., Sfikakis, P., Viswanathan, V., Kitas, G., Nicolaides, A., Gupta, A. & Suri, J.S. The present and future of deep learning in radiology. *European Journal of Radiology* 2019, *114*, 14–24.

Savola, R. M., Abie, H., & Sihvonen, M. Towards metrics-driven adaptive security management in e-health IoT applications. *BodyNets '12: Proceedings of the 7th International Conference on Body Area Networks*, ACM Digital Library, Brussels, 276–281, 2012. Doi:10.4108/icst.bodynets.2012.250241.

Scurlock, C. & D'Ambrosio, C. Telemedicine in the intensive care unit: State of the art. *Critical Care Clinics*, 2015, *31*, 2, 187–195, PMID: 25814449. Doi:10.1016/j.ccc.2014.12.001.

Shrimali, R. *How IoT is Transforming the Healthcare Industry*. June 30, 2020. https://embeddedcomputing.com/application/healthcare/telehealth-healthcare-iot/how-iot-is-transforming-the-healthcare-industry.

Sparaco, M., Lavorgna, L., Conforti, R., Tedeschi, G. & Bonavita, S. The role of wearable devices in multiple sclerosis, *Multiple Sclerosis International*, 2018, *2018*, 1–7, PMC: 6199873. Doi: 10.1155/2018/7627643.

Uyulan, Ç., Ergüzel, T. T., & Tarhan, N. The use of deep learning algorithms on EEG based signal analysis, *JNBS*, 2019, 6, 2, 108–124. Doi: 10.5455/JNBS.1553607558.

Valliani, A. A., Ranti, D., & Oermann, E. K. Deep learning and neurology: A systematic review, *Neurology and Therapy*, 2019, *8*, 351–365. Doi: https://doi.org/10.1007/s40120-019-00153-8.

Vergara, P. M., Cal, E., Villar, J. R., González, V. M. & Sedano, J. An IoT platform for epilepsy monitoring and supervising, *Journal of Sensors*, 2017, *2017*, 18, Article ID: 6043069. Doi: https://doi.org/10.1155/2017/6043069.

Vermesan, O., & Friess, P. *Internet of Things: Converging Technologies for Smart Environments and Integrated Ecosystems*, River Publishers, SINTEF, Norway & Belgium, 2013.

Wei, J. How wearables intersect with the cloud and the internet of things, considerations for the developers of wearables, *IEEE Consumer Electronics Magazine*, 2014, *3*, 53–56.

Zhang, B., Wang, W., Wang, S., Li, S., Liu, M., Wang, L., & Yang, C. Clinical study on electronic medical neuroelectric stimulation based on the internet of things to treat epilepsy patients with anxiety and depression, *Journal of Healthcare Engineering*, 2021, *2021*, 13, Article ID: 6667309. Doi: https://doi.org/10.1155/2021/6667309.

Zhao, W., Wang, C., & Nakahira, Y. Medical application on internet of things, *IET Conference*, 2011, IEEE, Beijing, China.

Index

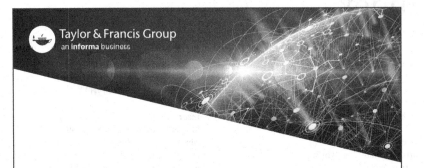